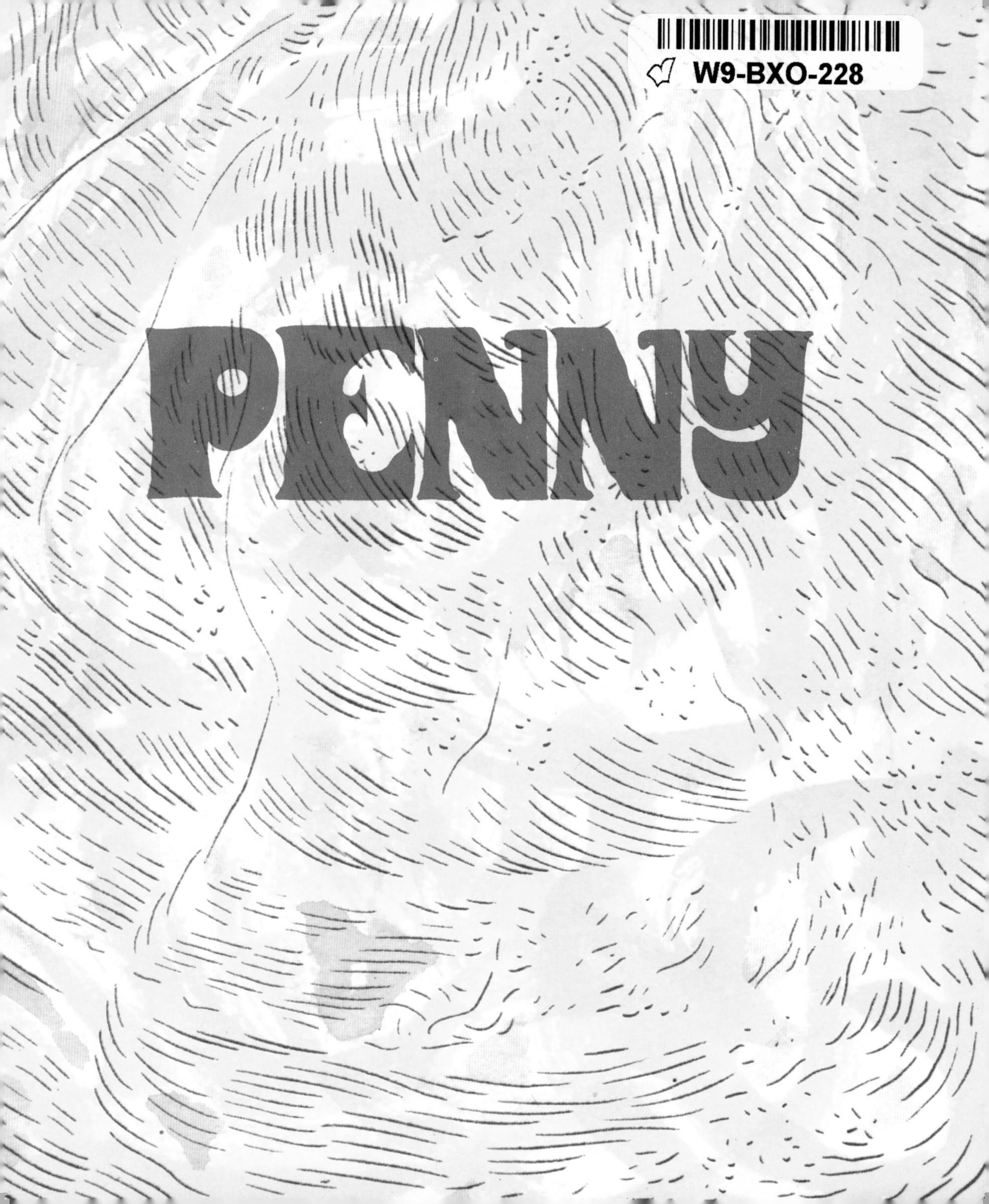
PENNY

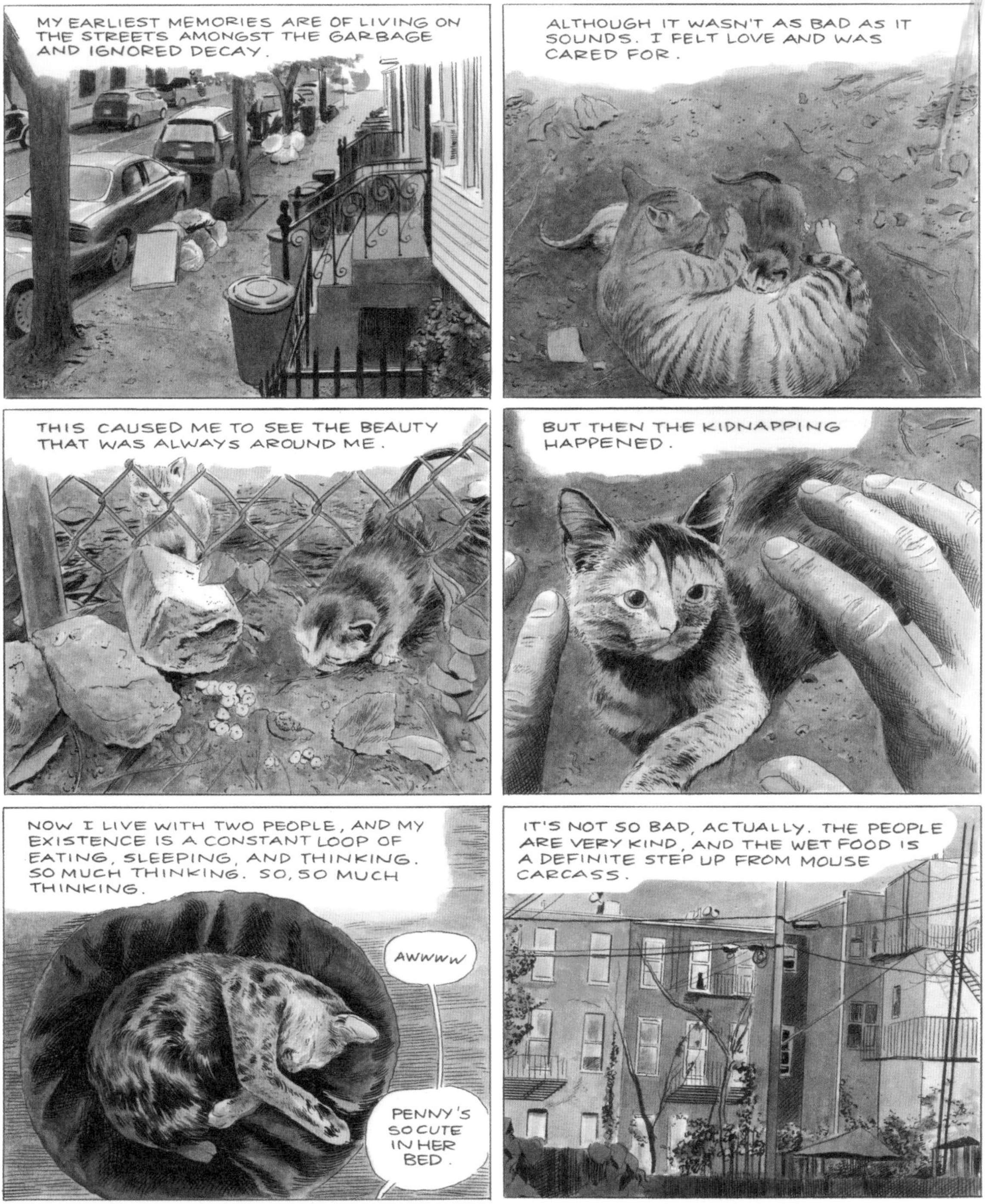
MY EARLIEST MEMORIES ARE OF LIVING ON THE STREETS AMONGST THE GARBAGE AND IGNORED DECAY.
ALTHOUGH IT WASN'T AS BAD AS IT SOUNDS. I FELT LOVE AND WAS CARED FOR.
THIS CAUSED ME TO SEE THE BEAUTY THAT WAS ALWAYS AROUND ME.
BUT THEN THE KIDNAPPING HAPPENED.
NOW I LIVE WITH TWO PEOPLE, AND MY EXISTENCE IS A CONSTANT LOOP OF EATING, SLEEPING, AND THINKING. SO MUCH THINKING. SO, SO MUCH THINKING.
AWWWW
PENNY'S SO CUTE IN HER BED.
IT'S NOT SO BAD, ACTUALLY. THE PEOPLE ARE VERY KIND, AND THE WET FOOD IS A DEFINITE STEP UP FROM MOUSE CARCASS.

Library of Congress Cataloging-in-Publication Data

Names: Stevens, Karl, 1978- author, artist.
Title: Penny : a graphic memoir / by Karl Stevens.
Description: San Francisco : Chronicle Books, 2021.
Identifiers: LCCN 2020041017 | ISBN 9781452183053 (paperback)
Subjects: LCSH: Cats--Comic books, strips, etc. | Self-perception–Comic books, strips, etc. | Graphic novels.
Classification: LCC PN6727.S6976 P46 2021 | DDC 741.5/973--dc23
LC record available at https://lccn.loc.gov/2020041017
ISBN 978-1-4521-8305-3

Manufactured in China.

FSC MIX Paper from responsible sources FSC™ C008047 www.fsc.org

Design by Kim Di Santo.

10 9 8 7 6 5 4 3 2 1

Chronicle Books LLC
680 Second Street
San Francisco, CA 94107
www.chroniclebooks.com

PENNY

A GRAPHIC MEMOIR
BY KARL STEVENS

CHRONICLE BOOKS

SAN FRANCISCO

To the memory of Tom Spurgeon

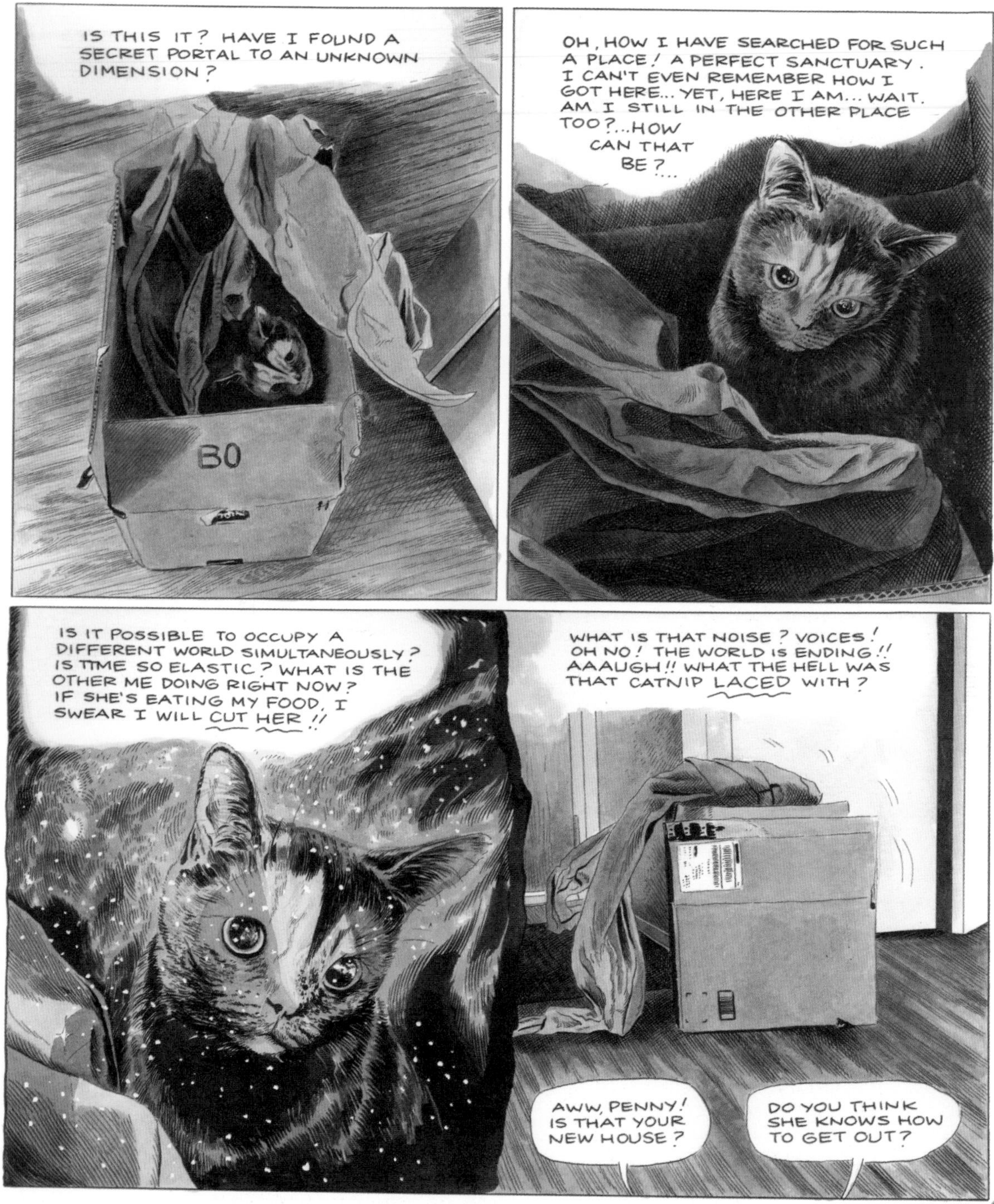
IS THIS IT? HAVE I FOUND A SECRET PORTAL TO AN UNKNOWN DIMENSION?
BO
OH, HOW I HAVE SEARCHED FOR SUCH A PLACE! A PERFECT SANCTUARY. I CAN'T EVEN REMEMBER HOW I GOT HERE... YET, HERE I AM... WAIT. AM I STILL IN THE OTHER PLACE TOO?...HOW CAN THAT BE?...
IS IT POSSIBLE TO OCCUPY A DIFFERENT WORLD SIMULTANEOUSLY? IS TIME SO ELASTIC? WHAT IS THE OTHER ME DOING RIGHT NOW? IF SHE'S EATING MY FOOD, I SWEAR I WILL CUT HER!!
WHAT IS THAT NOISE? VOICES! OH NO! THE WORLD IS ENDING!! AAAUGH!! WHAT THE HELL WAS THAT CATNIP LACED WITH?
AWW, PENNY! IS THAT YOUR NEW HOUSE?
DO YOU THINK SHE KNOWS HOW TO GET OUT?

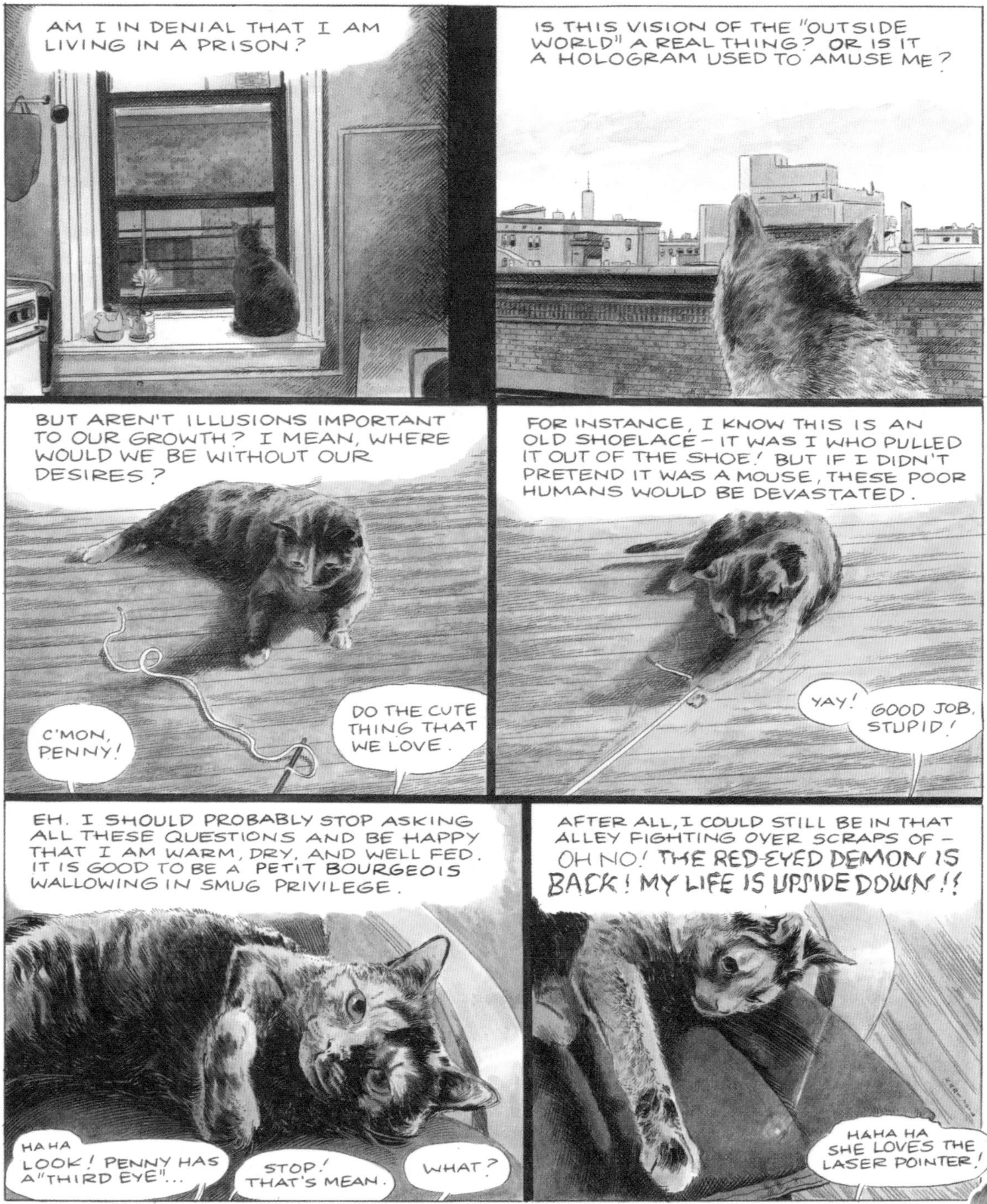
AM I IN DENIAL THAT I AM LIVING IN A PRISON?
IS THIS VISION OF THE "OUTSIDE WORLD" A REAL THING? OR IS IT A HOLOGRAM USED TO AMUSE ME?
BUT AREN'T ILLUSIONS IMPORTANT TO OUR GROWTH? I MEAN, WHERE WOULD WE BE WITHOUT OUR DESIRES?
C'MON, PENNY!
DO THE CUTE THING THAT WE LOVE.
FOR INSTANCE, I KNOW THIS IS AN OLD SHOELACE – IT WAS I WHO PULLED IT OUT OF THE SHOE! BUT IF I DIDN'T PRETEND IT WAS A MOUSE, THESE POOR HUMANS WOULD BE DEVASTATED.
YAY!
GOOD JOB, STUPID!
EH. I SHOULD PROBABLY STOP ASKING ALL THESE QUESTIONS AND BE HAPPY THAT I AM WARM, DRY, AND WELL FED. IT IS GOOD TO BE A PETIT BOURGEOIS WALLOWING IN SMUG PRIVILEGE.
HA HA LOOK! PENNY HAS A "THIRD EYE"...
STOP! THAT'S MEAN.
WHAT?
AFTER ALL, I COULD STILL BE IN THAT ALLEY FIGHTING OVER SCRAPS OF – OH NO! THE RED-EYED DEMON IS BACK! MY LIFE IS UPSIDE DOWN!!
HAHA HA SHE LOVES THE LASER POINTER!

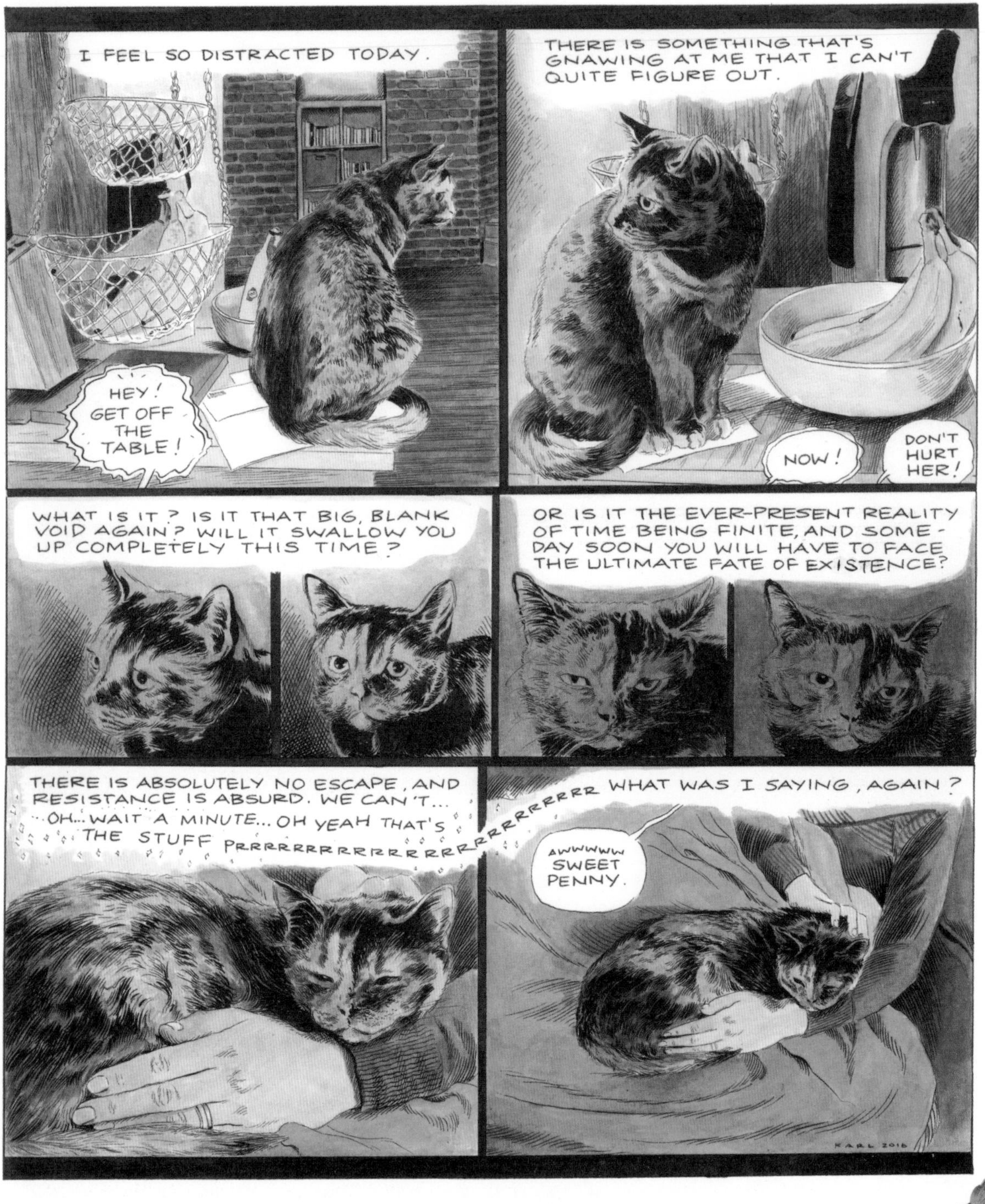
I FEEL SO DISTRACTED TODAY.
HEY! GET OFF THE TABLE!
THERE IS SOMETHING THAT'S GNAWING AT ME THAT I CAN'T QUITE FIGURE OUT.
NOW!
DON'T HURT HER!
WHAT IS IT? IS IT THAT BIG, BLANK VOID AGAIN? WILL IT SWALLOW YOU UP COMPLETELY THIS TIME?
OR IS IT THE EVER-PRESENT REALITY OF TIME BEING FINITE, AND SOME-DAY SOON YOU WILL HAVE TO FACE THE ULTIMATE FATE OF EXISTENCE?
THERE IS ABSOLUTELY NO ESCAPE, AND RESISTANCE IS ABSURD. WE CAN'T...
...OH... WAIT A MINUTE... OH YEAH THAT'S THE STUFF PRRRRRRRRRRRRRRRRRRRRRRRRRRRRRRR
WHAT WAS I SAYING, AGAIN?
AWWWWW SWEET PENNY.
KARL 2016

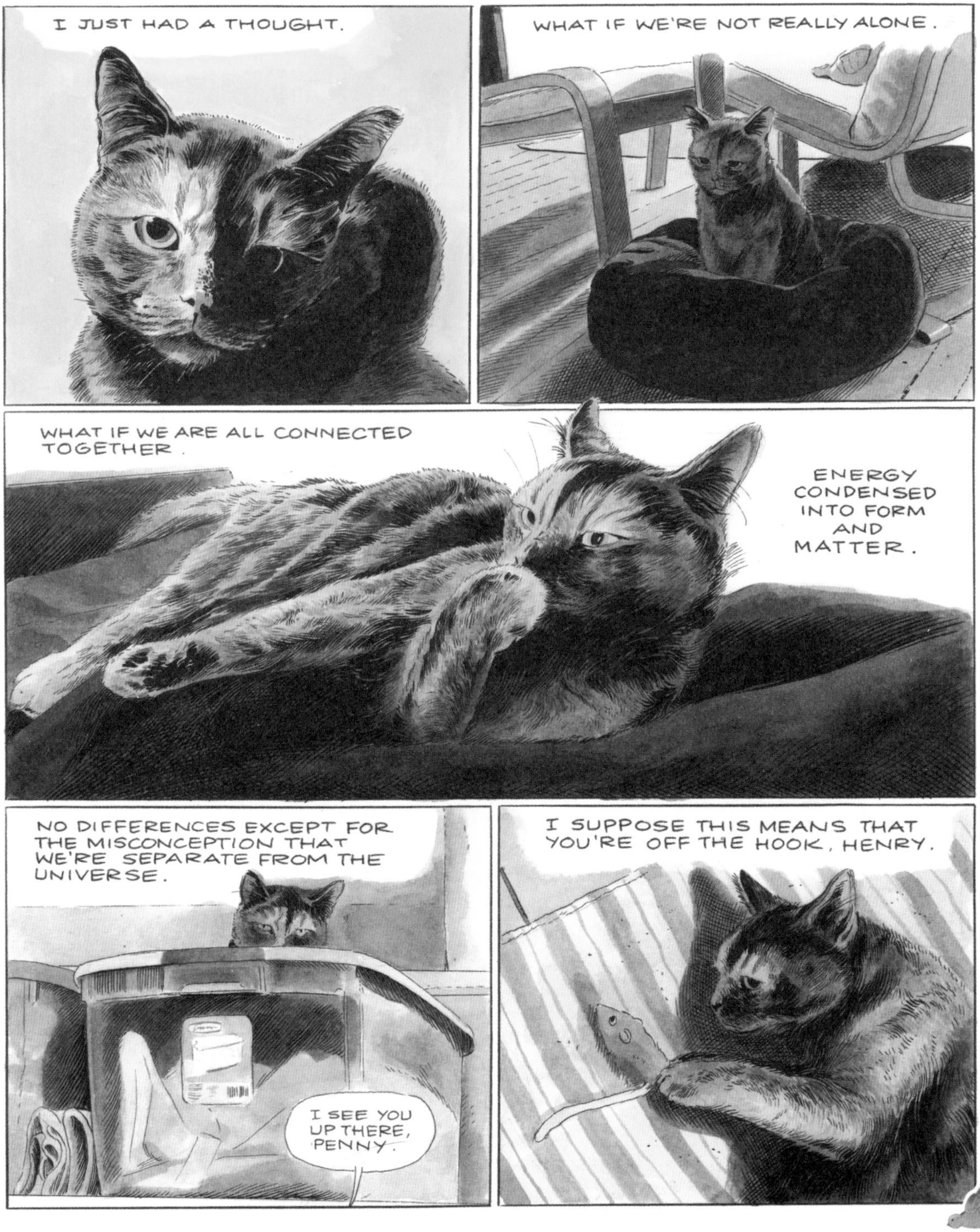
I JUST HAD A THOUGHT.
WHAT IF WE'RE NOT REALLY ALONE.
WHAT IF WE ARE ALL CONNECTED TOGETHER.
ENERGY CONDENSED INTO FORM AND MATTER.
NO DIFFERENCES EXCEPT FOR THE MISCONCEPTION THAT WE'RE SEPARATE FROM THE UNIVERSE.
I SEE YOU UP THERE, PENNY.
I SUPPOSE THIS MEANS THAT YOU'RE OFF THE HOOK, HENRY.

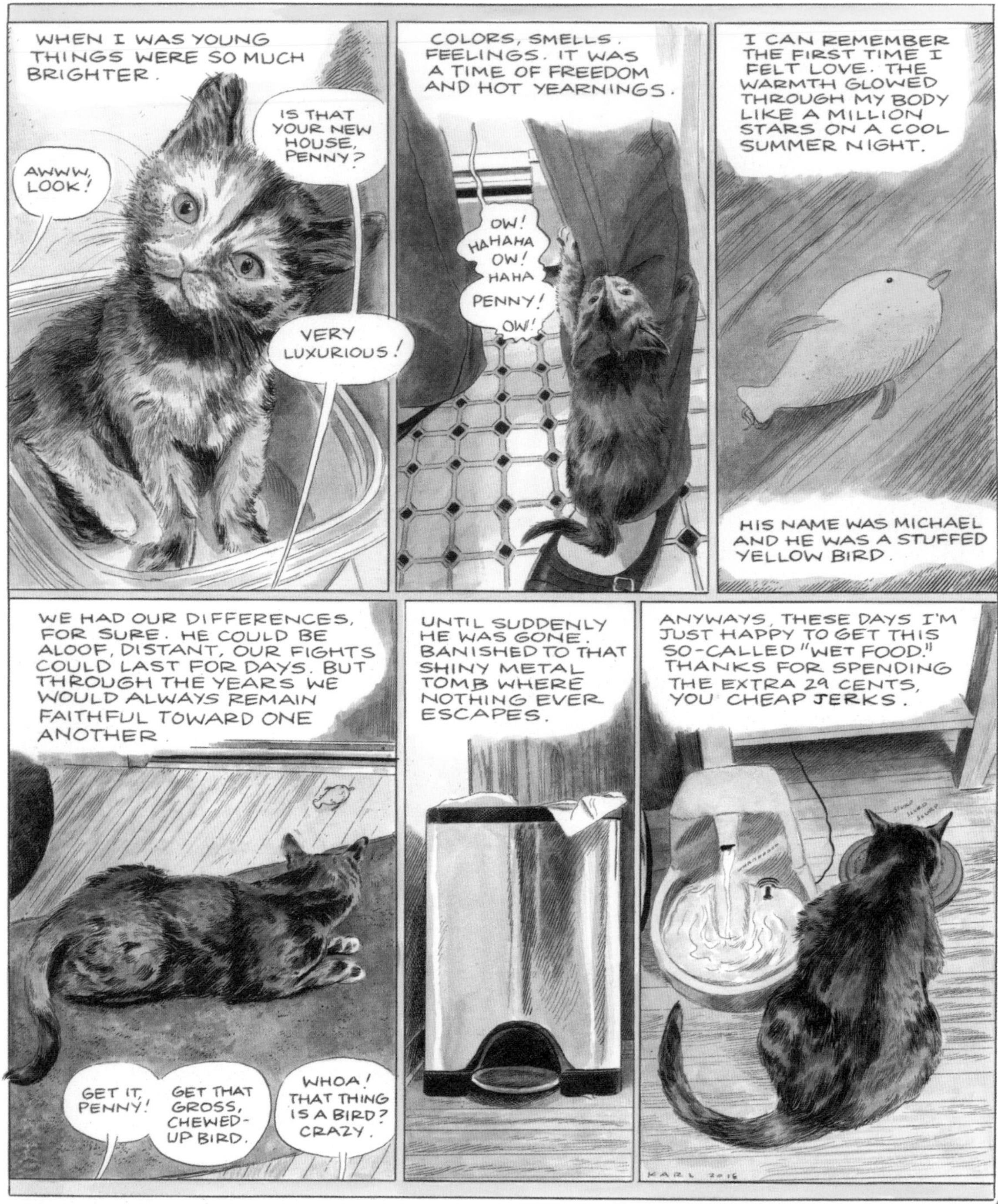

WHEN I WAS YOUNG THINGS WERE SO MUCH BRIGHTER.
AWWW, LOOK!
IS THAT YOUR NEW HOUSE, PENNY?
VERY LUXURIOUS!
COLORS, SMELLS. FEELINGS. IT WAS A TIME OF FREEDOM AND HOT YEARNINGS.
OW! HAHAHA OW! HAHA PENNY! OW!
I CAN REMEMBER THE FIRST TIME I FELT LOVE. THE WARMTH GLOWED THROUGH MY BODY LIKE A MILLION STARS ON A COOL SUMMER NIGHT.
HIS NAME WAS MICHAEL AND HE WAS A STUFFED YELLOW BIRD.
WE HAD OUR DIFFERENCES, FOR SURE. HE COULD BE ALOOF, DISTANT, OUR FIGHTS COULD LAST FOR DAYS. BUT THROUGH THE YEARS WE WOULD ALWAYS REMAIN FAITHFUL TOWARD ONE ANOTHER.
GET IT, PENNY!
GET THAT GROSS, CHEWED-UP BIRD.
WHOA! THAT THING IS A BIRD? CRAZY.
UNTIL SUDDENLY HE WAS GONE. BANISHED TO THAT SHINY METAL TOMB WHERE NOTHING EVER ESCAPES.
ANYWAYS, THESE DAYS I'M JUST HAPPY TO GET THIS SO-CALLED "WET FOOD." THANKS FOR SPENDING THE EXTRA 29 CENTS, YOU CHEAP JERKS.
KARL 2016

WITHOUT FANTASY THERE IS NO REALITY.

PRRRRRRRRR

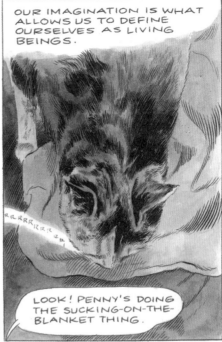

OUR IMAGINATION IS WHAT ALLOWS US TO DEFINE OURSELVES AS LIVING BEINGS.

RRRRRRR

LOOK! PENNY'S DOING THE SUCKING-ON-THE-BLANKET THING.

IT IS THROUGH THIS ACT THAT OUR SOCIETY WAS BUILT. WITHOUT IT, THE WORLD IS MERELY A SERIES OF INSTINCTUAL REACTIONS.

PRRRRRRRRR

DON'T LOOK AT ME.

SO CUTE.

RRRRRRRRRRRRRRRRRRR

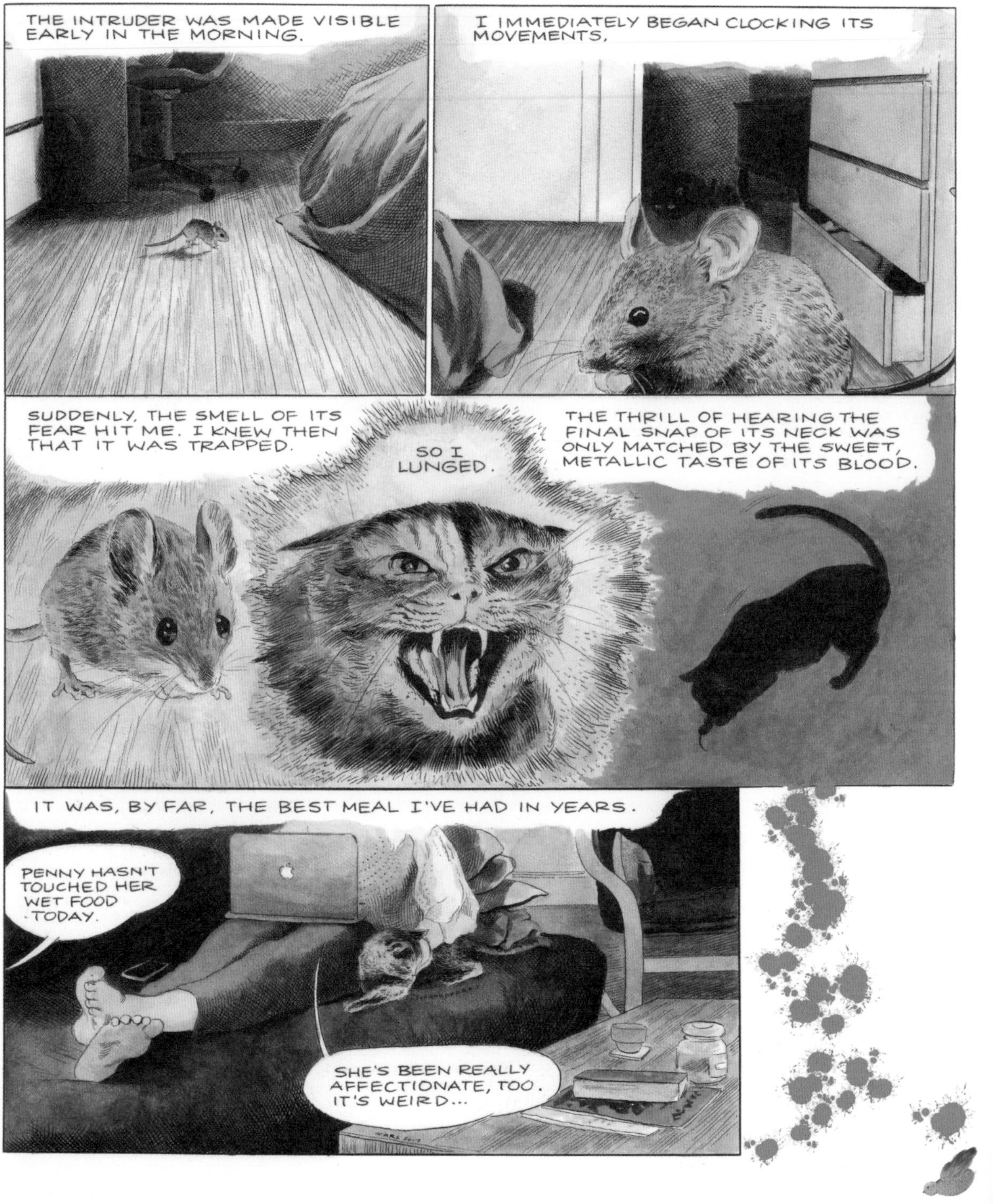
THE INTRUDER WAS MADE VISIBLE EARLY IN THE MORNING.
I IMMEDIATELY BEGAN CLOCKING ITS MOVEMENTS.
SUDDENLY, THE SMELL OF ITS FEAR HIT ME. I KNEW THEN THAT IT WAS TRAPPED.
SO I LUNGED.
THE THRILL OF HEARING THE FINAL SNAP OF ITS NECK WAS ONLY MATCHED BY THE SWEET, METALLIC TASTE OF ITS BLOOD.
IT WAS, BY FAR, THE BEST MEAL I'VE HAD IN YEARS.
PENNY HASN'T TOUCHED HER WET FOOD TODAY.
SHE'S BEEN REALLY AFFECTIONATE, TOO. IT'S WEIRD...

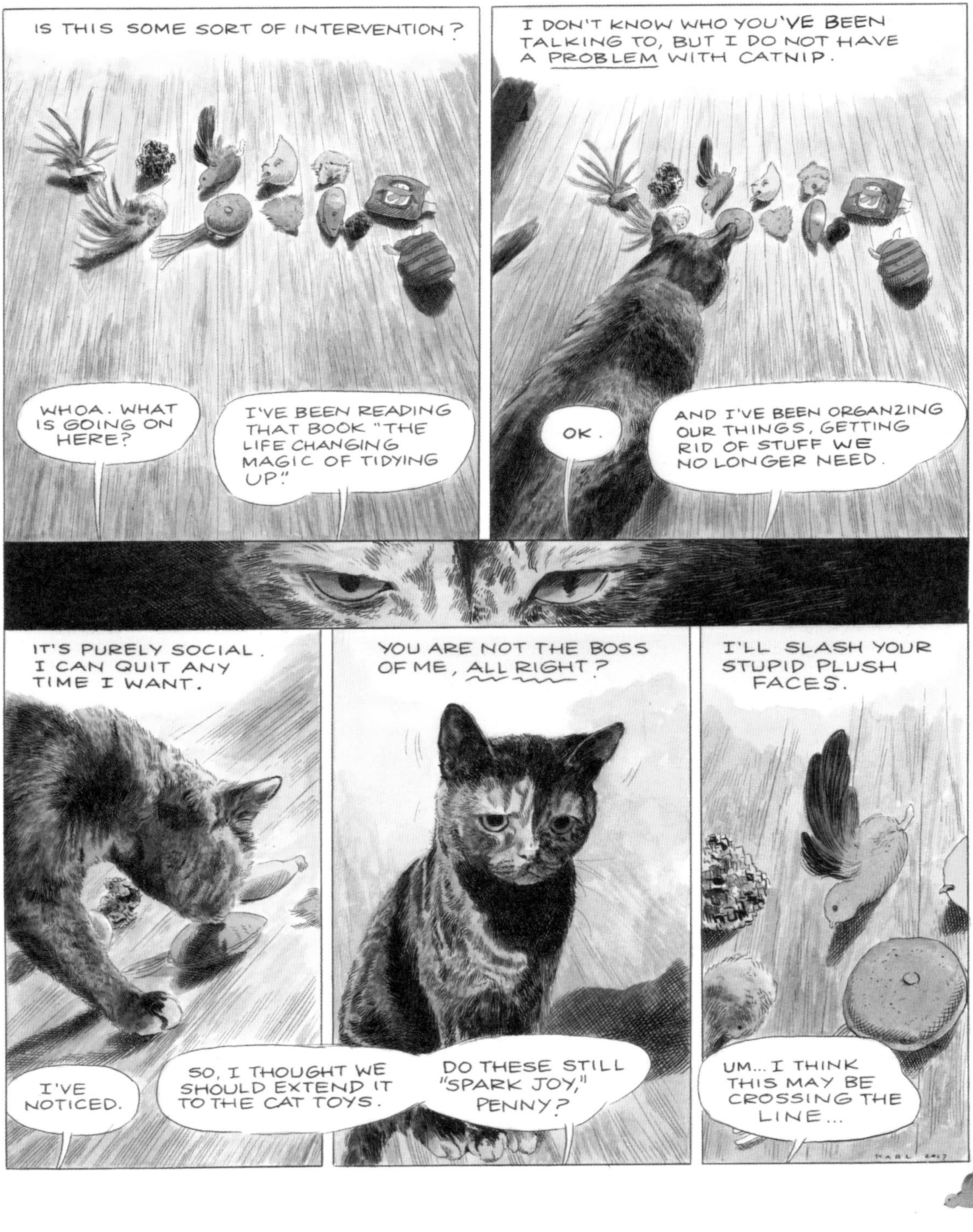
IS THIS SOME SORT OF INTERVENTION?
WHOA. WHAT IS GOING ON HERE?
I'VE BEEN READING THAT BOOK "THE LIFE CHANGING MAGIC OF TIDYING UP."
I DON'T KNOW WHO YOU'VE BEEN TALKING TO, BUT I DO NOT HAVE A PROBLEM WITH CATNIP.
OK.
AND I'VE BEEN ORGANZING OUR THINGS, GETTING RID OF STUFF WE NO LONGER NEED.
IT'S PURELY SOCIAL. I CAN QUIT ANY TIME I WANT.
I'VE NOTICED.
YOU ARE NOT THE BOSS OF ME, ALL RIGHT?
SO, I THOUGHT WE SHOULD EXTEND IT TO THE CAT TOYS.
DO THESE STILL "SPARK JOY," PENNY?
I'LL SLASH YOUR STUPID PLUSH FACES.
UM... I THINK THIS MAY BE CROSSING THE LINE...
KARL 2017

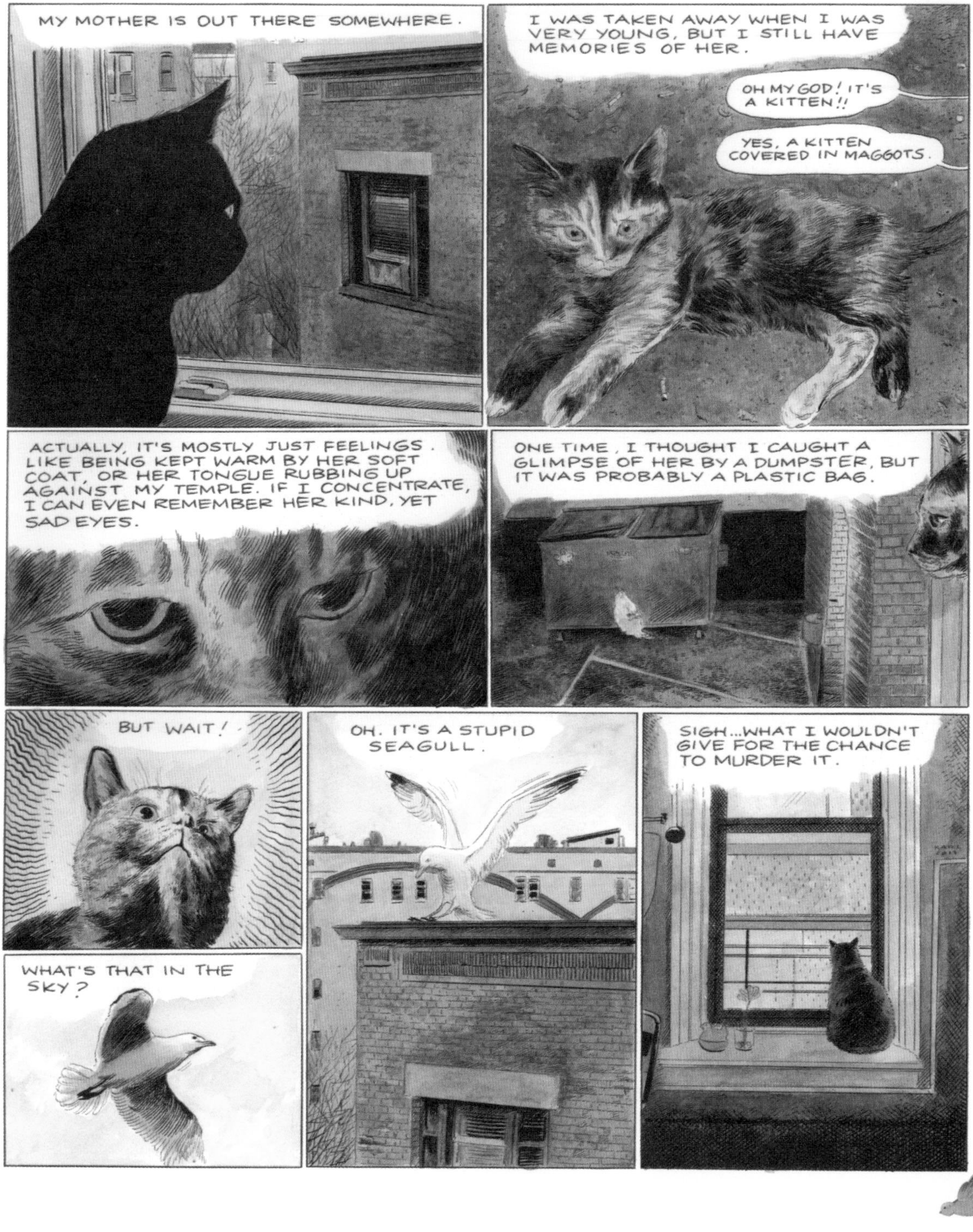
MY MOTHER IS OUT THERE SOMEWHERE.
I WAS TAKEN AWAY WHEN I WAS VERY YOUNG, BUT I STILL HAVE MEMORIES OF HER.
OH MY GOD! IT'S A KITTEN!!
YES, A KITTEN COVERED IN MAGGOTS.
ACTUALLY, IT'S MOSTLY JUST FEELINGS. LIKE BEING KEPT WARM BY HER SOFT COAT, OR HER TONGUE RUBBING UP AGAINST MY TEMPLE. IF I CONCENTRATE, I CAN EVEN REMEMBER HER KIND, YET SAD EYES.
ONE TIME, I THOUGHT I CAUGHT A GLIMPSE OF HER BY A DUMPSTER, BUT IT WAS PROBABLY A PLASTIC BAG.
BUT WAIT!
WHAT'S THAT IN THE SKY?
OH. IT'S A STUPID SEAGULL.
SIGH...WHAT I WOULDN'T GIVE FOR THE CHANCE TO MURDER IT.

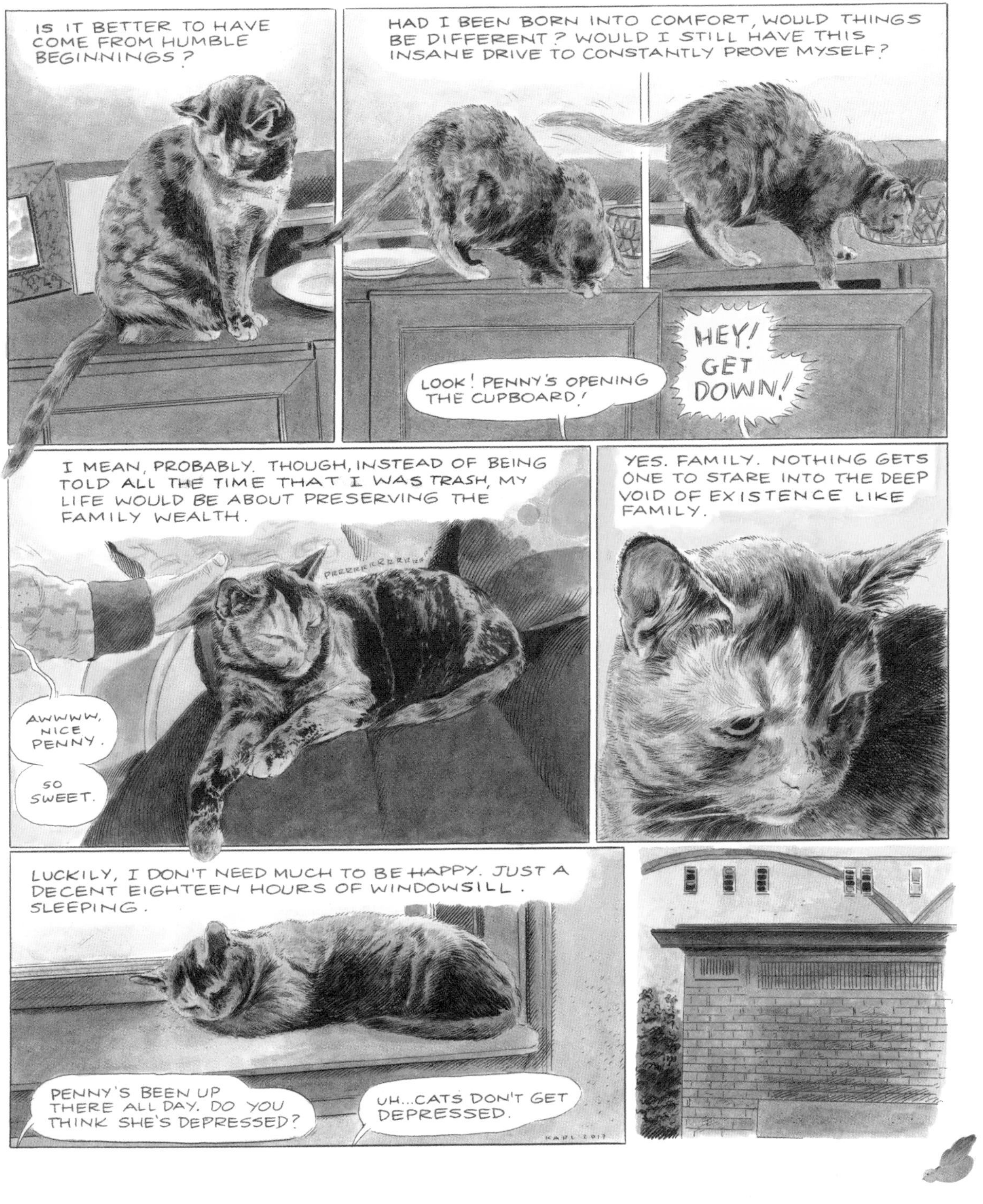
IS IT BETTER TO HAVE COME FROM HUMBLE BEGINNINGS?
HAD I BEEN BORN INTO COMFORT, WOULD THINGS BE DIFFERENT? WOULD I STILL HAVE THIS INSANE DRIVE TO CONSTANTLY PROVE MYSELF?
LOOK! PENNY'S OPENING THE CUPBOARD!
HEY! GET DOWN!
I MEAN, PROBABLY. THOUGH, INSTEAD OF BEING TOLD ALL THE TIME THAT I WAS TRASH, MY LIFE WOULD BE ABOUT PRESERVING THE FAMILY WEALTH.
AWWWW, NICE PENNY.
SO SWEET.
YES. FAMILY. NOTHING GETS ONE TO STARE INTO THE DEEP VOID OF EXISTENCE LIKE FAMILY.
LUCKILY, I DON'T NEED MUCH TO BE HAPPY. JUST A DECENT EIGHTEEN HOURS OF WINDOWSILL SLEEPING.
PENNY'S BEEN UP THERE ALL DAY. DO YOU THINK SHE'S DEPRESSED?
UH...CATS DON'T GET DEPRESSED.
KARL 2017

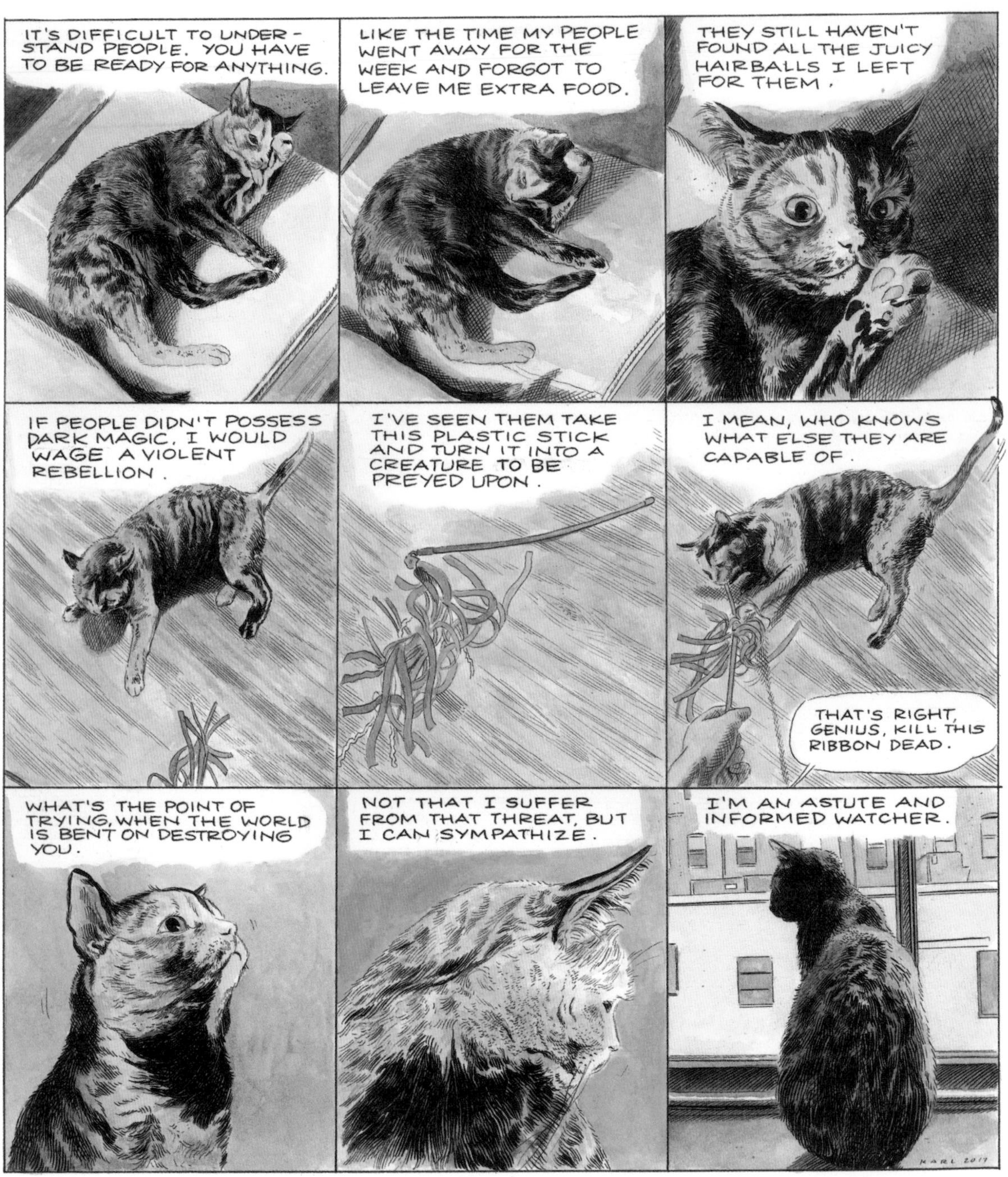
IT'S DIFFICULT TO UNDER-STAND PEOPLE. YOU HAVE TO BE READY FOR ANYTHING.
LIKE THE TIME MY PEOPLE WENT AWAY FOR THE WEEK AND FORGOT TO LEAVE ME EXTRA FOOD.
THEY STILL HAVEN'T FOUND ALL THE JUICY HAIRBALLS I LEFT FOR THEM.
IF PEOPLE DIDN'T POSSESS DARK MAGIC, I WOULD WAGE A VIOLENT REBELLION.
I'VE SEEN THEM TAKE THIS PLASTIC STICK AND TURN IT INTO A CREATURE TO BE PREYED UPON.
I MEAN, WHO KNOWS WHAT ELSE THEY ARE CAPABLE OF.
THAT'S RIGHT, GENIUS, KILL THIS RIBBON DEAD.
WHAT'S THE POINT OF TRYING, WHEN THE WORLD IS BENT ON DESTROYING YOU.
NOT THAT I SUFFER FROM THAT THREAT, BUT I CAN SYMPATHIZE.
I'M AN ASTUTE AND INFORMED WATCHER.
KARL 2017

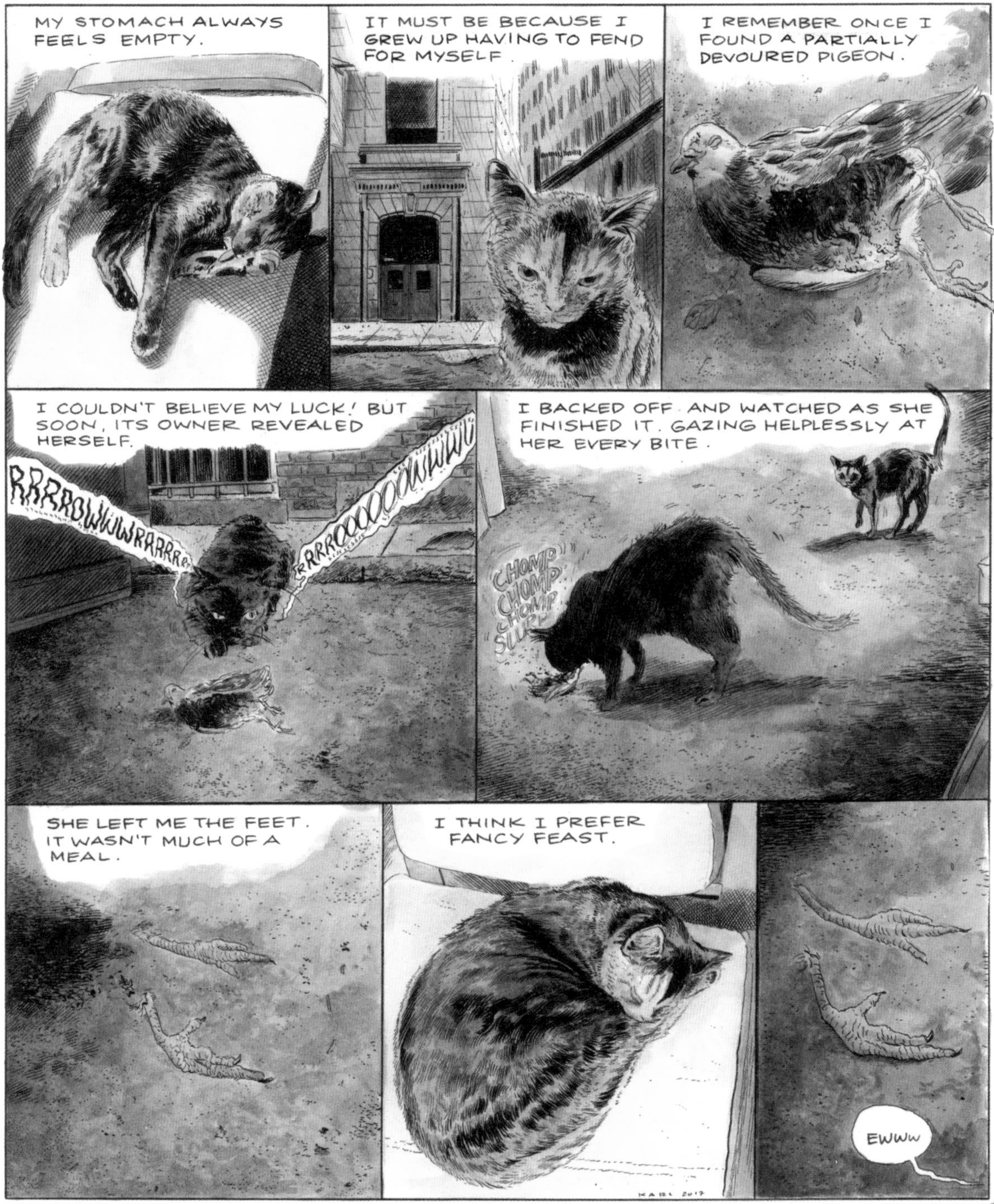
MY STOMACH ALWAYS FEELS EMPTY.
IT MUST BE BECAUSE I GREW UP HAVING TO FEND FOR MYSELF.
I REMEMBER ONCE I FOUND A PARTIALLY DEVOURED PIGEON.
I COULDN'T BELIEVE MY LUCK! BUT SOON, ITS OWNER REVEALED HERSELF.
RRRROWWWWRRRRRR
RRRROOOOOOOWWWW
I BACKED OFF AND WATCHED AS SHE FINISHED IT. GAZING HELPLESSLY AT HER EVERY BITE.
CHOMP CHOMP CHOMP
SHE LEFT ME THE FEET. IT WASN'T MUCH OF A MEAL.
I THINK I PREFER FANCY FEAST.
EWWW

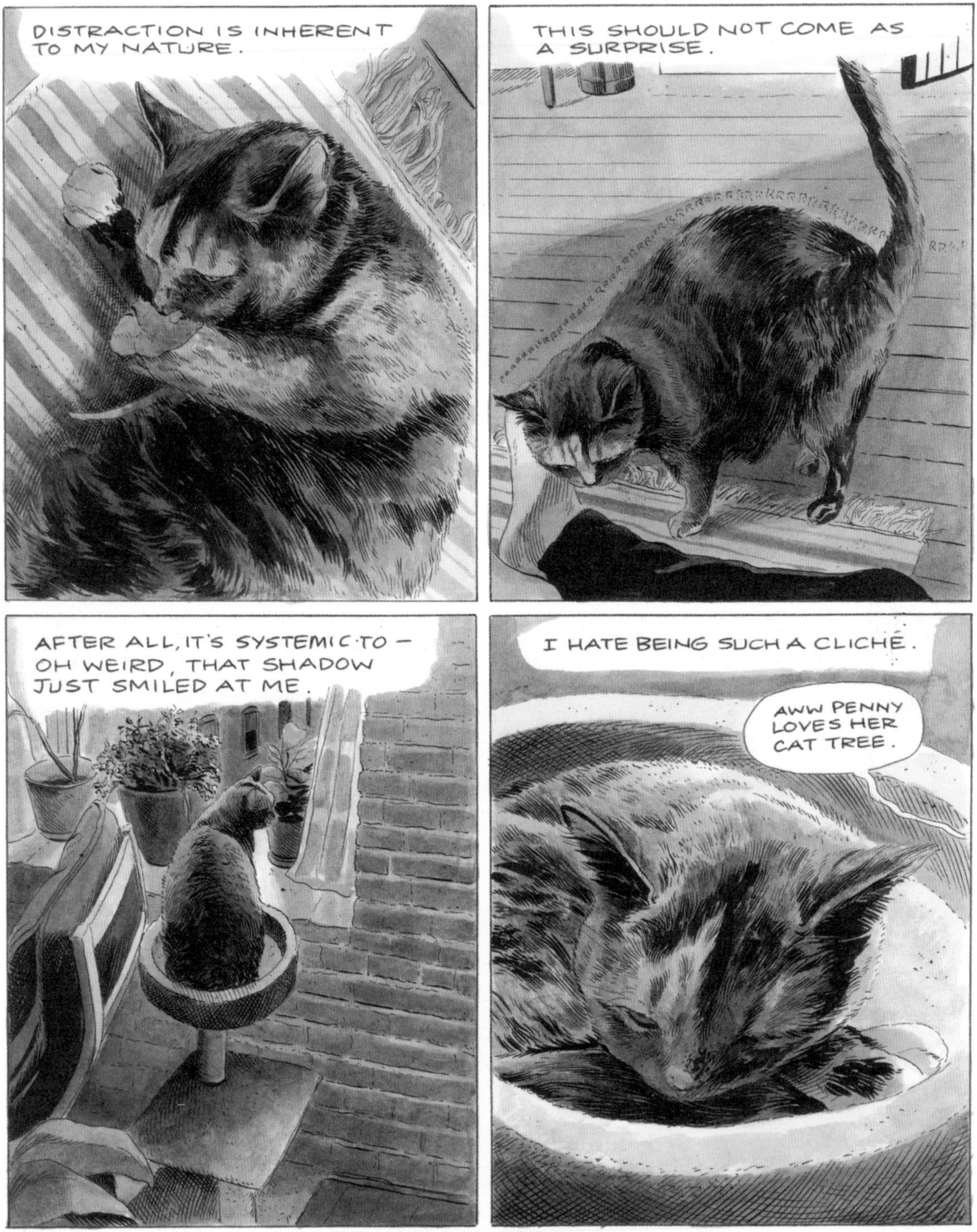
DISTRACTION IS INHERENT TO MY NATURE.
THIS SHOULD NOT COME AS A SURPRISE.
AFTER ALL, IT'S SYSTEMIC TO — OH WEIRD, THAT SHADOW JUST SMILED AT ME.
I HATE BEING SUCH A CLICHÉ.
AWW PENNY LOVES HER CAT TREE.

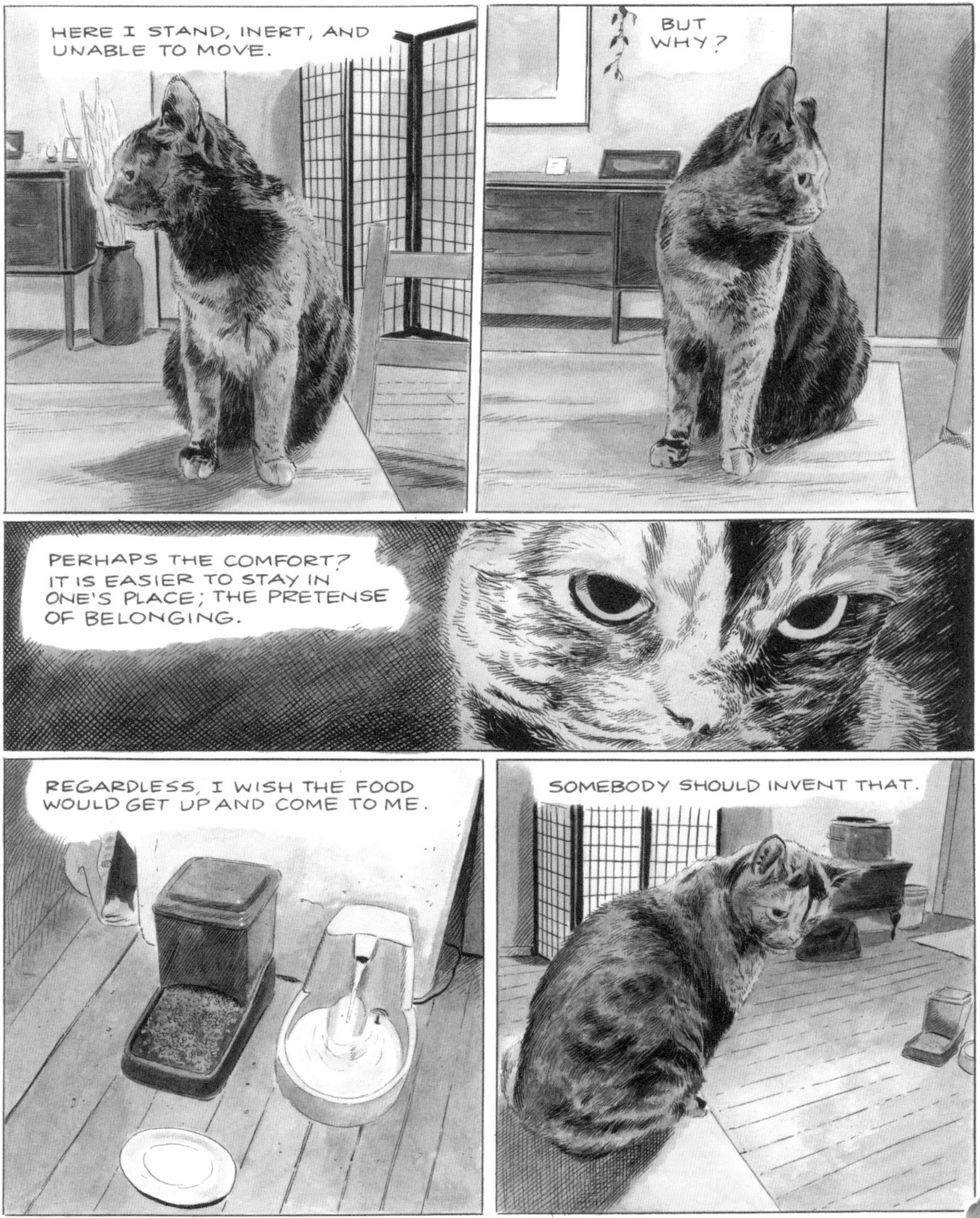
HERE I STAND, INERT, AND UNABLE TO MOVE.
BUT WHY?
PERHAPS THE COMFORT? IT IS EASIER TO STAY IN ONE'S PLACE; THE PRETENSE OF BELONGING.
REGARDLESS, I WISH THE FOOD WOULD GET UP AND COME TO ME.
SOMEBODY SHOULD INVENT THAT.

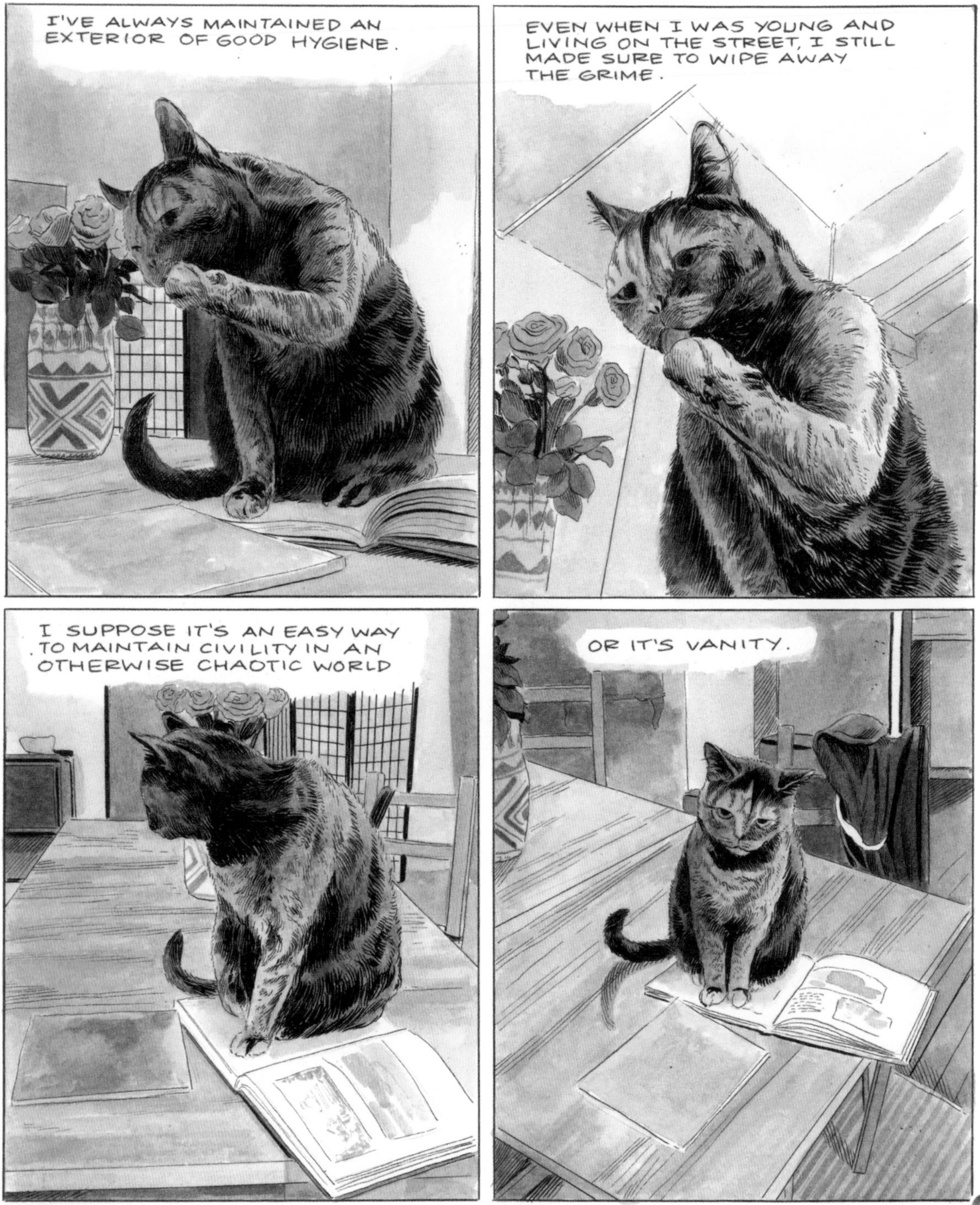
I'VE ALWAYS MAINTAINED AN EXTERIOR OF GOOD HYGIENE.
EVEN WHEN I WAS YOUNG AND LIVING ON THE STREET, I STILL MADE SURE TO WIPE AWAY THE GRIME.
I SUPPOSE IT'S AN EASY WAY TO MAINTAIN CIVILITY IN AN OTHERWISE CHAOTIC WORLD
OR IT'S VANITY.

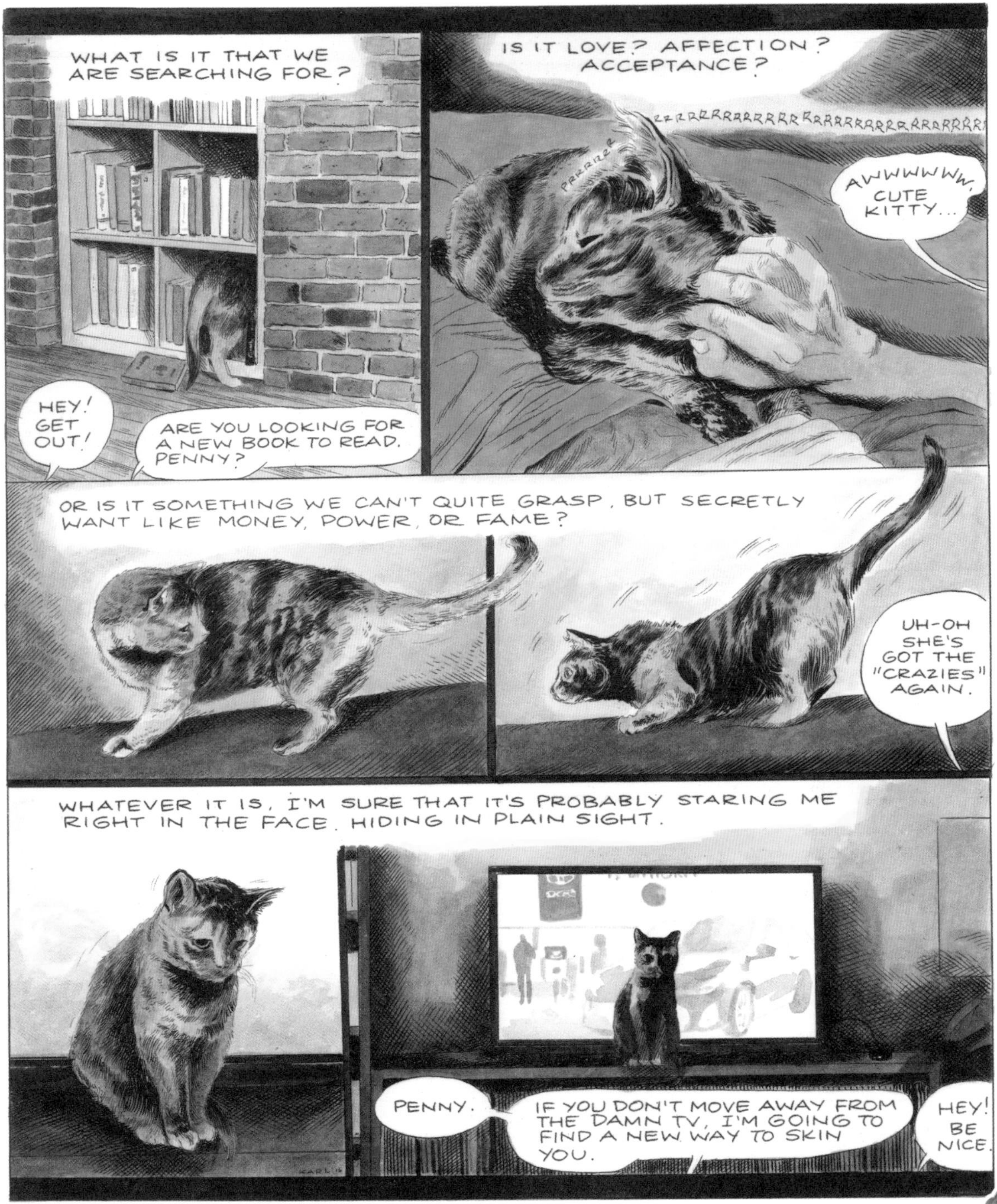
WHAT IS IT THAT WE ARE SEARCHING FOR?
HEY! GET OUT!
ARE YOU LOOKING FOR A NEW BOOK TO READ, PENNY?
IS IT LOVE? AFFECTION? ACCEPTANCE?
PRRRRR
AWWWWWW, CUTE KITTY...
OR IS IT SOMETHING WE CAN'T QUITE GRASP, BUT SECRETLY WANT LIKE MONEY, POWER, OR FAME?
UH-OH SHE'S GOT THE "CRAZIES" AGAIN.
WHATEVER IT IS, I'M SURE THAT IT'S PROBABLY STARING ME RIGHT IN THE FACE, HIDING IN PLAIN SIGHT.
PENNY.
IF YOU DON'T MOVE AWAY FROM THE DAMN TV, I'M GOING TO FIND A NEW WAY TO SKIN YOU.
HEY! BE NICE.

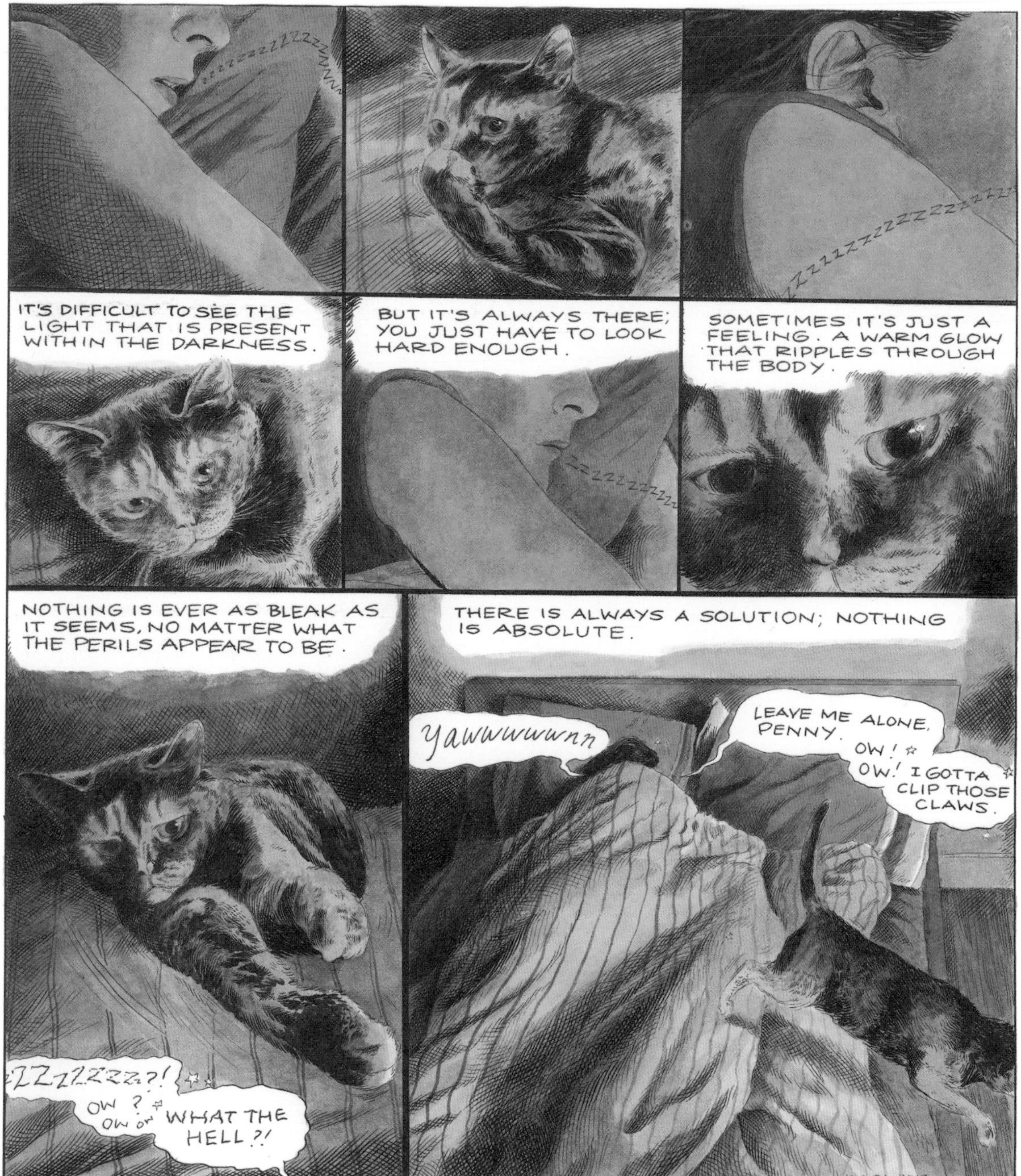
IT'S DIFFICULT TO SEE THE LIGHT THAT IS PRESENT WITHIN THE DARKNESS.
BUT IT'S ALWAYS THERE; YOU JUST HAVE TO LOOK HARD ENOUGH.
SOMETIMES IT'S JUST A FEELING. A WARM GLOW THAT RIPPLES THROUGH THE BODY.
NOTHING IS EVER AS BLEAK AS IT SEEMS, NO MATTER WHAT THE PERILS APPEAR TO BE.
ZZZZZZZZ?!
OW? OW OW WHAT THE HELL?!
THERE IS ALWAYS A SOLUTION; NOTHING IS ABSOLUTE.
Yawwwwwnn
LEAVE ME ALONE, PENNY.
OW! OW! I GOTTA CLIP THOSE CLAWS.
KARL 2017

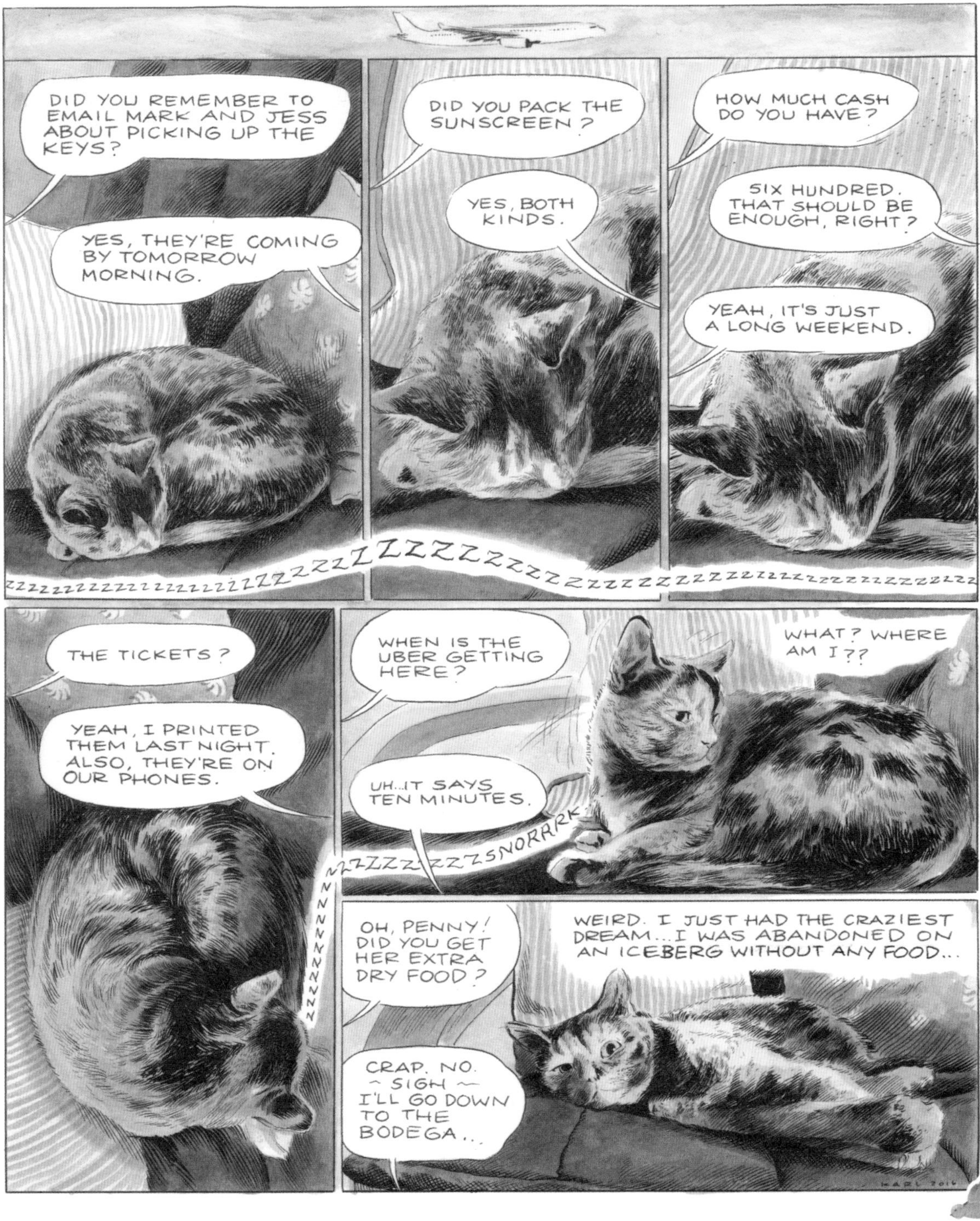
DID YOU REMEMBER TO EMAIL MARK AND JESS ABOUT PICKING UP THE KEYS?
YES, THEY'RE COMING BY TOMORROW MORNING.
DID YOU PACK THE SUNSCREEN?
YES, BOTH KINDS.
HOW MUCH CASH DO YOU HAVE?
SIX HUNDRED. THAT SHOULD BE ENOUGH, RIGHT?
YEAH, IT'S JUST A LONG WEEKEND.
ZZZZZZZZZZZZZZZZZZZZZZZZZZZZZZZZZZZZZZZZZZZZZZZZZZZZZZZZZZZZZZZZZZZZZZZZ
THE TICKETS?
YEAH, I PRINTED THEM LAST NIGHT. ALSO, THEY'RE ON OUR PHONES.
NNNNNNNNNNNNNNZZZZZZZZZSNORRRRK
WHEN IS THE UBER GETTING HERE?
UH...IT SAYS TEN MINUTES.
WHAT? WHERE AM I??
OH, PENNY! DID YOU GET HER EXTRA DRY FOOD?
CRAP. NO. ~SIGH~ I'LL GO DOWN TO THE BODEGA...
WEIRD. I JUST HAD THE CRAZIEST DREAM...I WAS ABANDONED ON AN ICEBERG WITHOUT ANY FOOD...
KARL 2016

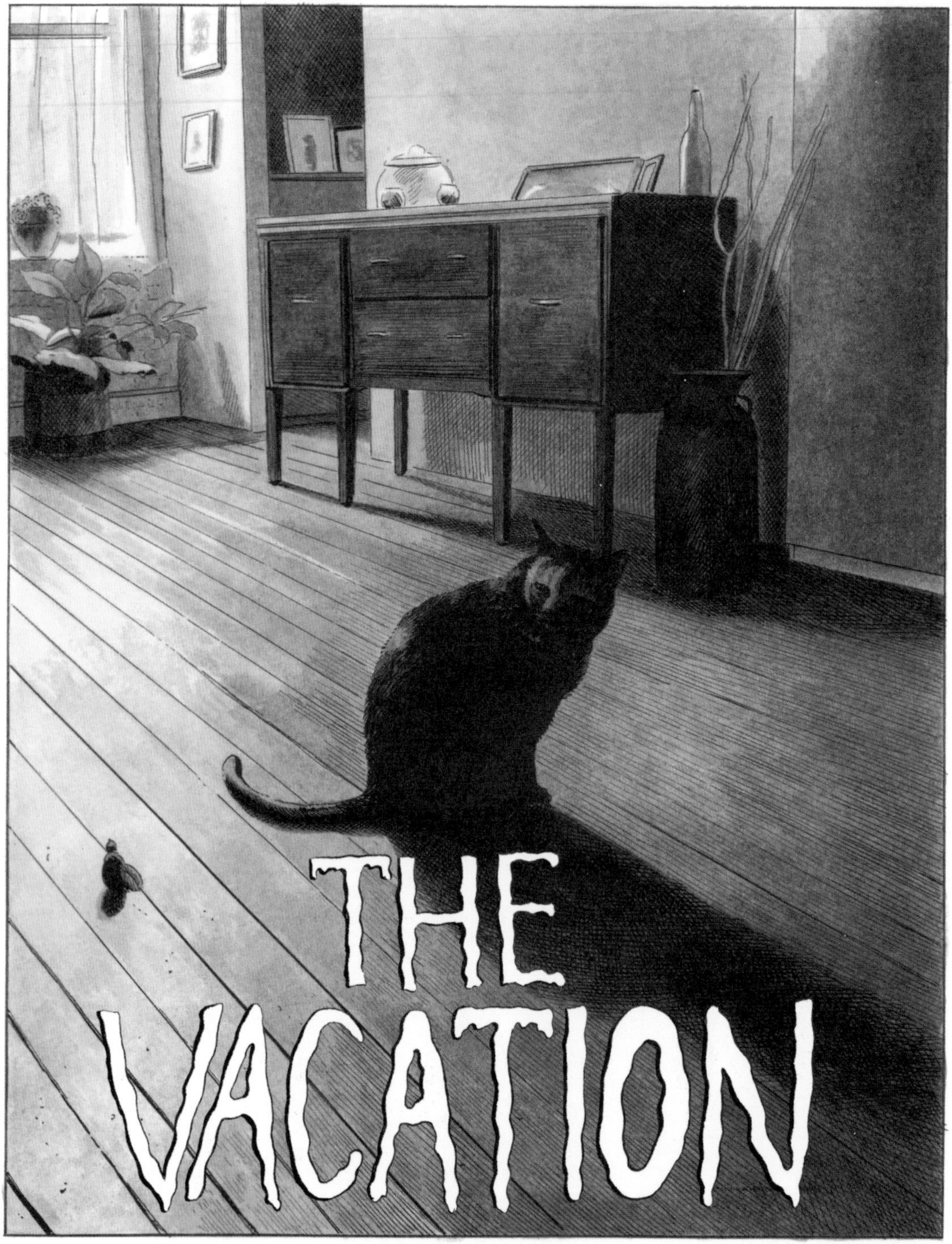
THE
VACATION

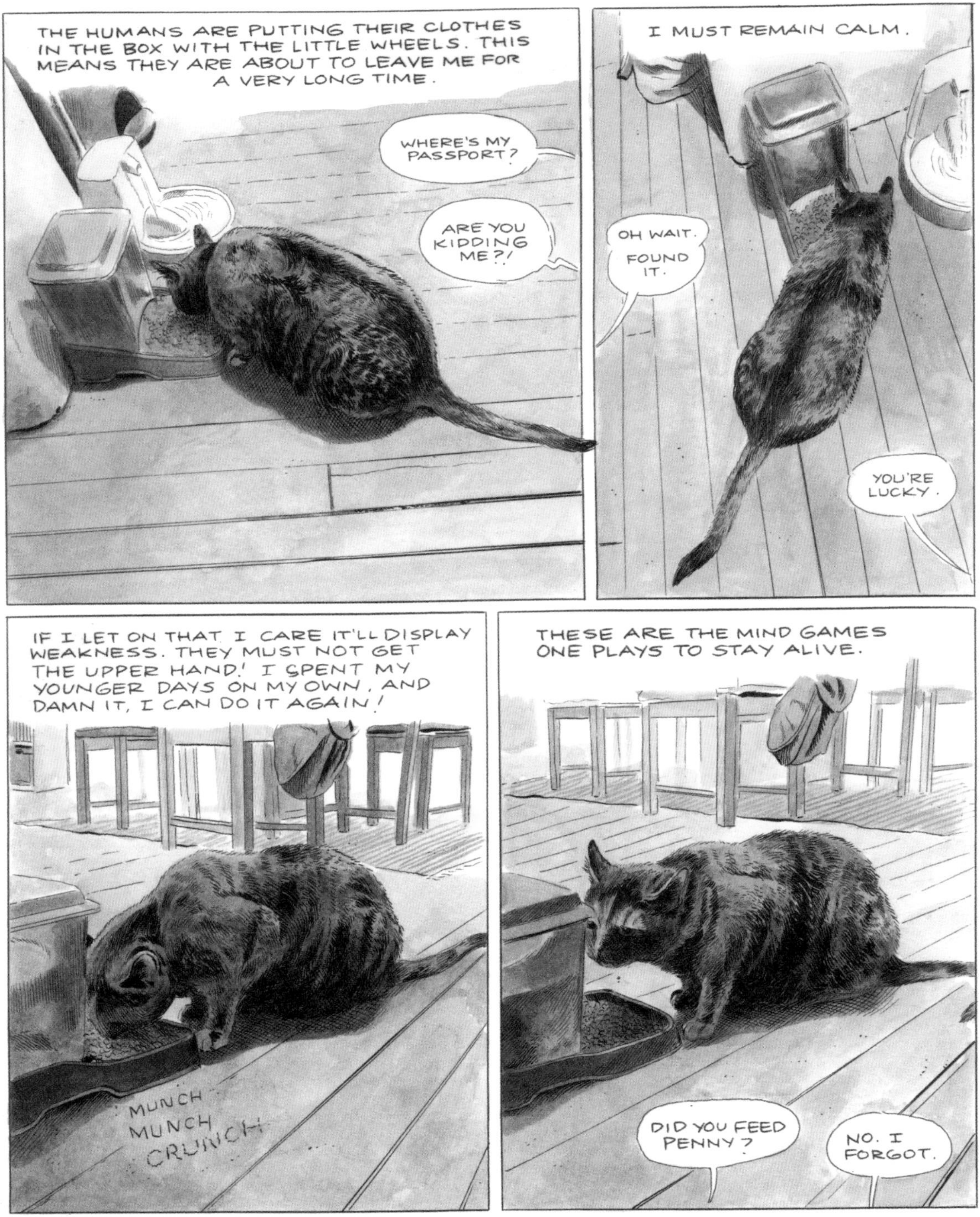
THE HUMANS ARE PUTTING THEIR CLOTHES IN THE BOX WITH THE LITTLE WHEELS. THIS MEANS THEY ARE ABOUT TO LEAVE ME FOR A VERY LONG TIME.
WHERE'S MY PASSPORT?
ARE YOU KIDDING ME?!
I MUST REMAIN CALM.
OH WAIT. FOUND IT.
YOU'RE LUCKY.
IF I LET ON THAT I CARE IT'LL DISPLAY WEAKNESS. THEY MUST NOT GET THE UPPER HAND! I SPENT MY YOUNGER DAYS ON MY OWN, AND DAMN IT, I CAN DO IT AGAIN!
MUNCH MUNCH CRUNCH
THESE ARE THE MIND GAMES ONE PLAYS TO STAY ALIVE.
DID YOU FEED PENNY?
NO. I FORGOT.

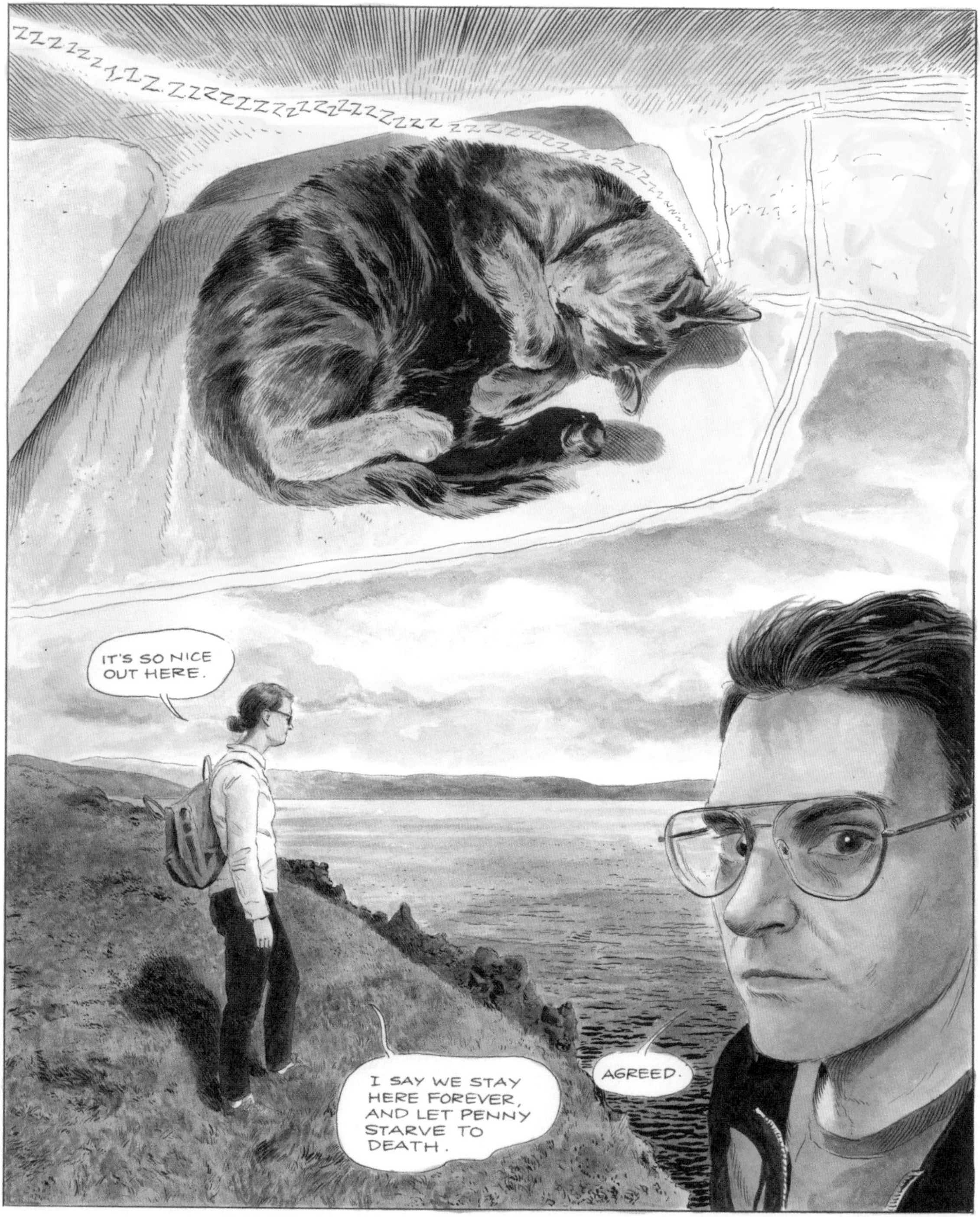
ZZZZZZZZZZZZZZZZZZZZZZZZZZZZZZZZZZZZZZZZZZ
IT'S SO NICE OUT HERE.
I SAY WE STAY HERE FOREVER, AND LET PENNY STARVE TO DEATH.
AGREED.

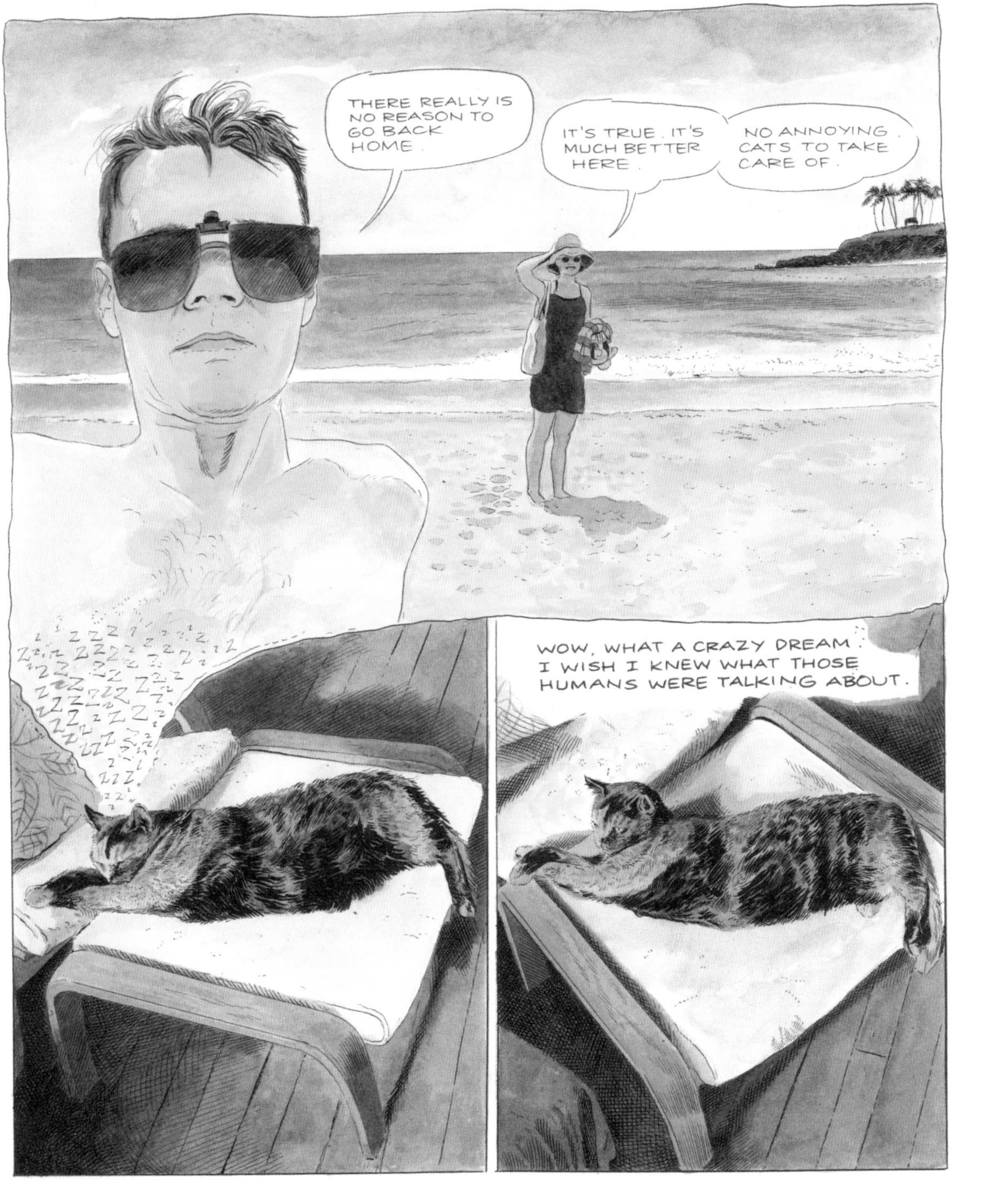
THERE REALLY IS NO REASON TO GO BACK HOME.
IT'S TRUE. IT'S MUCH BETTER HERE.
NO ANNOYING CATS TO TAKE CARE OF.
WOW, WHAT A CRAZY DREAM. I WISH I KNEW WHAT THOSE HUMANS WERE TALKING ABOUT.

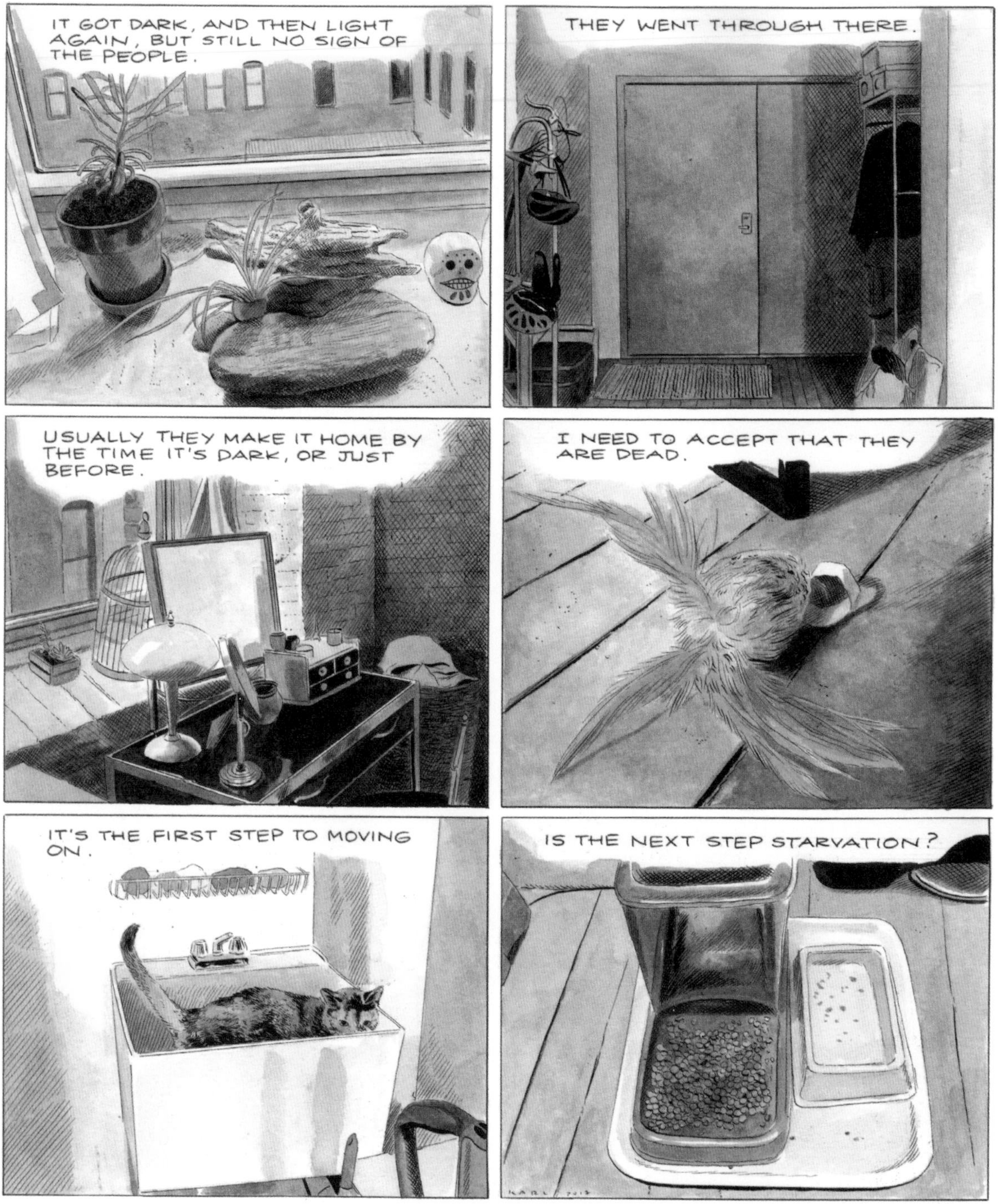
IT GOT DARK, AND THEN LIGHT AGAIN, BUT STILL NO SIGN OF THE PEOPLE.
THEY WENT THROUGH THERE.
USUALLY THEY MAKE IT HOME BY THE TIME IT'S DARK, OR JUST BEFORE.
I NEED TO ACCEPT THAT THEY ARE DEAD.
IT'S THE FIRST STEP TO MOVING ON.
IS THE NEXT STEP STARVATION?

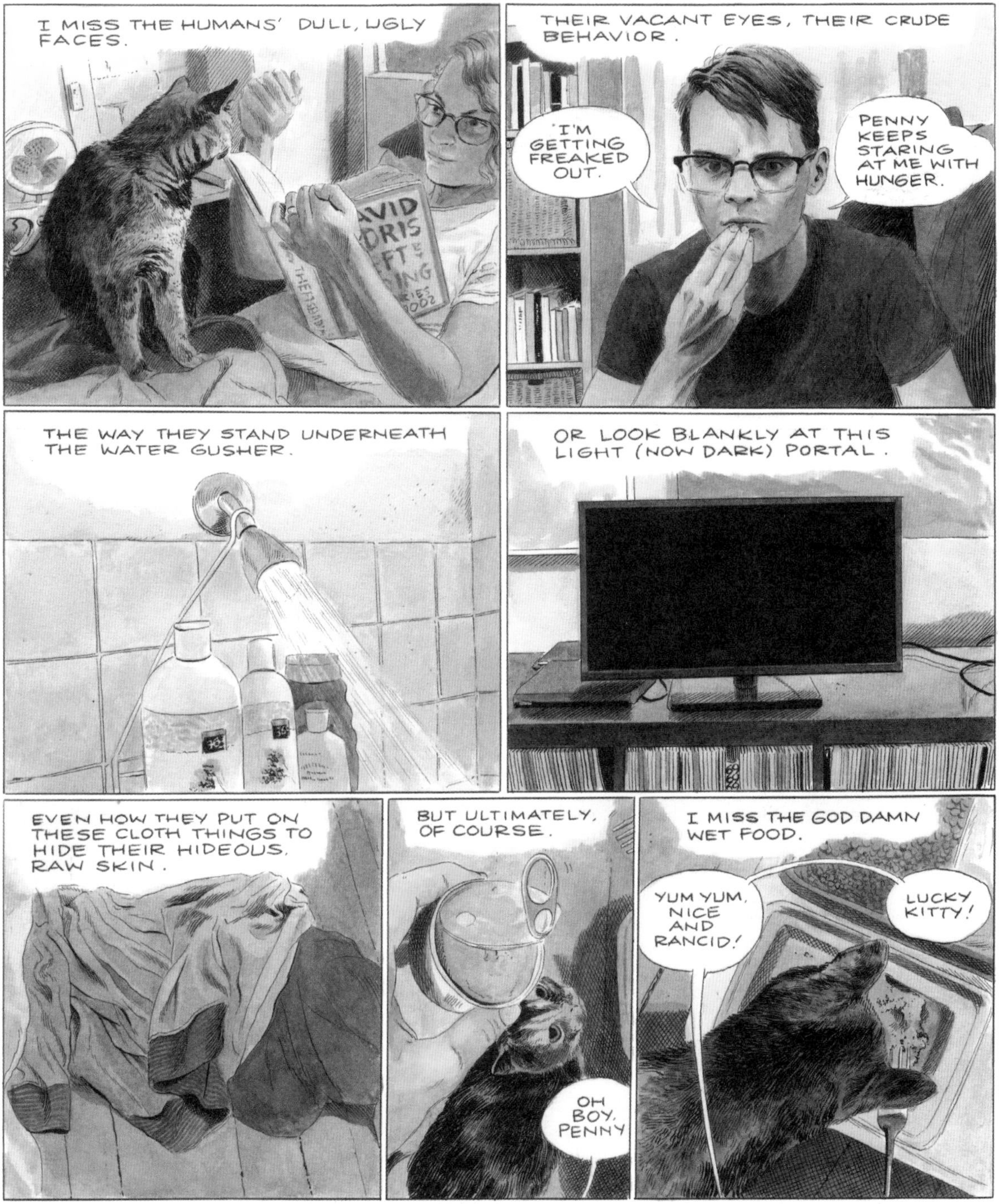
I MISS THE HUMANS' DULL, UGLY FACES.
THEIR VACANT EYES, THEIR CRUDE BEHAVIOR.
I'M GETTING FREAKED OUT.
PENNY KEEPS STARING AT ME WITH HUNGER.
THE WAY THEY STAND UNDERNEATH THE WATER GUSHER.
OR LOOK BLANKLY AT THIS LIGHT (NOW DARK) PORTAL.
EVEN HOW THEY PUT ON THESE CLOTH THINGS TO HIDE THEIR HIDEOUS, RAW SKIN.
BUT ULTIMATELY, OF COURSE.
OH BOY, PENNY
I MISS THE GOD DAMN WET FOOD.
YUM YUM, NICE AND RANCID!
LUCKY KITTY!

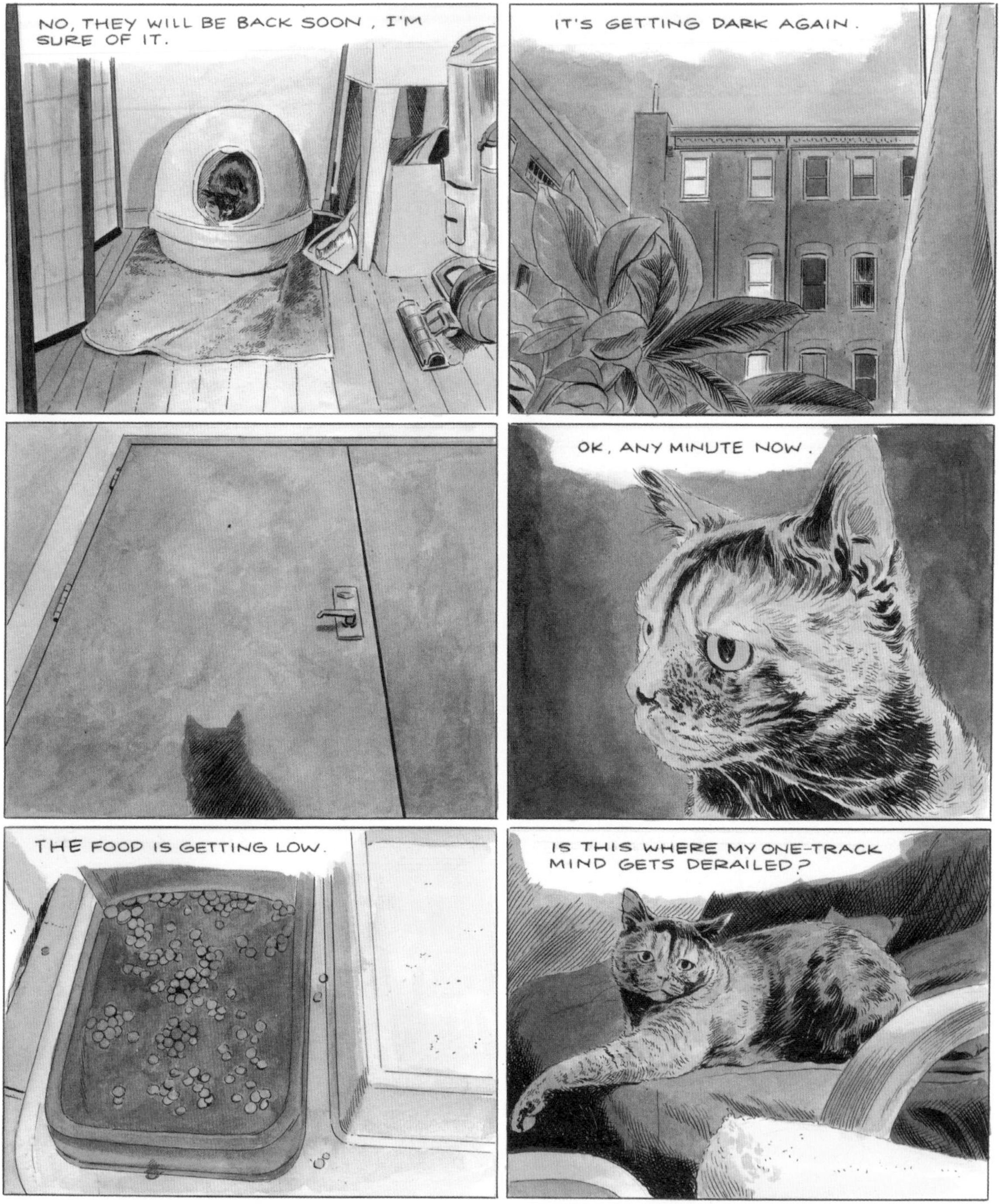
NO, THEY WILL BE BACK SOON, I'M SURE OF IT.
IT'S GETTING DARK AGAIN.
OK, ANY MINUTE NOW.
THE FOOD IS GETTING LOW.
IS THIS WHERE MY ONE-TRACK MIND GETS DERAILED?

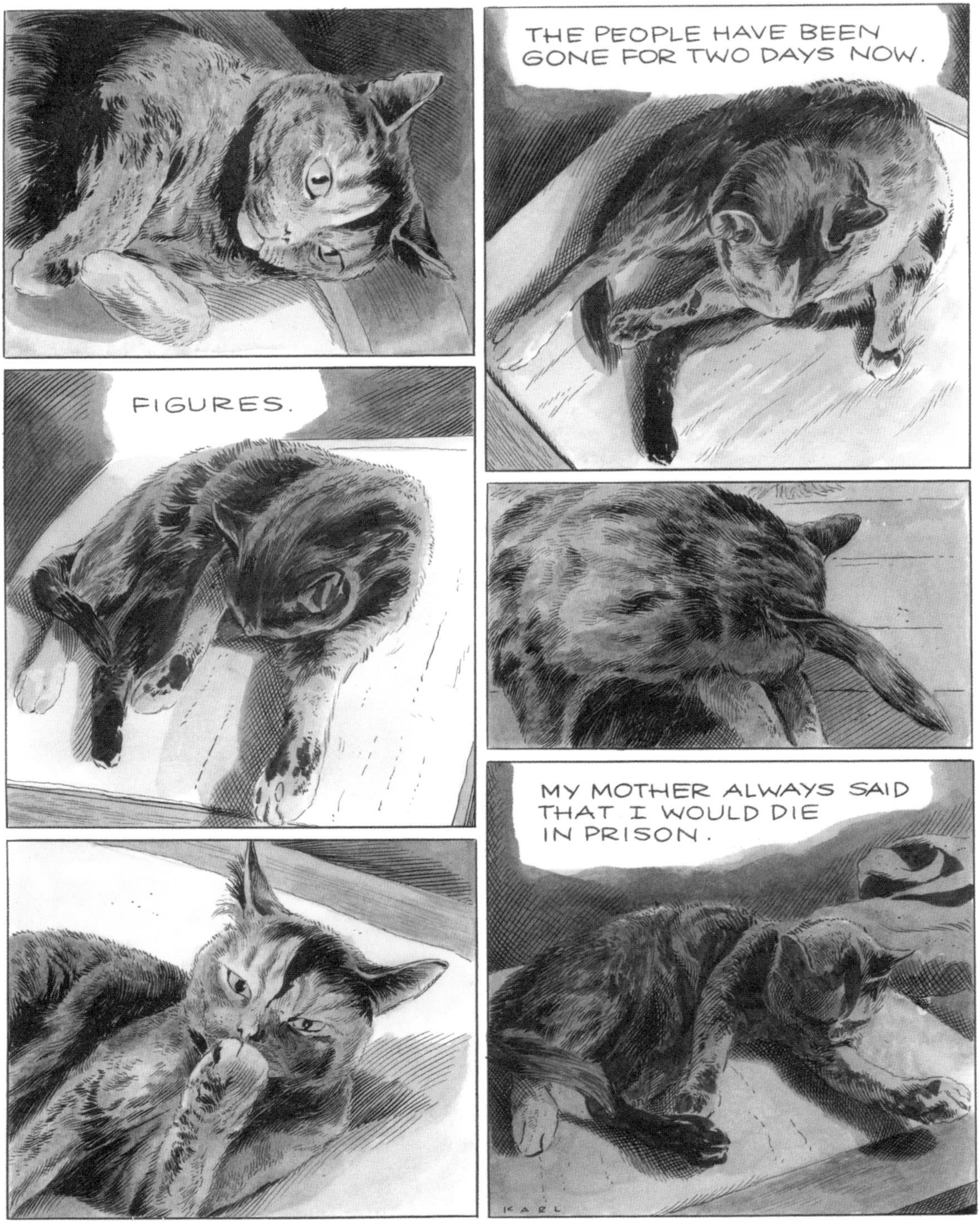
THE PEOPLE HAVE BEEN GONE FOR TWO DAYS NOW.
FIGURES.
MY MOTHER ALWAYS SAID THAT I WOULD DIE IN PRISON.
KARL

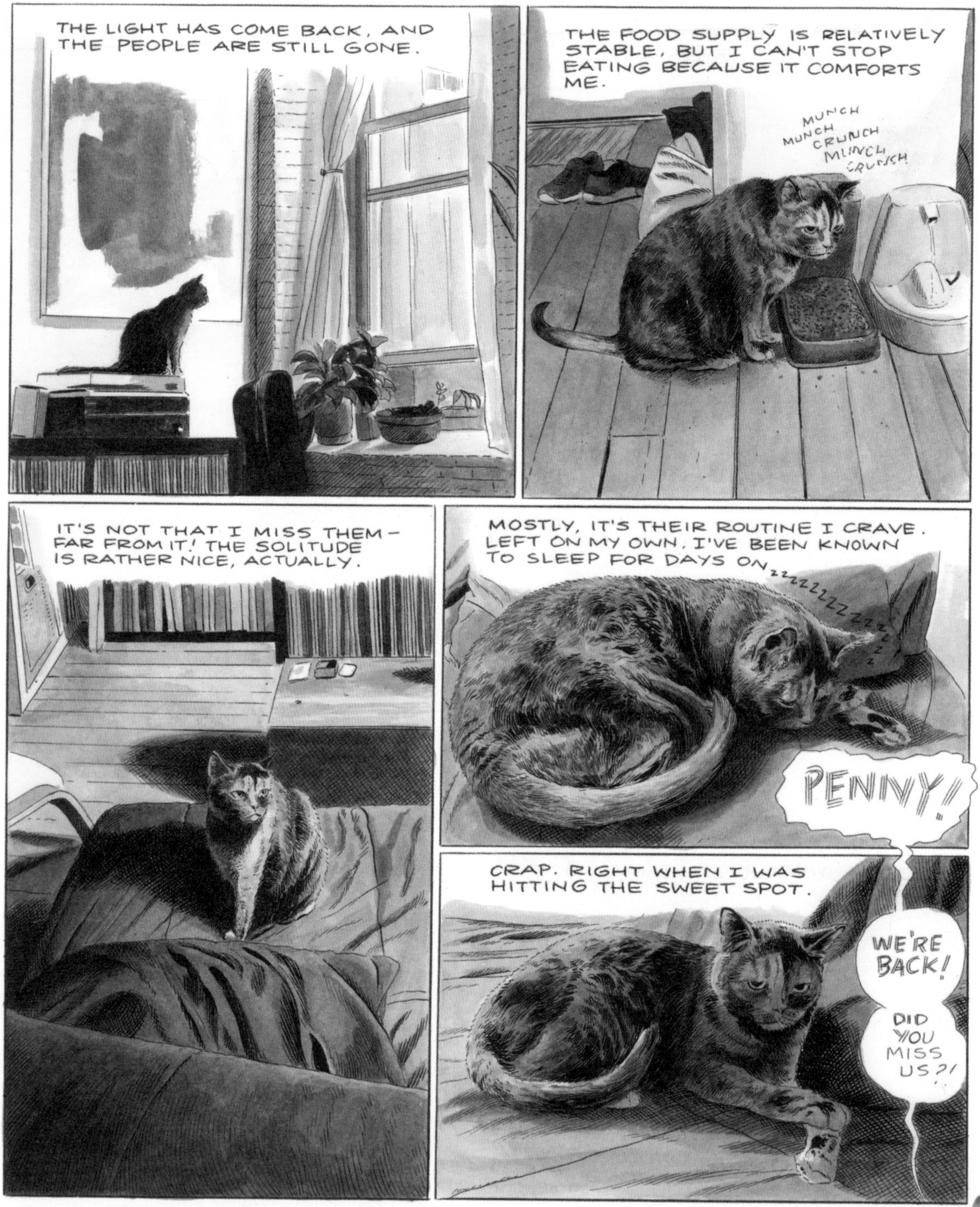
THE LIGHT HAS COME BACK, AND THE PEOPLE ARE STILL GONE.
THE FOOD SUPPLY IS RELATIVELY STABLE, BUT I CAN'T STOP EATING BECAUSE IT COMFORTS ME.
MUNCH MUNCH CRUNCH MUNCH CRUNCH
IT'S NOT THAT I MISS THEM — FAR FROM IT! THE SOLITUDE IS RATHER NICE, ACTUALLY.
MOSTLY, IT'S THEIR ROUTINE I CRAVE. LEFT ON MY OWN, I'VE BEEN KNOWN TO SLEEP FOR DAYS ON
ZZZZZZZZZZZ
PENNY!
CRAP. RIGHT WHEN I WAS HITTING THE SWEET SPOT.
WE'RE BACK!
DID YOU MISS US?!

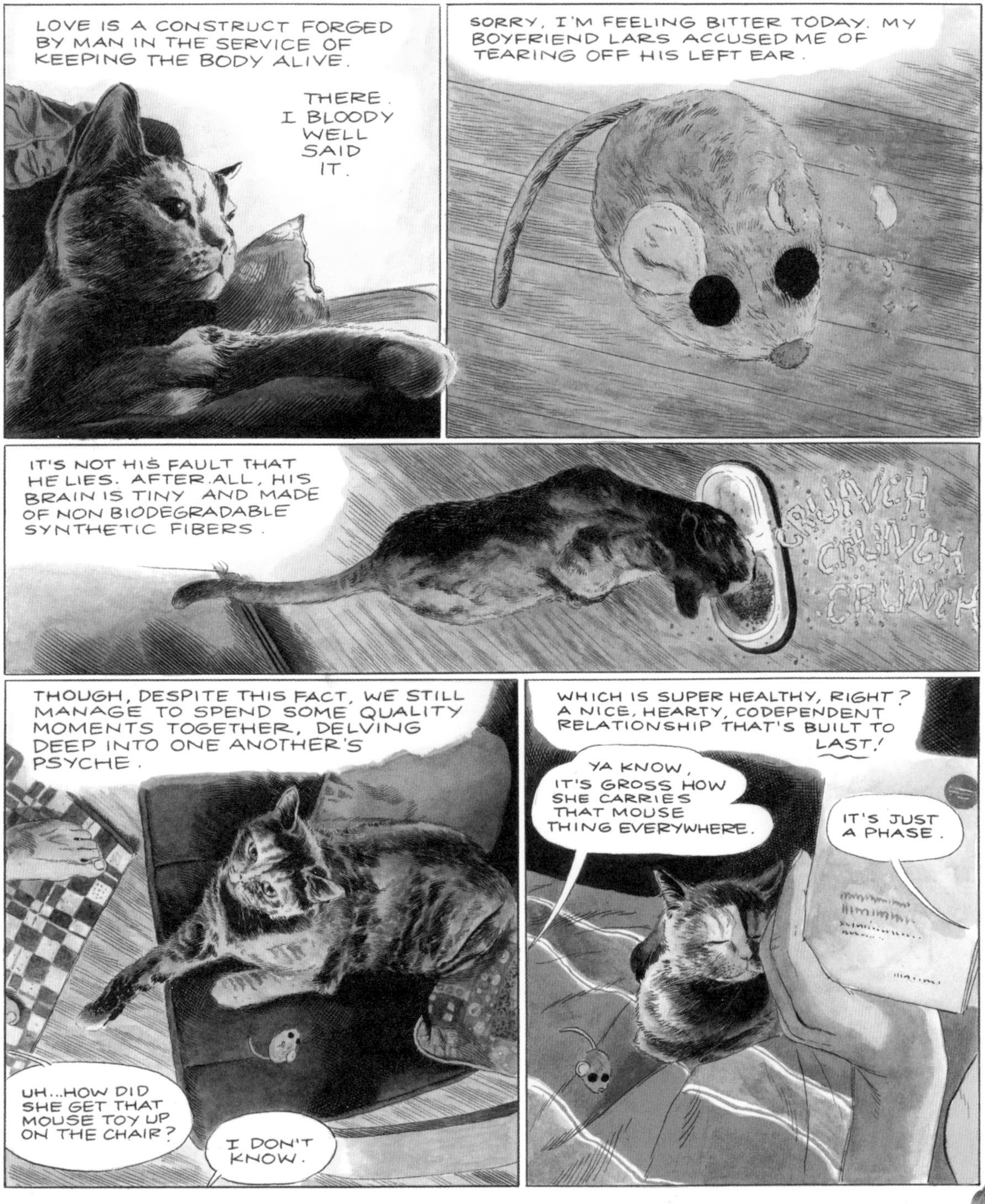
LOVE IS A CONSTRUCT FORGED BY MAN IN THE SERVICE OF KEEPING THE BODY ALIVE.
THERE. I BLOODY WELL SAID IT.
SORRY, I'M FEELING BITTER TODAY. MY BOYFRIEND LARS ACCUSED ME OF TEARING OFF HIS LEFT EAR.
IT'S NOT HIS FAULT THAT HE LIES. AFTER ALL, HIS BRAIN IS TINY AND MADE OF NON BIODEGRADABLE SYNTHETIC FIBERS.
CRUNCH CRUNCH CRUNCH
THOUGH, DESPITE THIS FACT, WE STILL MANAGE TO SPEND SOME QUALITY MOMENTS TOGETHER, DELVING DEEP INTO ONE ANOTHER'S PSYCHE.
UH...HOW DID SHE GET THAT MOUSE TOY UP ON THE CHAIR?
I DON'T KNOW.
WHICH IS SUPER HEALTHY, RIGHT? A NICE, HEARTY, CODEPENDENT RELATIONSHIP THAT'S BUILT TO LAST!
YA KNOW, IT'S GROSS HOW SHE CARRIES THAT MOUSE THING EVERYWHERE.
IT'S JUST A PHASE.

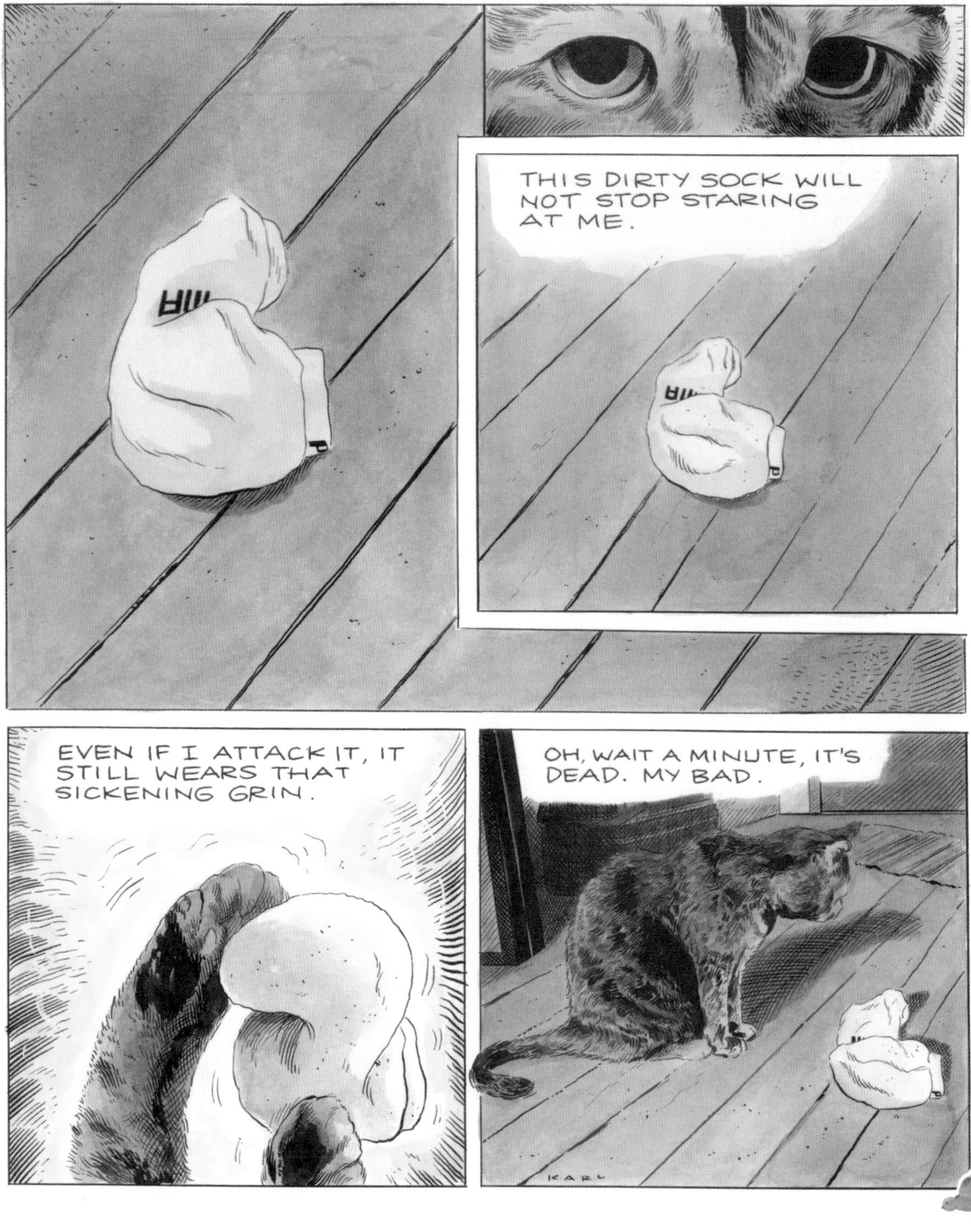
THIS DIRTY SOCK WILL NOT STOP STARING AT ME.
EVEN IF I ATTACK IT, IT STILL WEARS THAT SICKENING GRIN.
OH, WAIT A MINUTE, IT'S DEAD. MY BAD.
KARL

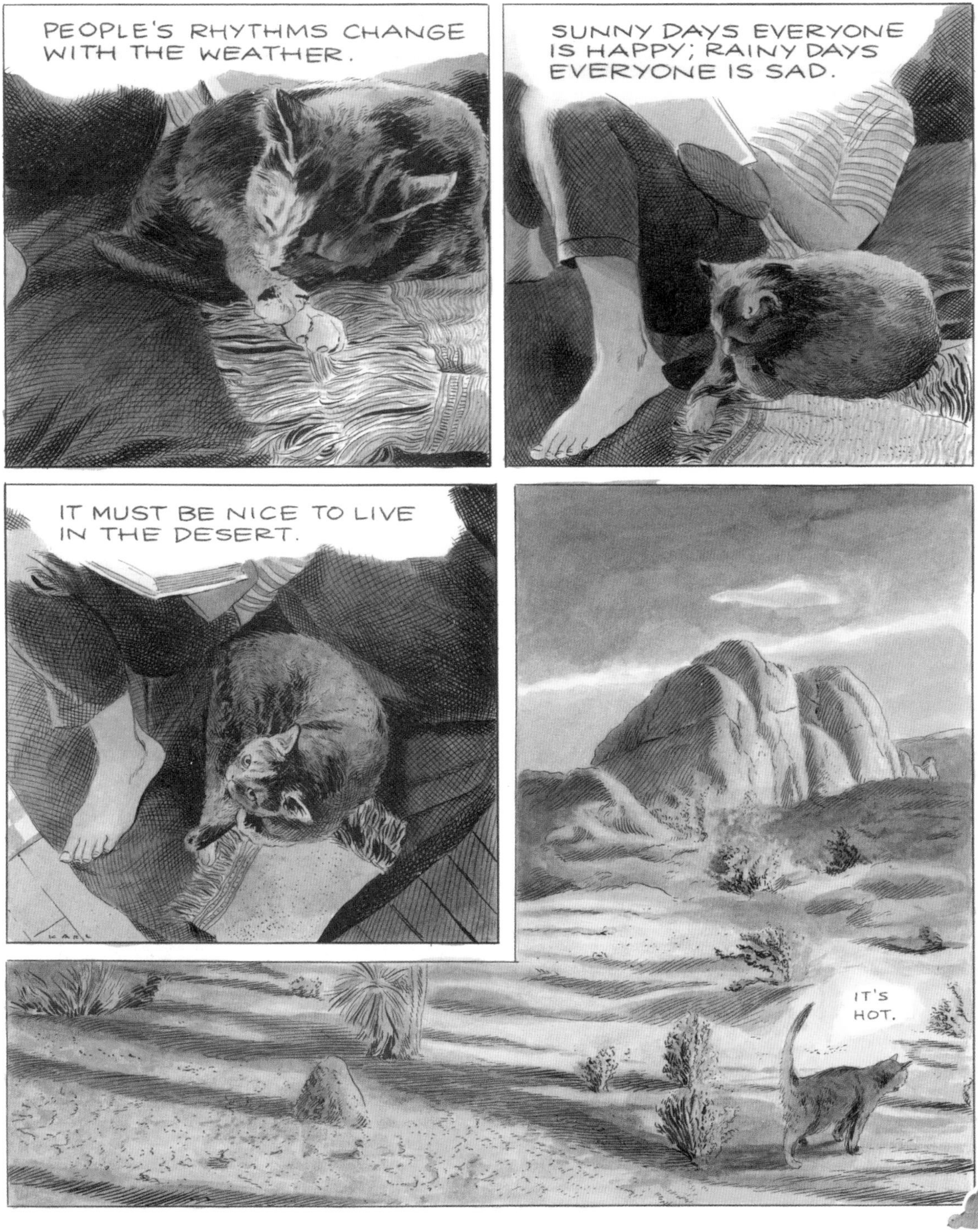
PEOPLE'S RHYTHMS CHANGE WITH THE WEATHER.
SUNNY DAYS EVERYONE IS HAPPY; RAINY DAYS EVERYONE IS SAD.
IT MUST BE NICE TO LIVE IN THE DESERT.
IT'S HOT.

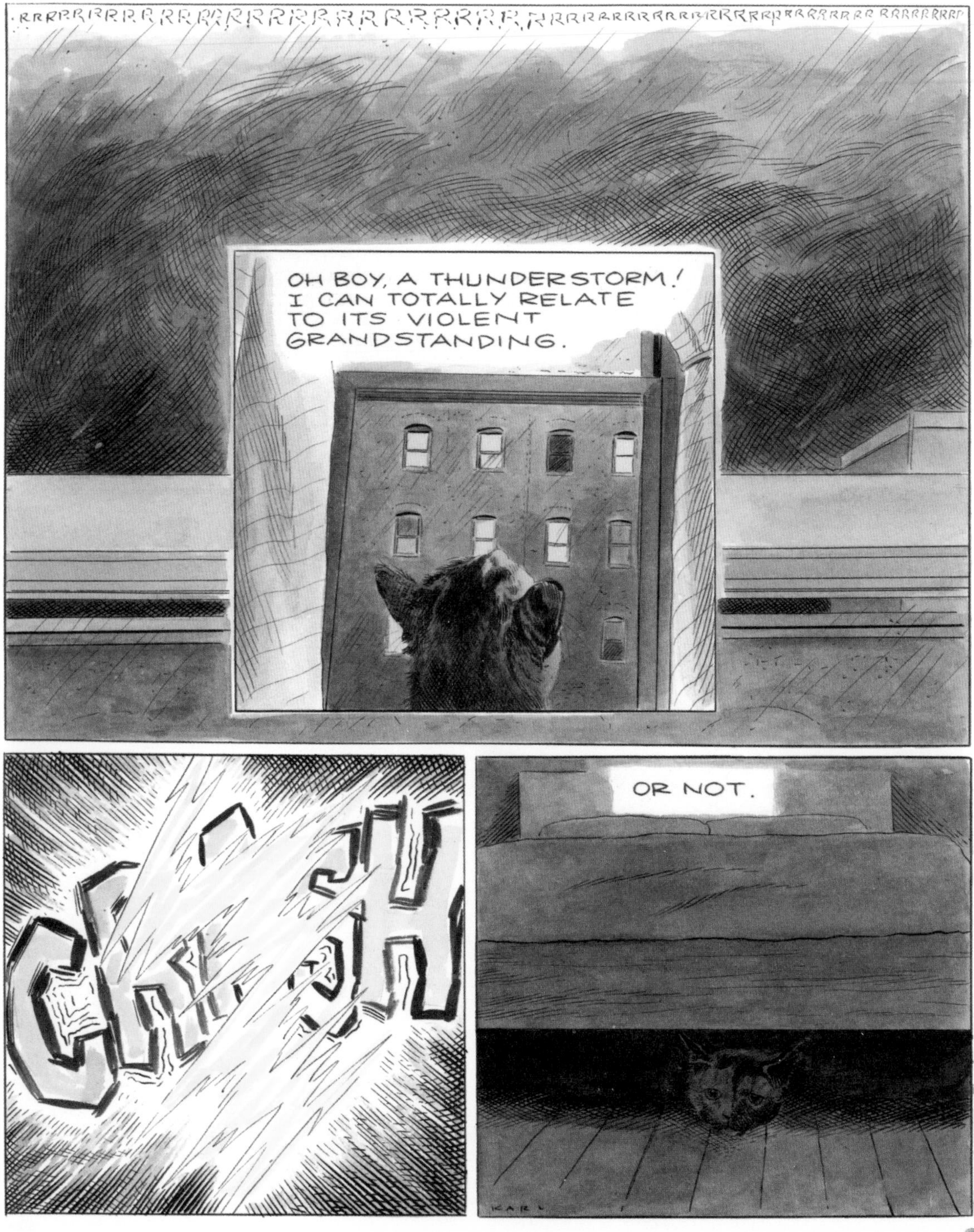
RRRRRRRRRRRRRRRRRRRRRRRRRRRRRRRRRRRRRRRRRRRRRRRRRRRRRRRRRRRRRRRR
OH BOY, A THUNDERSTORM! I CAN TOTALLY RELATE TO ITS VIOLENT GRANDSTANDING.
OR NOT.
KARL

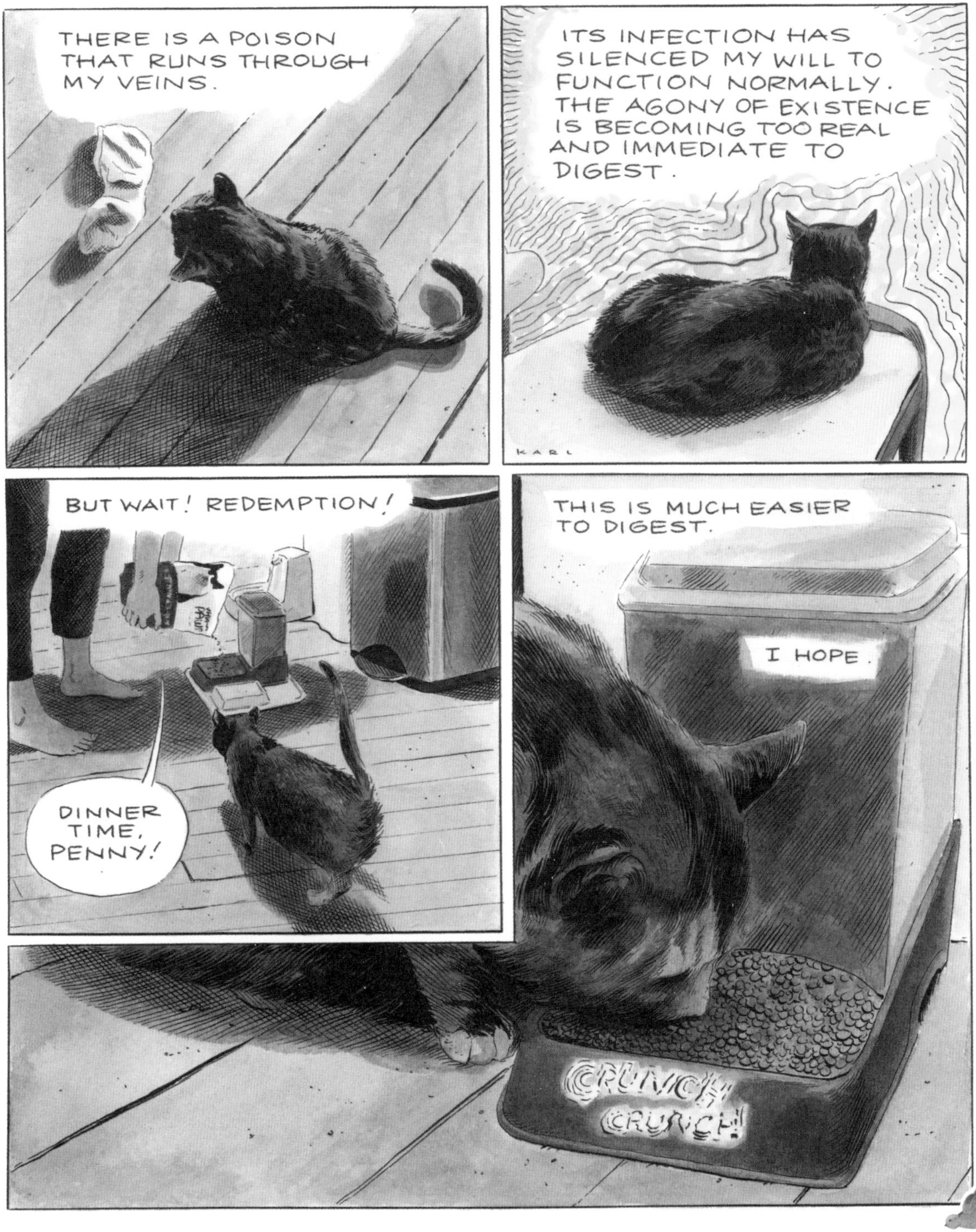
THERE IS A POISON THAT RUNS THROUGH MY VEINS.
ITS INFECTION HAS SILENCED MY WILL TO FUNCTION NORMALLY. THE AGONY OF EXISTENCE IS BECOMING TOO REAL AND IMMEDIATE TO DIGEST.
KARL
BUT WAIT! REDEMPTION!
DINNER TIME, PENNY!
THIS IS MUCH EASIER TO DIGEST.
I HOPE.
CRUNCH CRUNCH!

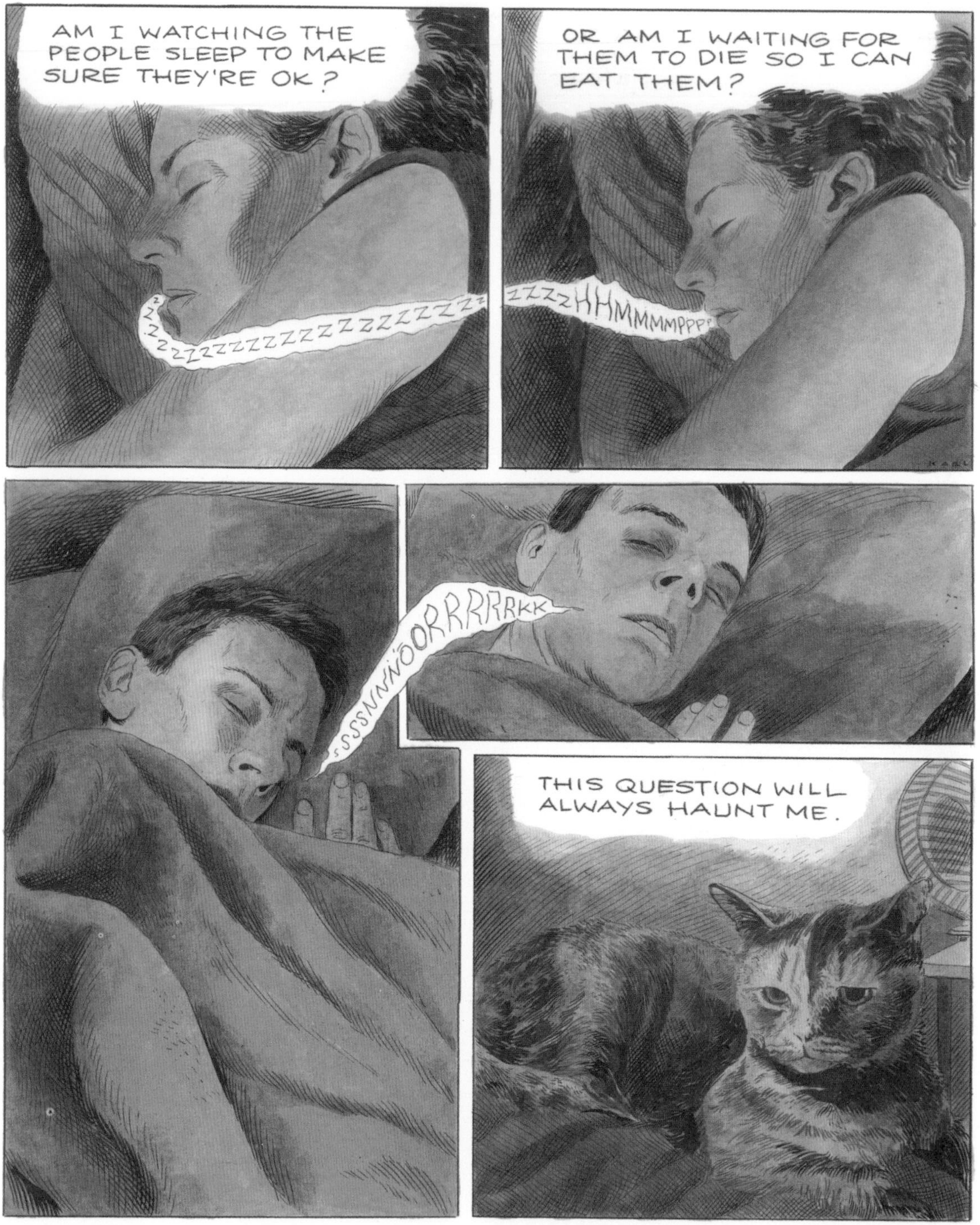
AM I WATCHING THE PEOPLE SLEEP TO MAKE SURE THEY'RE OK?
ZZZZZZZZZZZZZZZZZZZZZZZZZZZ
OR AM I WAITING FOR THEM TO DIE SO I CAN EAT THEM?
ZZZZHHMMMMPPP
SSSNNNÖORRRRRRKK
THIS QUESTION WILL ALWAYS HAUNT ME.

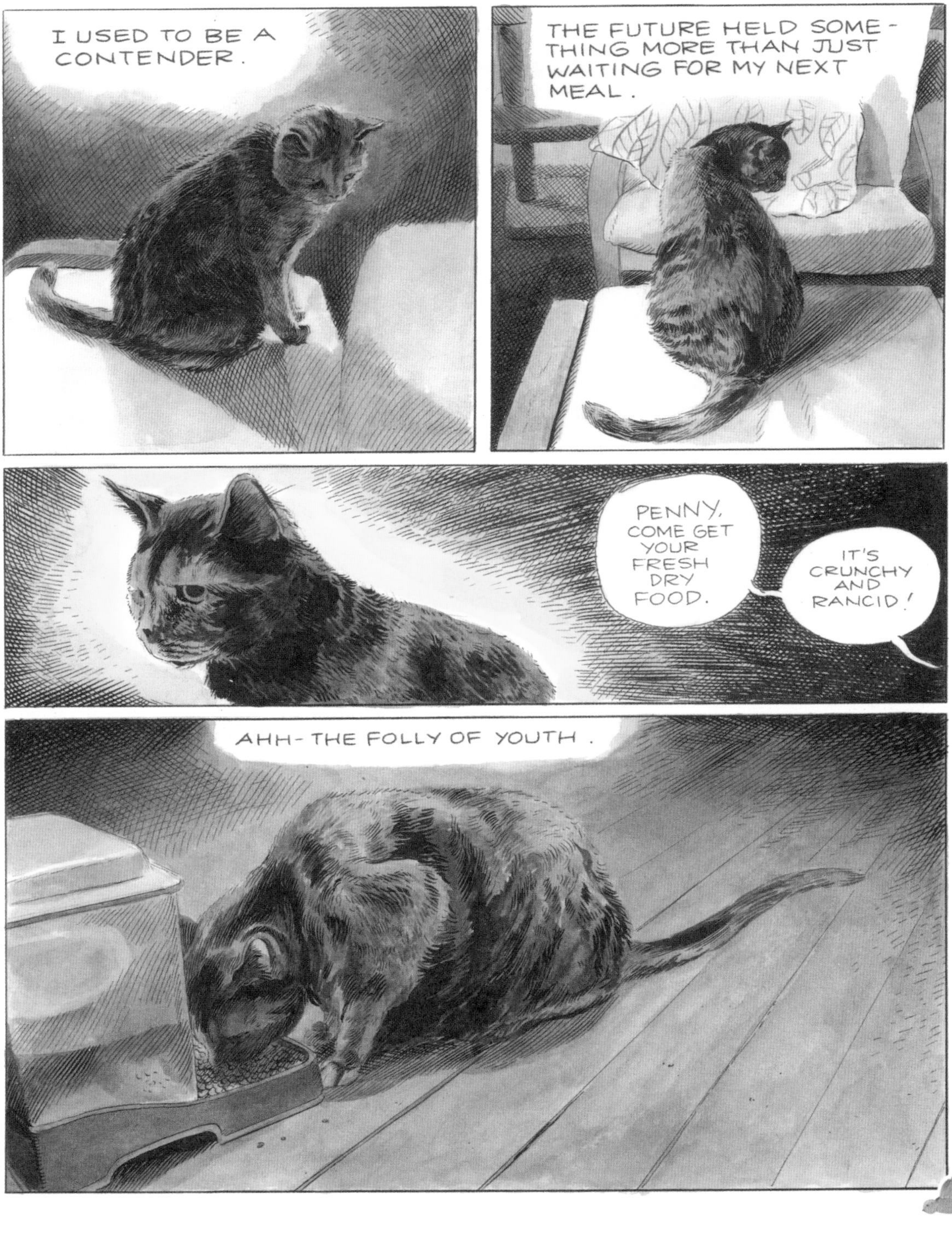
I USED TO BE A CONTENDER.
THE FUTURE HELD SOMETHING MORE THAN JUST WAITING FOR MY NEXT MEAL.
PENNY, COME GET YOUR FRESH DRY FOOD.
IT'S CRUNCHY AND RANCID!
AHH - THE FOLLY OF YOUTH.

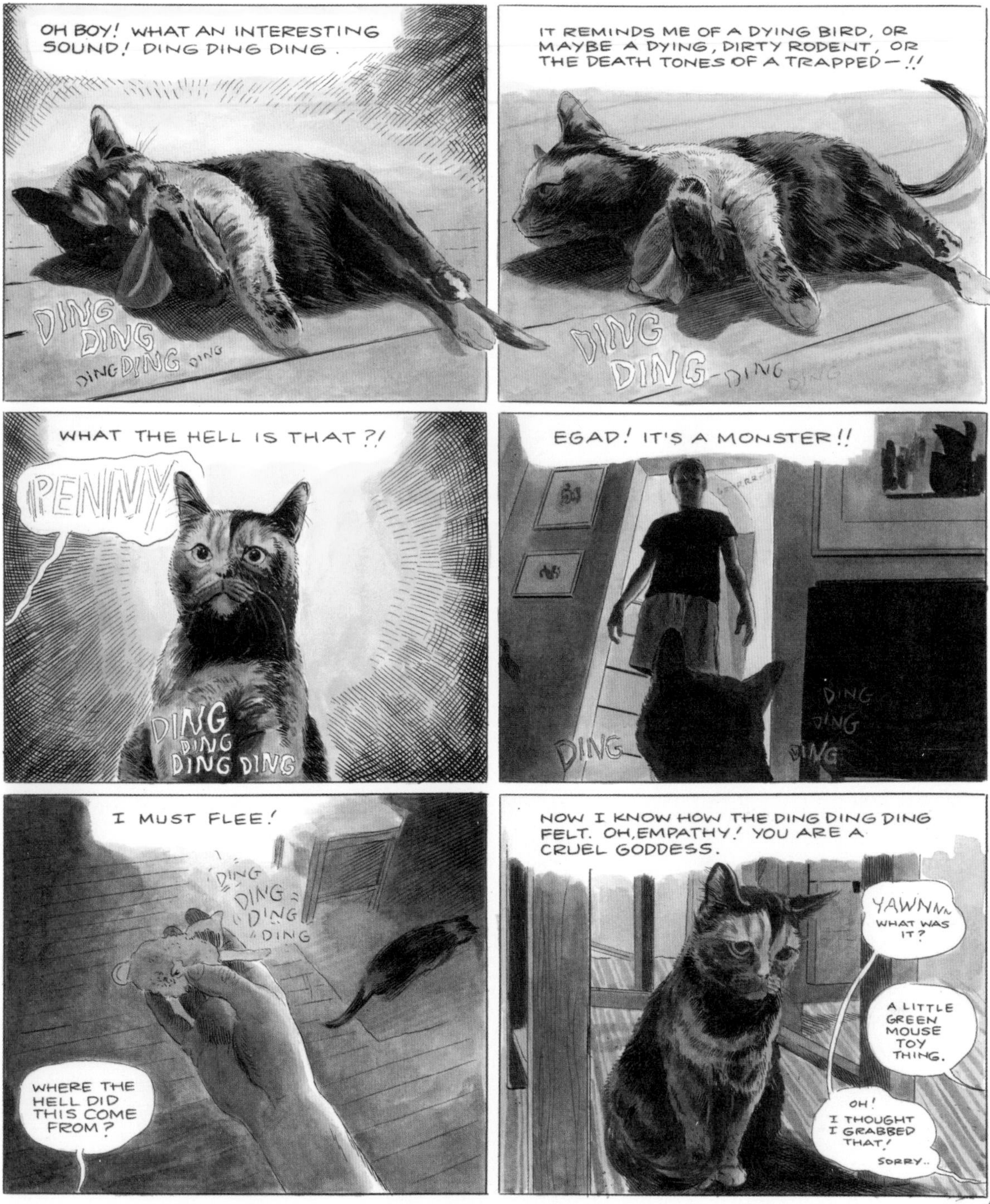
OH BOY! WHAT AN INTERESTING SOUND! DING DING DING.
DING DING DING DING DING
IT REMINDS ME OF A DYING BIRD, OR MAYBE A DYING, DIRTY RODENT, OR THE DEATH TONES OF A TRAPPED—!!
DING DING-DING DING
WHAT THE HELL IS THAT?!
PENNY
DING DING DING DING
EGAD! IT'S A MONSTER!!
DING DING DING DING
I MUST FLEE!
DING DING DING DING
WHERE THE HELL DID THIS COME FROM?
NOW I KNOW HOW THE DING DING DING FELT. OH, EMPATHY! YOU ARE A CRUEL GODDESS.
YAWNNN WHAT WAS IT?
A LITTLE GREEN MOUSE TOY THING.
OH! I THOUGHT I GRABBED THAT! SORRY..

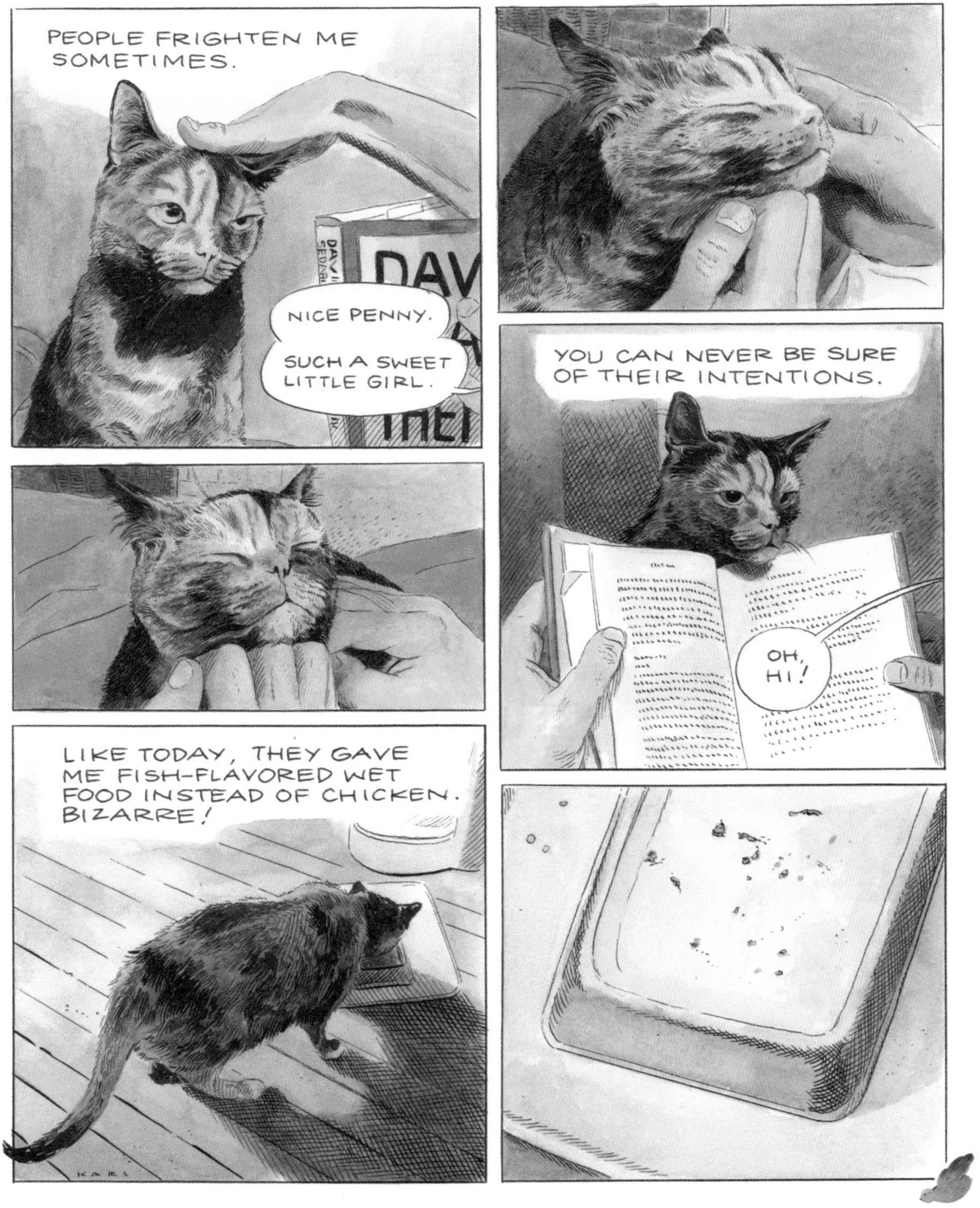
PEOPLE FRIGHTEN ME SOMETIMES.
NICE PENNY.
SUCH A SWEET LITTLE GIRL.
YOU CAN NEVER BE SURE OF THEIR INTENTIONS.
OH, HI!
LIKE TODAY, THEY GAVE ME FISH-FLAVORED WET FOOD INSTEAD OF CHICKEN. BIZARRE!

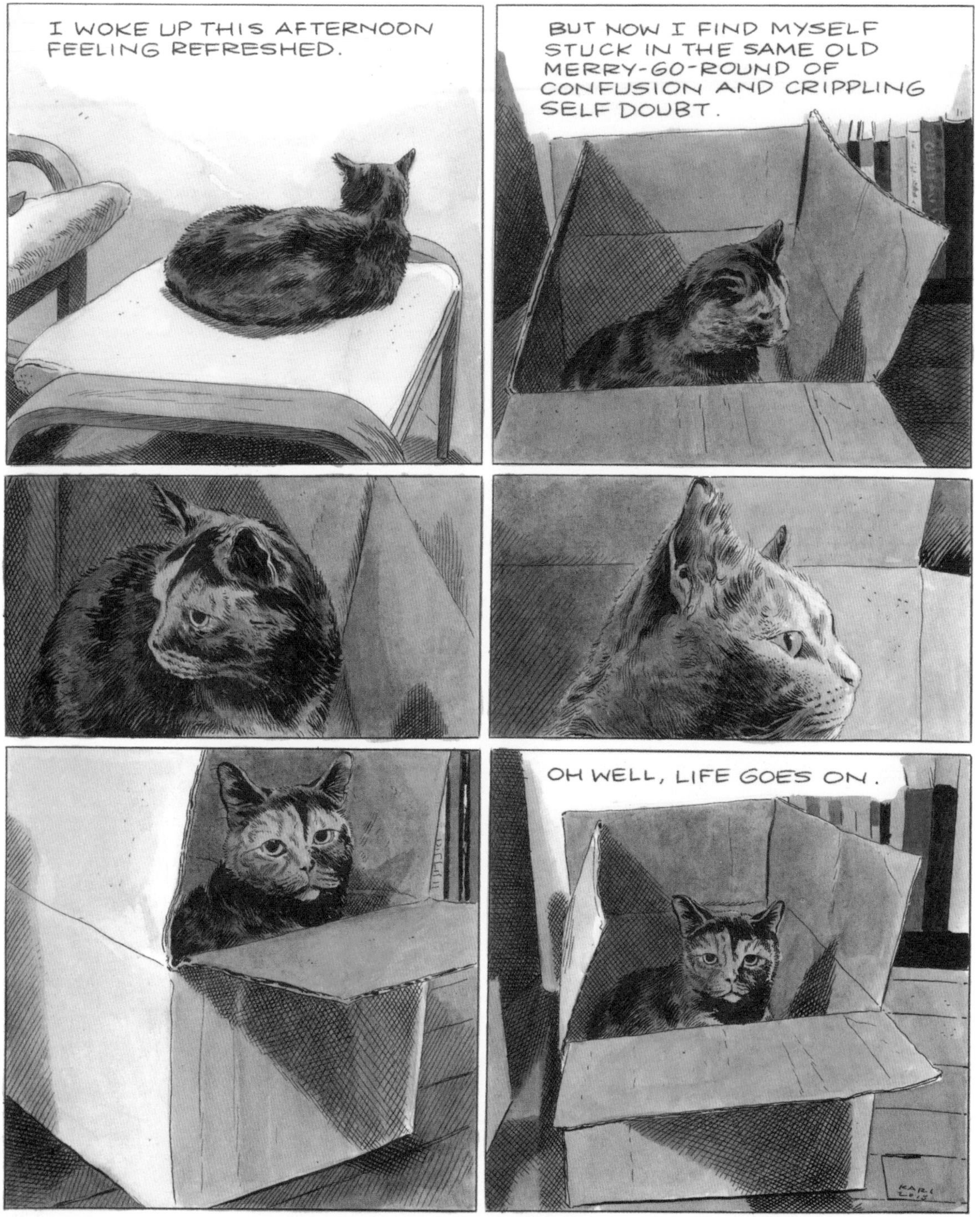
I WOKE UP THIS AFTERNOON FEELING REFRESHED.
BUT NOW I FIND MYSELF STUCK IN THE SAME OLD MERRY-GO-ROUND OF CONFUSION AND CRIPPLING SELF DOUBT.
OH WELL, LIFE GOES ON.

WHAT THE — ?!

A PORTAL OF SOME KIND HAS OPENED UP AROUND HENRY'S CARCASS.

ITS VELVETY-SMOOTH INCANTATIONS ARE TEMPTING ME TO ENTER IT.

BUT HOW COULD I ABANDON THIS LIFE OF COMFORT AND STABILITY? ISN'T THIS WHAT IT'S ALL ABOUT?

AWWW, LOOK! PENNY'S BEING AFFECTIONATE.

WHY ARE YOU SITTING ON THE FLOOR?

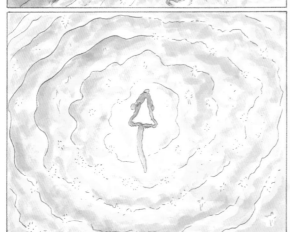

I'M NO GOOD AT THE BIG DECISIONS.

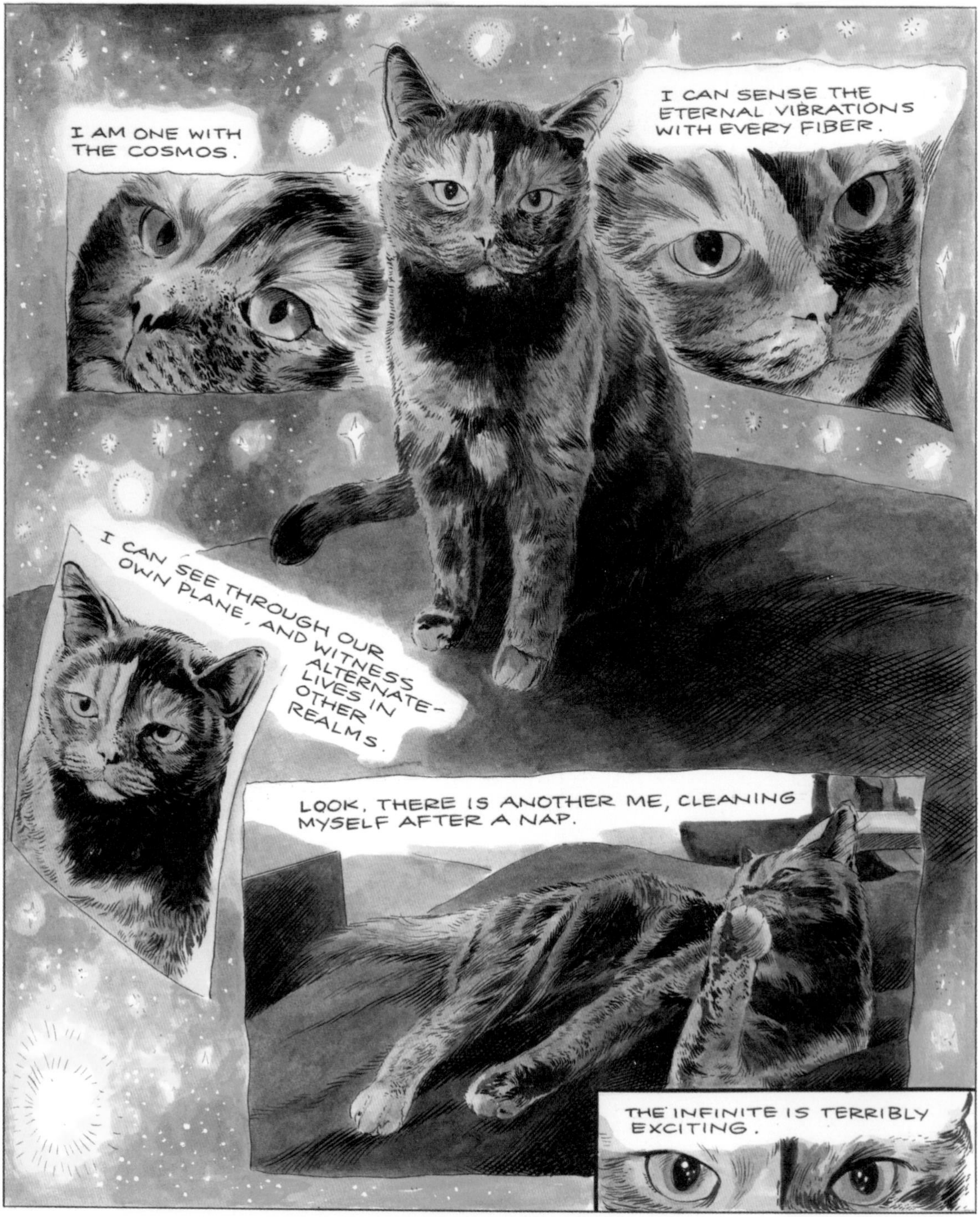
I AM ONE WITH THE COSMOS.
I CAN SENSE THE ETERNAL VIBRATIONS WITH EVERY FIBER.
I CAN SEE THROUGH OUR OWN PLANE, AND WITNESS ALTERNATE-LIVES IN OTHER REALMS.
LOOK. THERE IS ANOTHER ME, CLEANING MYSELF AFTER A NAP.
THE INFINITE IS TERRIBLY EXCITING.

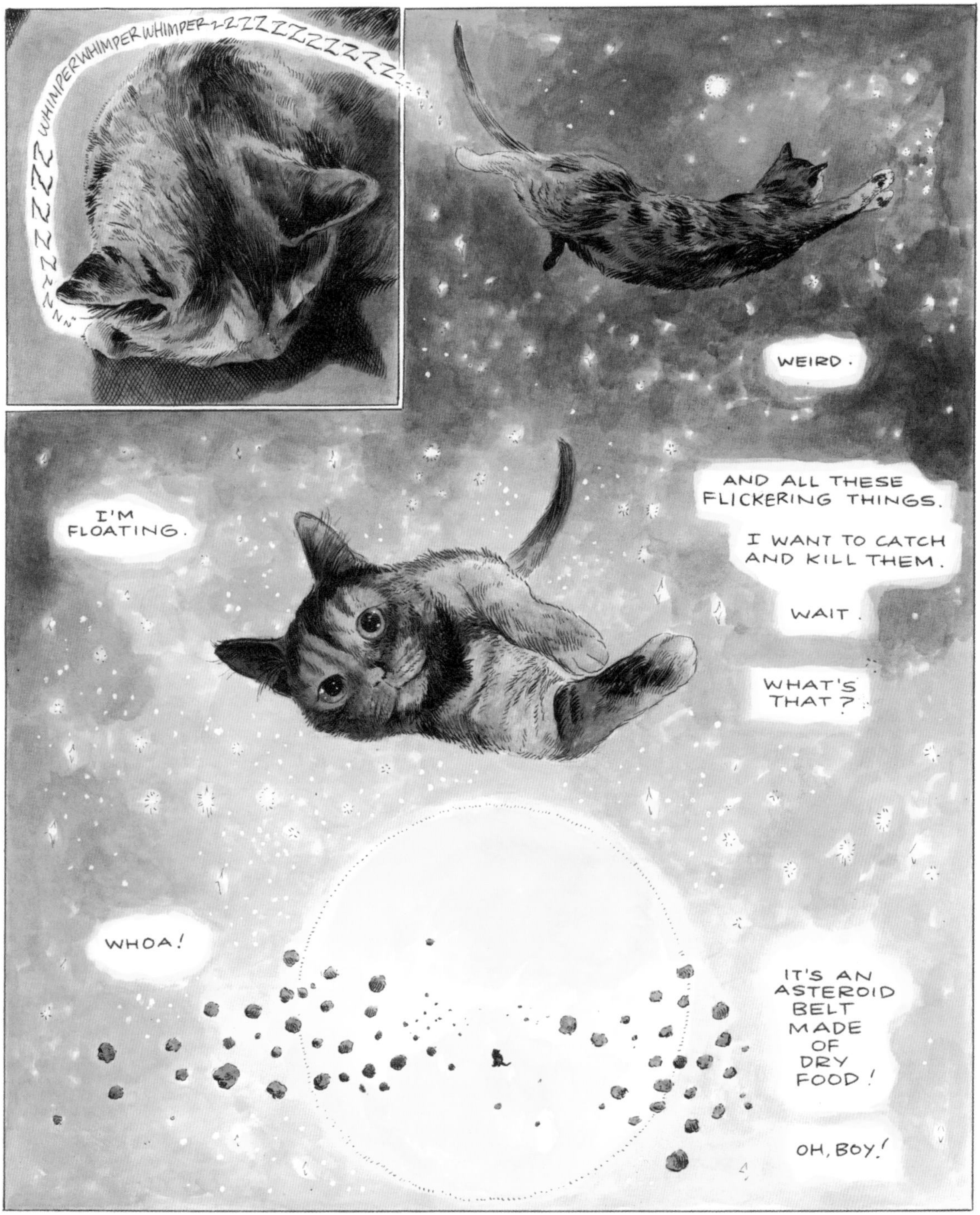
WHIMPERWHIMPERWHIMPER-Z-ZZZZZZZZZZZZ
WEIRD.
I'M FLOATING.
AND ALL THESE FLICKERING THINGS.
I WANT TO CATCH AND KILL THEM.
WAIT.
WHAT'S THAT?
WHOA!
IT'S AN ASTEROID BELT MADE OF DRY FOOD!
OH, BOY!

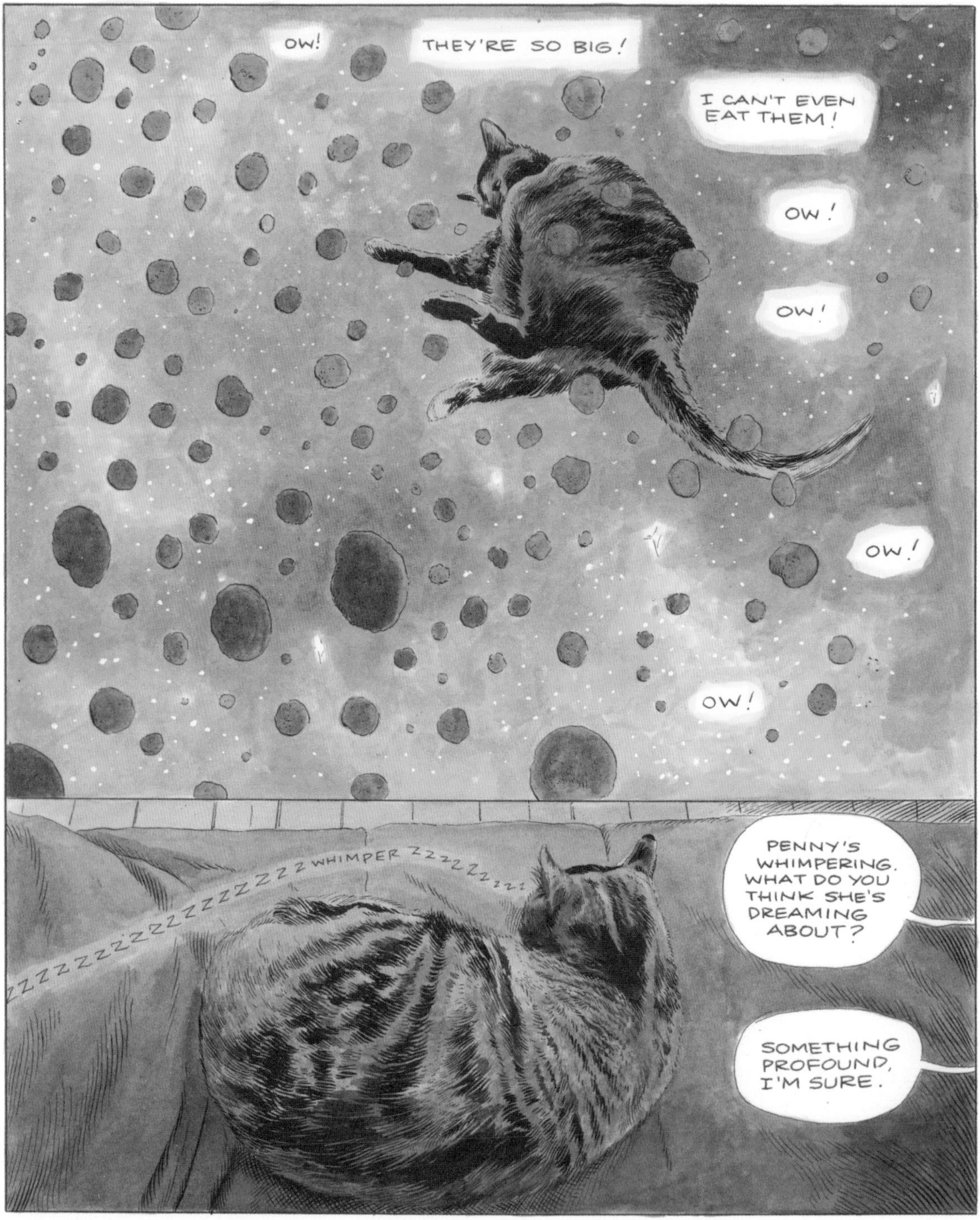
OW!
THEY'RE SO BIG!
I CAN'T EVEN EAT THEM!
OW!
OW!
OW!
OW!
ZZZZZZZZZZZZZZZZZZZZZZZZZWHIMPER ZZZZZZZZZZ
PENNY'S WHIMPERING. WHAT DO YOU THINK SHE'S DREAMING ABOUT?
SOMETHING PROFOUND, I'M SURE.

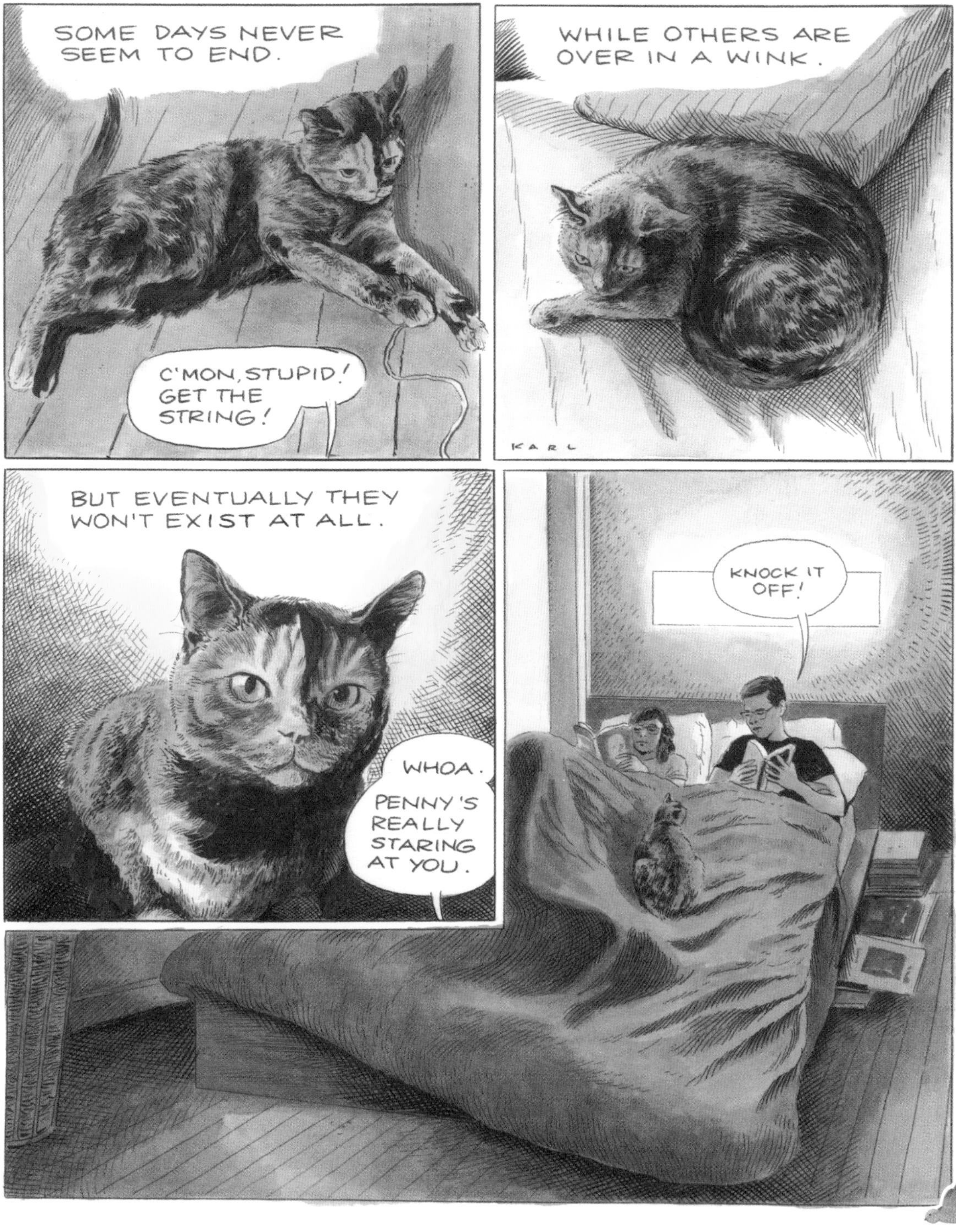
SOME DAYS NEVER SEEM TO END.
C'MON, STUPID! GET THE STRING!
WHILE OTHERS ARE OVER IN A WINK.
KARL
BUT EVENTUALLY THEY WON'T EXIST AT ALL.
WHOA.
PENNY'S REALLY STARING AT YOU.
KNOCK IT OFF!

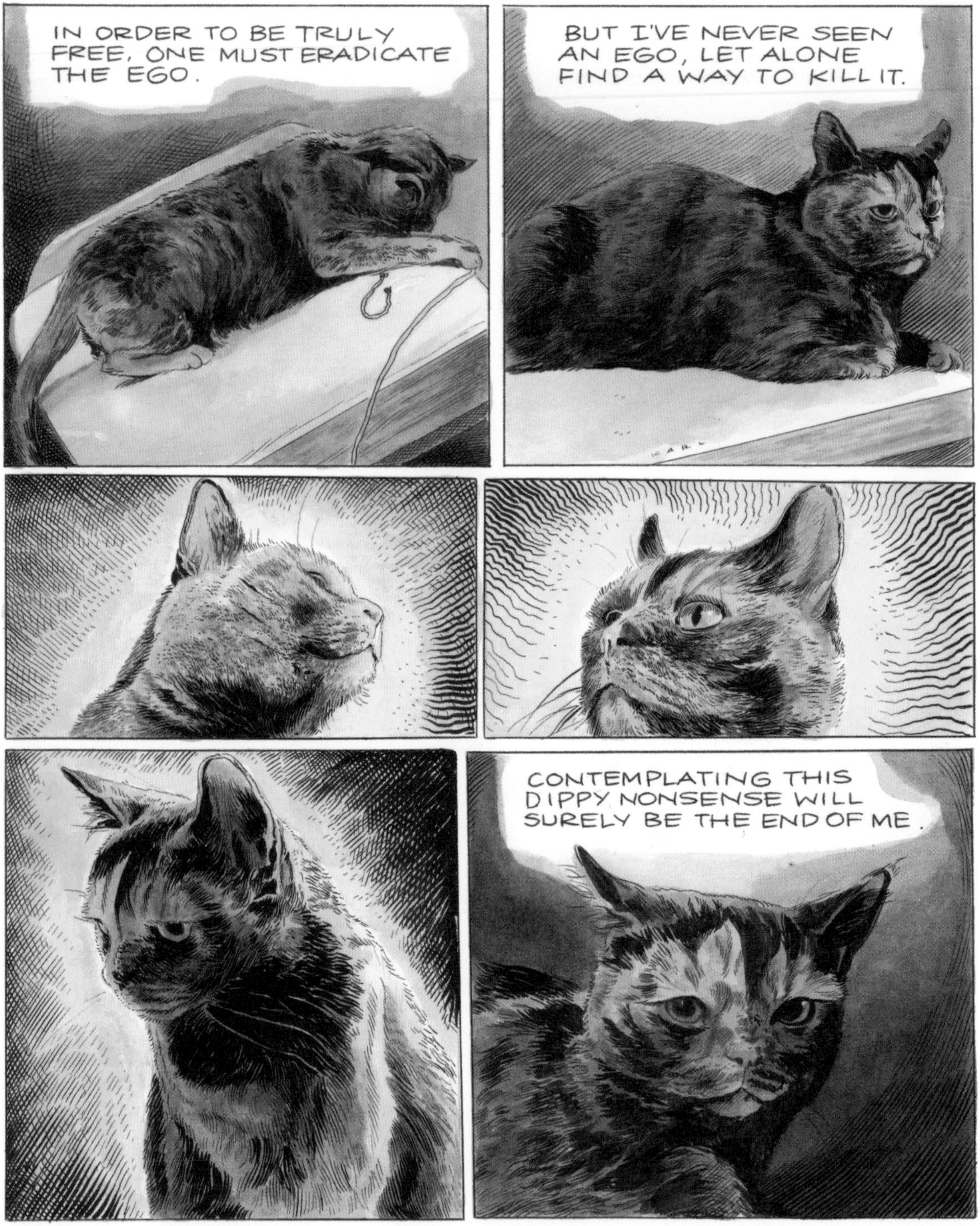
IN ORDER TO BE TRULY FREE, ONE MUST ERADICATE THE EGO.
BUT I'VE NEVER SEEN AN EGO, LET ALONE FIND A WAY TO KILL IT.
CONTEMPLATING THIS DIPPY NONSENSE WILL SURELY BE THE END OF ME.

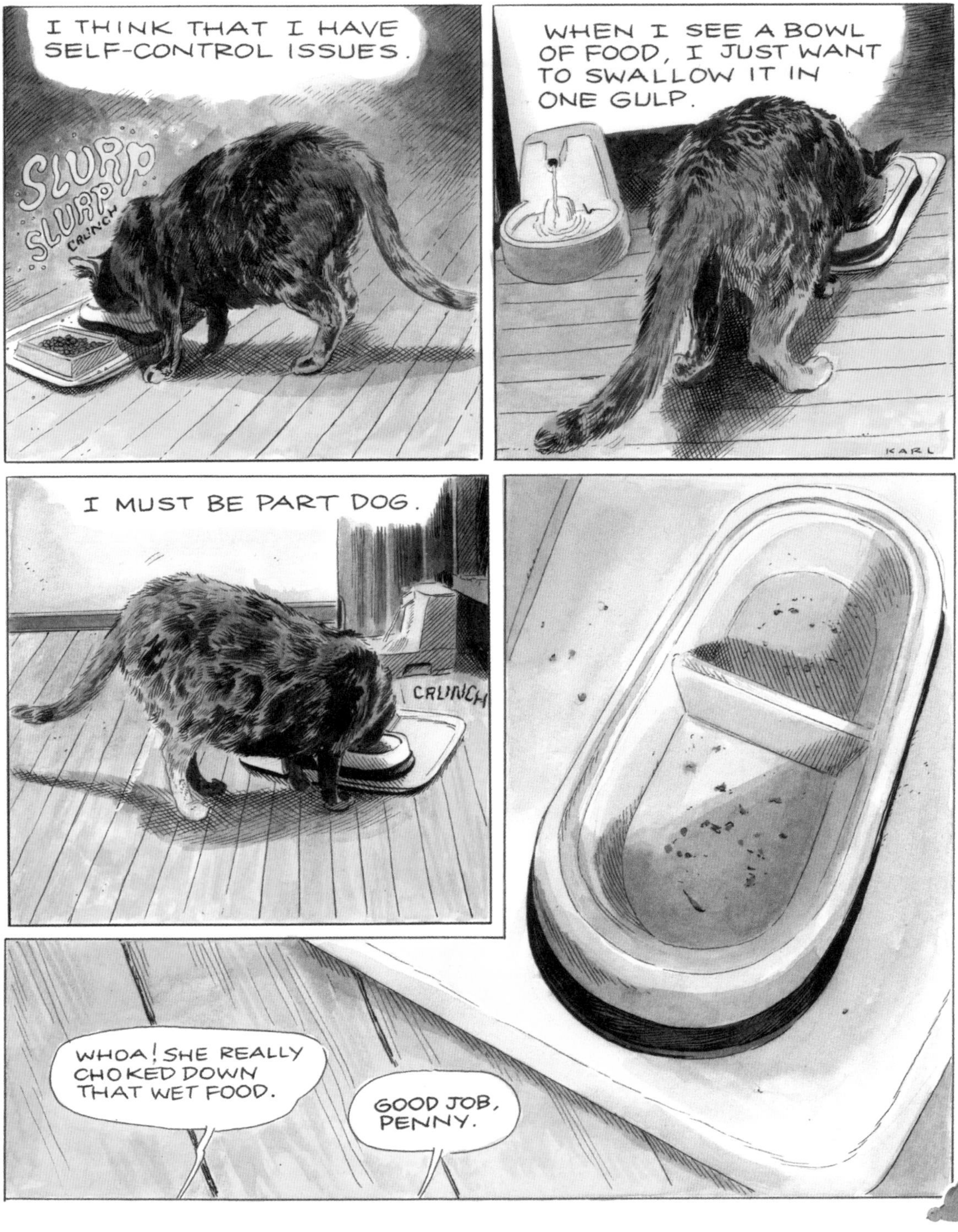
I THINK THAT I HAVE SELF-CONTROL ISSUES.
SLURP
SLURP
CRUNCH
WHEN I SEE A BOWL OF FOOD, I JUST WANT TO SWALLOW IT IN ONE GULP.
KARL
I MUST BE PART DOG.
CRUNCH
WHOA! SHE REALLY CHOKED DOWN THAT WET FOOD.
GOOD JOB, PENNY.

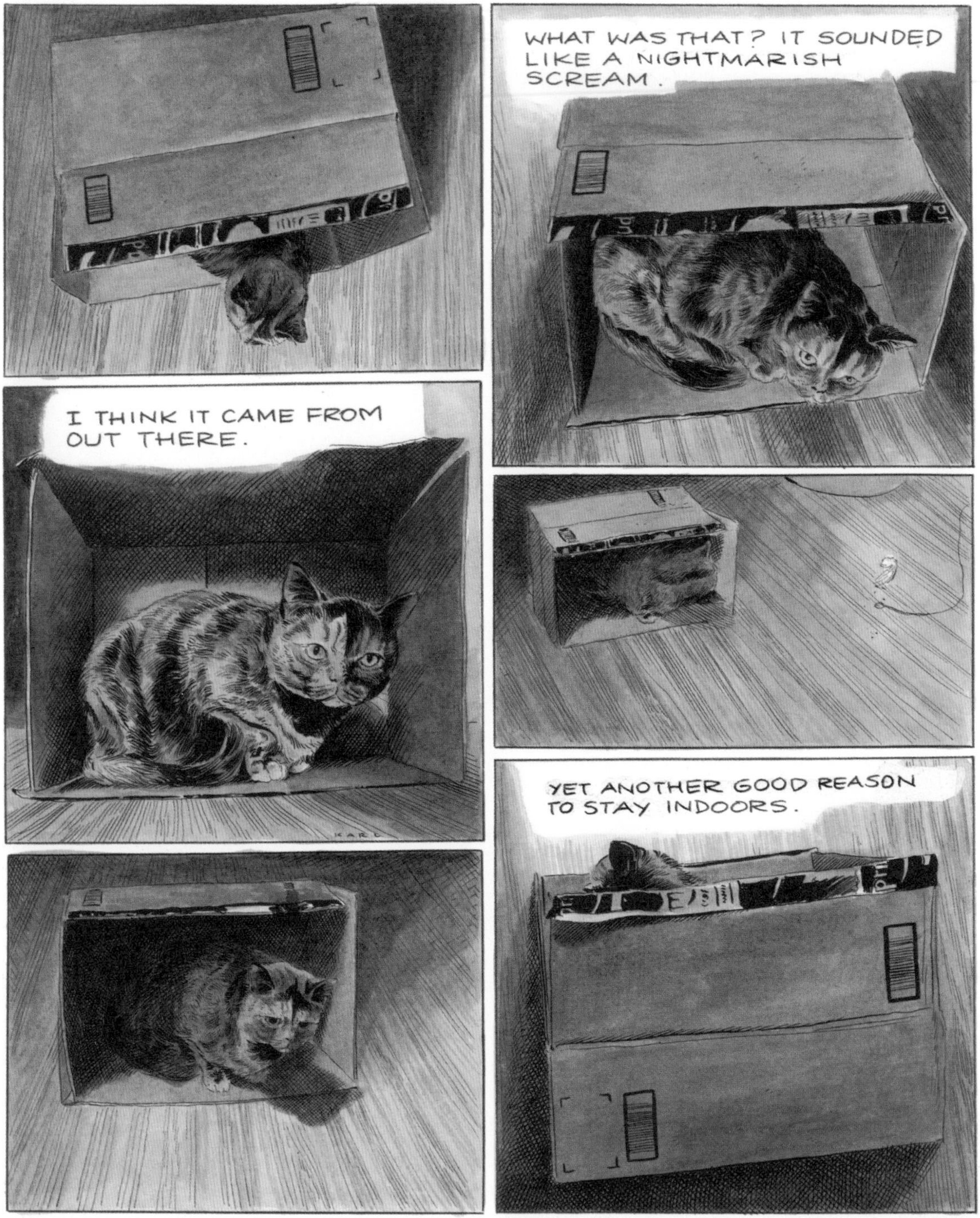
WHAT WAS THAT? IT SOUNDED LIKE A NIGHTMARISH SCREAM.
I THINK IT CAME FROM OUT THERE.
YET ANOTHER GOOD REASON TO STAY INDOORS.

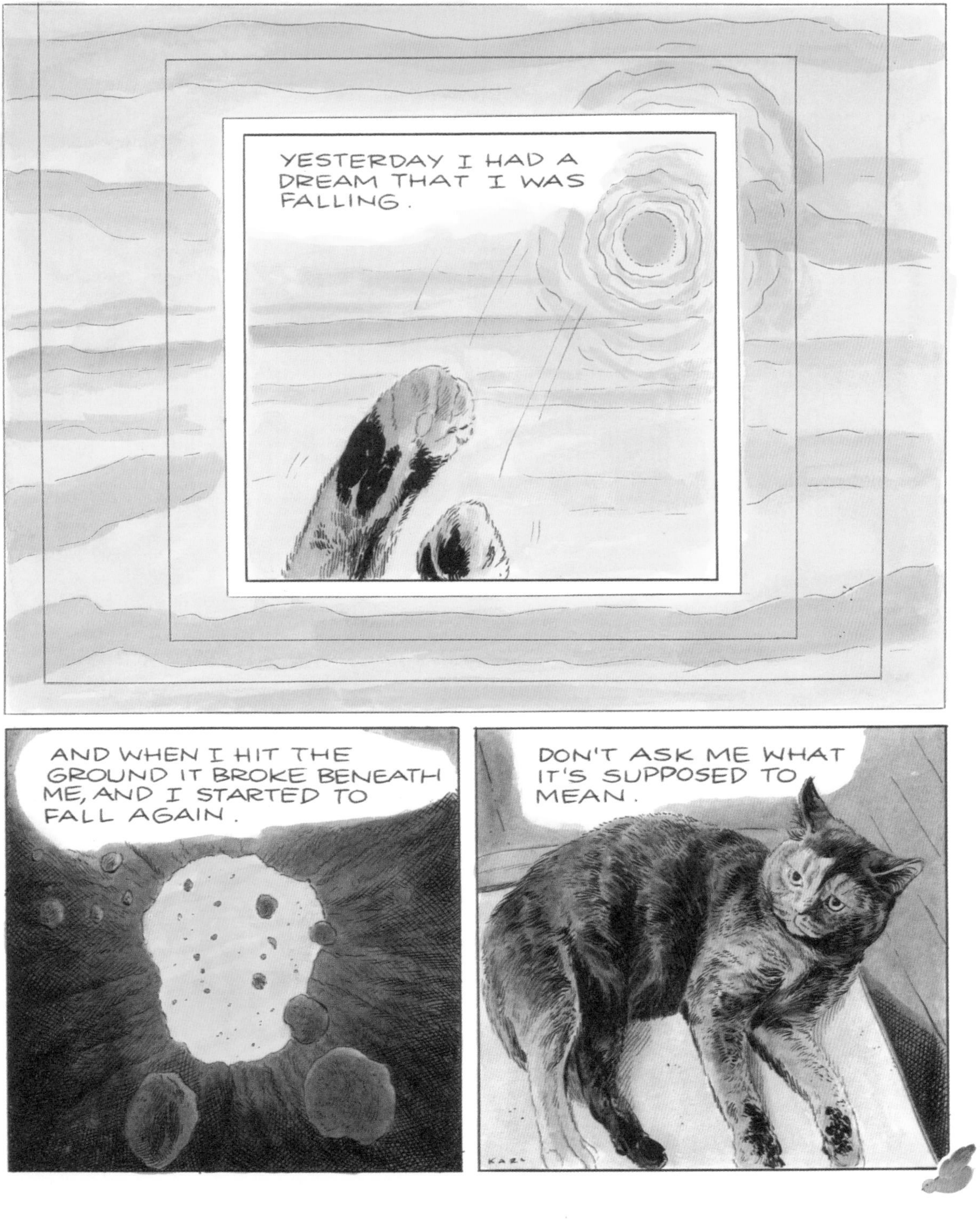
YESTERDAY I HAD A DREAM THAT I WAS FALLING.
AND WHEN I HIT THE GROUND IT BROKE BENEATH ME, AND I STARTED TO FALL AGAIN.
DON'T ASK ME WHAT IT'S SUPPOSED TO MEAN.

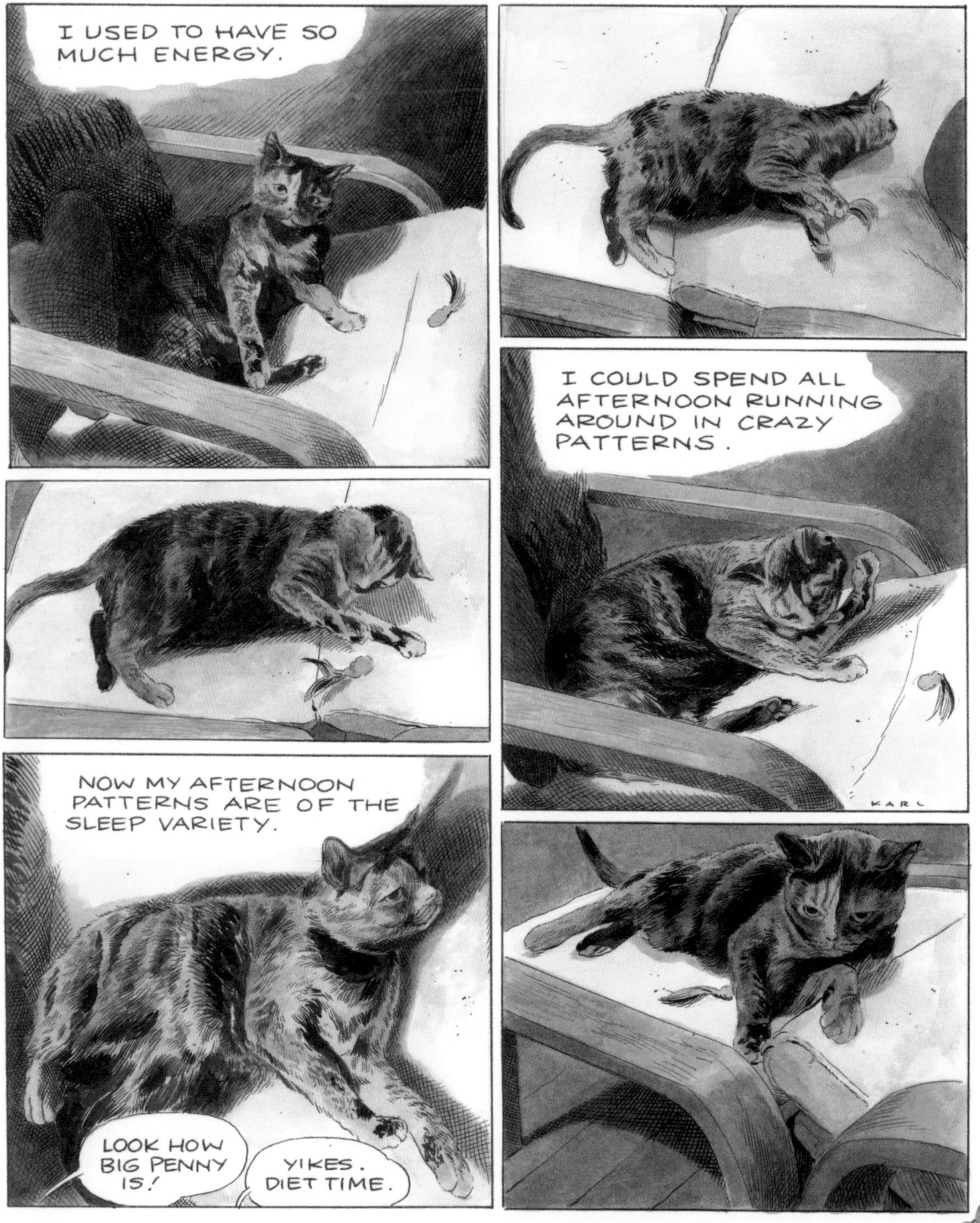
I USED TO HAVE SO MUCH ENERGY.
I COULD SPEND ALL AFTERNOON RUNNING AROUND IN CRAZY PATTERNS.
KARL
NOW MY AFTERNOON PATTERNS ARE OF THE SLEEP VARIETY.
LOOK HOW BIG PENNY IS!
YIKES. DIET TIME.

I NEED THREE THINGS IN LIFE.

FOOD IN MY DISH, A CLEAN TOILET BOX, AND SOME PEOPLE SERVANTS TO TAKE CARE OF THOSE THINGS.

ALL CLEAN FOR POOPING, PENNY.

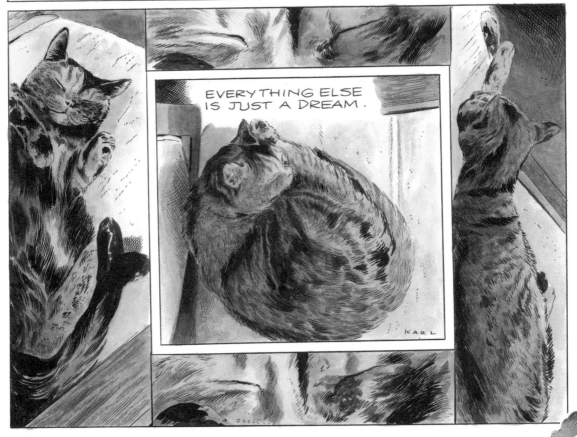

EVERYTHING ELSE IS JUST A DREAM.

KARL

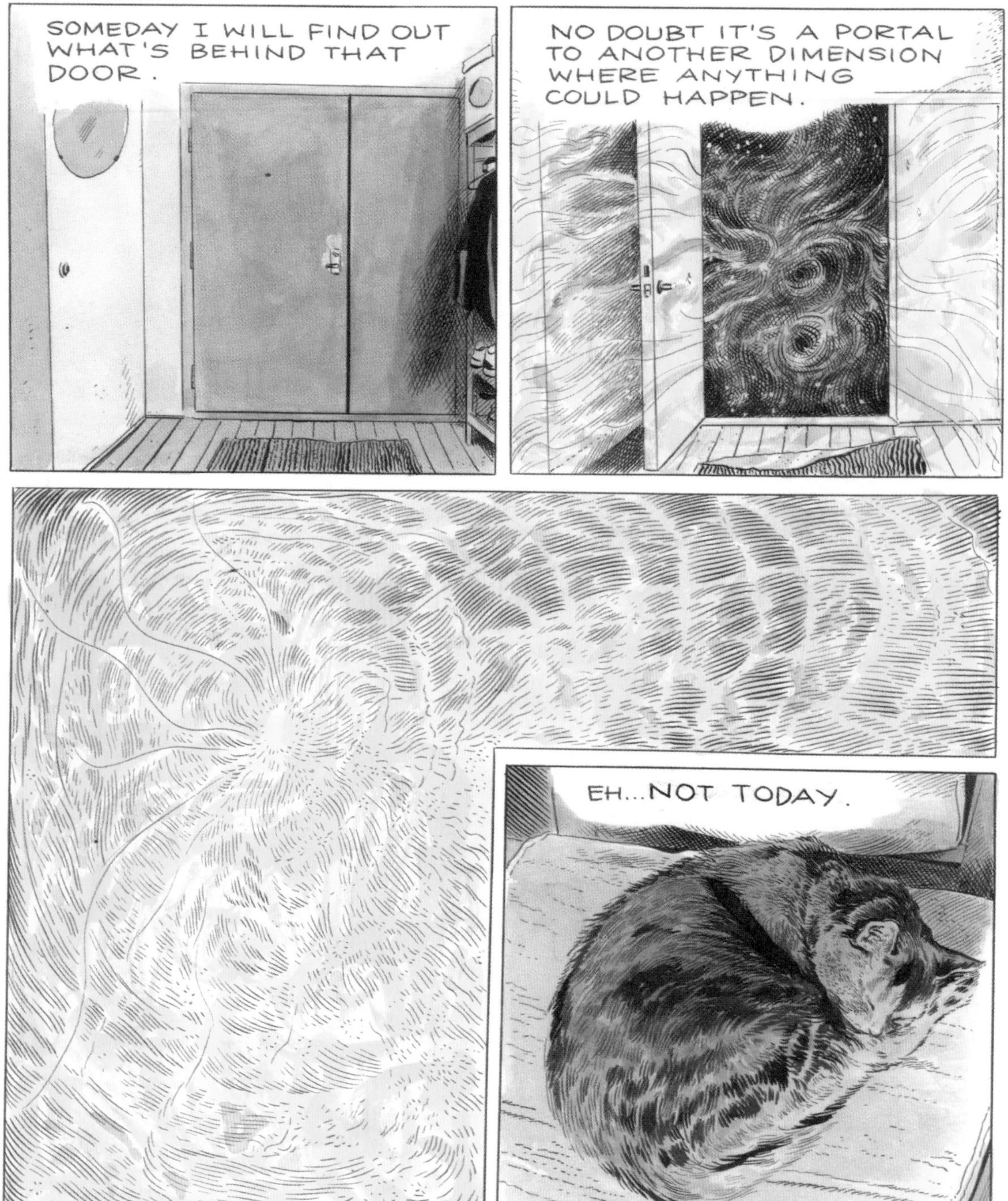
SOMEDAY I WILL FIND OUT WHAT'S BEHIND THAT DOOR.
NO DOUBT IT'S A PORTAL TO ANOTHER DIMENSION WHERE ANYTHING COULD HAPPEN.
EH...NOT TODAY.
KARL

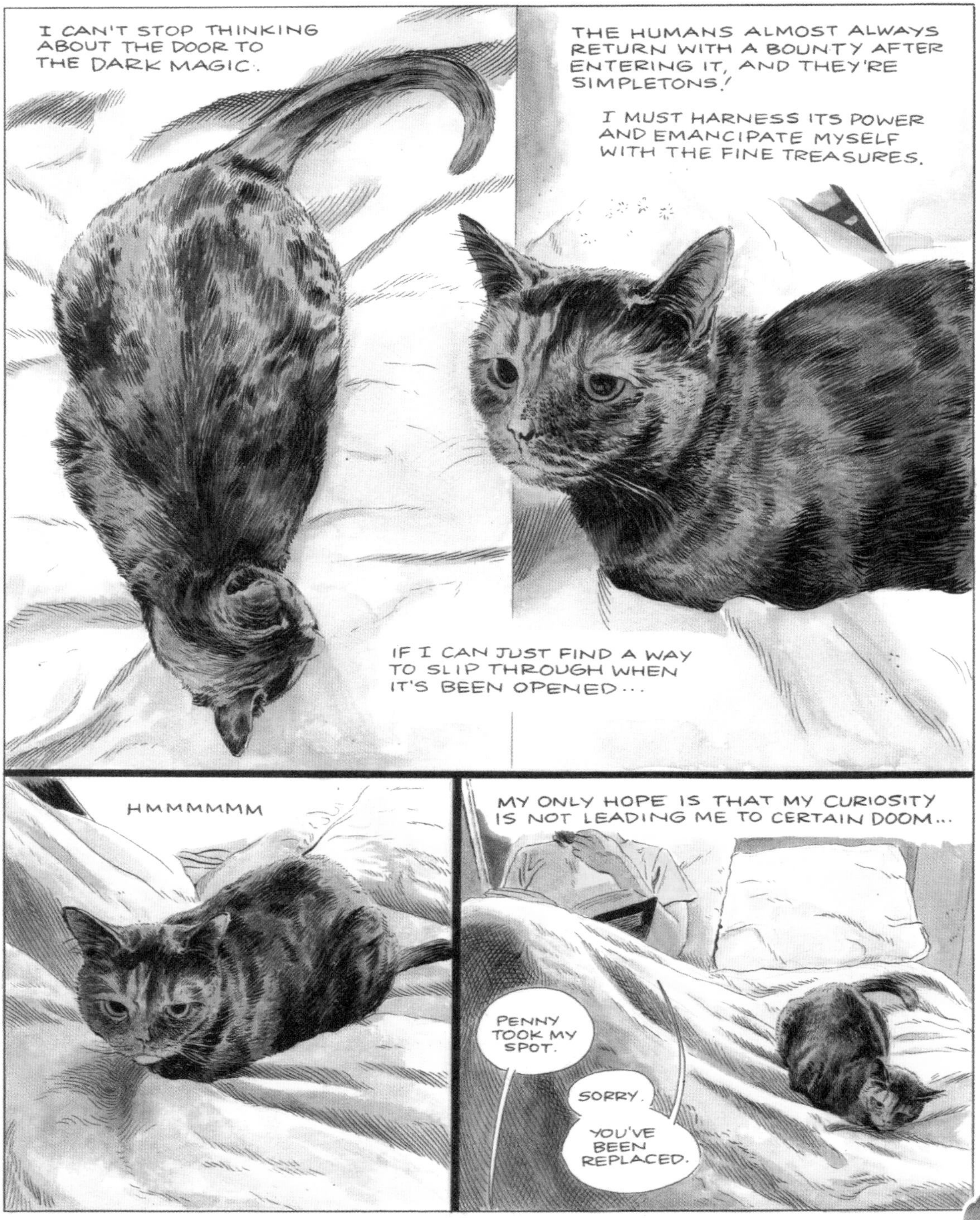
I CAN'T STOP THINKING ABOUT THE DOOR TO THE DARK MAGIC.
THE HUMANS ALMOST ALWAYS RETURN WITH A BOUNTY AFTER ENTERING IT, AND THEY'RE SIMPLETONS!
I MUST HARNESS ITS POWER AND EMANCIPATE MYSELF WITH THE FINE TREASURES.
IF I CAN JUST FIND A WAY TO SLIP THROUGH WHEN IT'S BEEN OPENED...
HMMMMMM
MY ONLY HOPE IS THAT MY CURIOSITY IS NOT LEADING ME TO CERTAIN DOOM...
PENNY TOOK MY SPOT.
SORRY.
YOU'VE BEEN REPLACED.

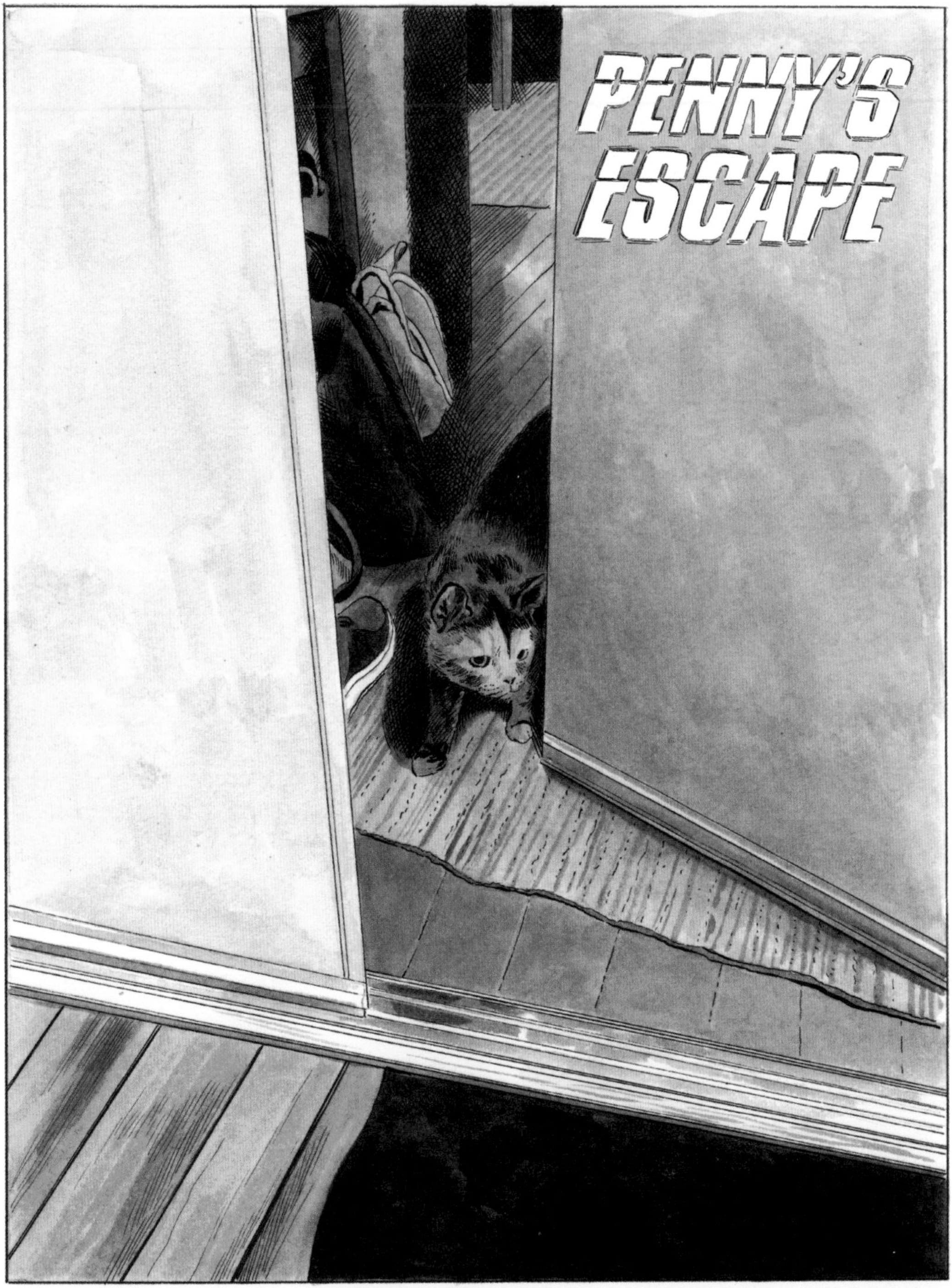
PENNY'S ESCAPE

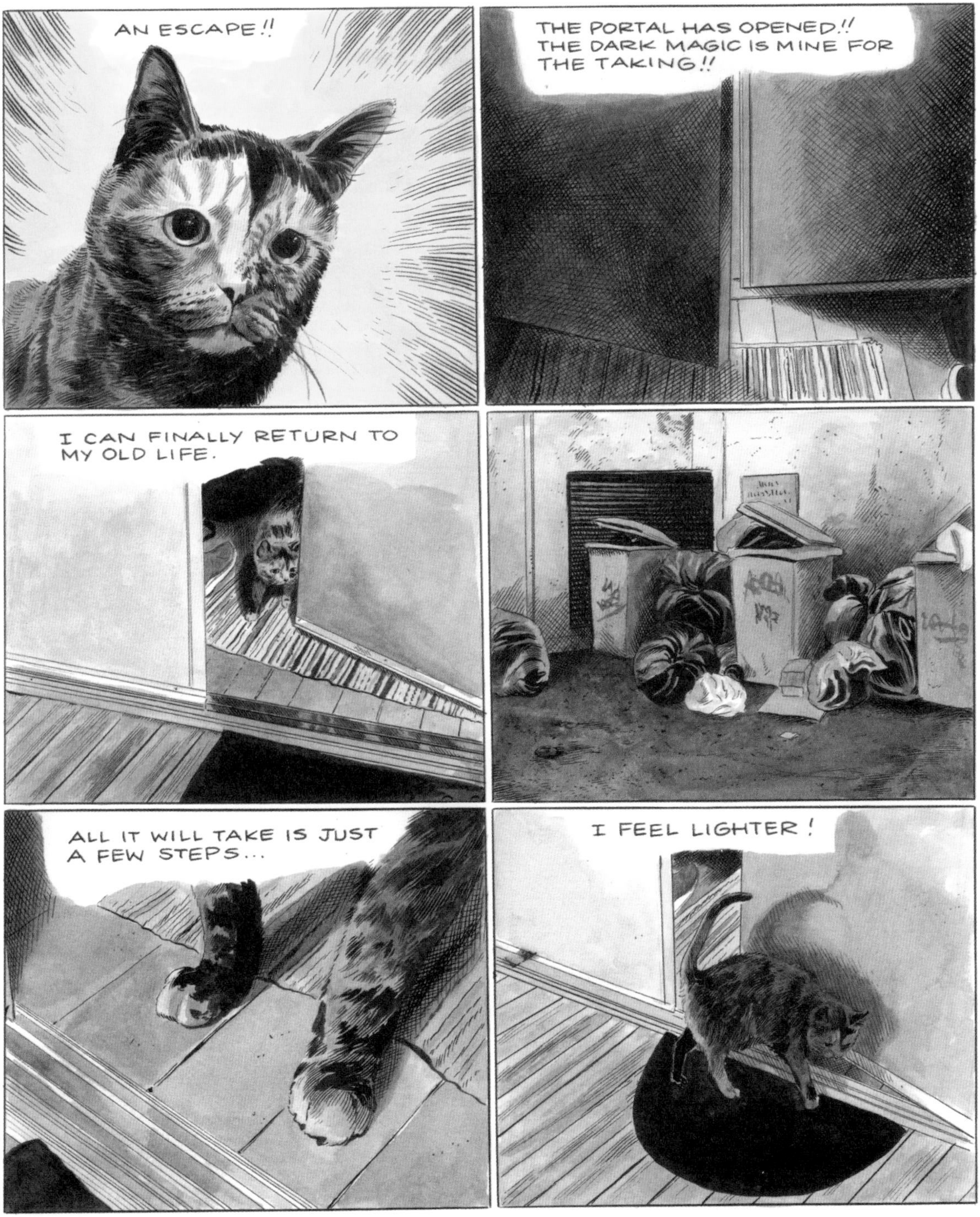
AN ESCAPE!!
THE PORTAL HAS OPENED!! THE DARK MAGIC IS MINE FOR THE TAKING!!
I CAN FINALLY RETURN TO MY OLD LIFE.
ALL IT WILL TAKE IS JUST A FEW STEPS...
I FEEL LIGHTER!

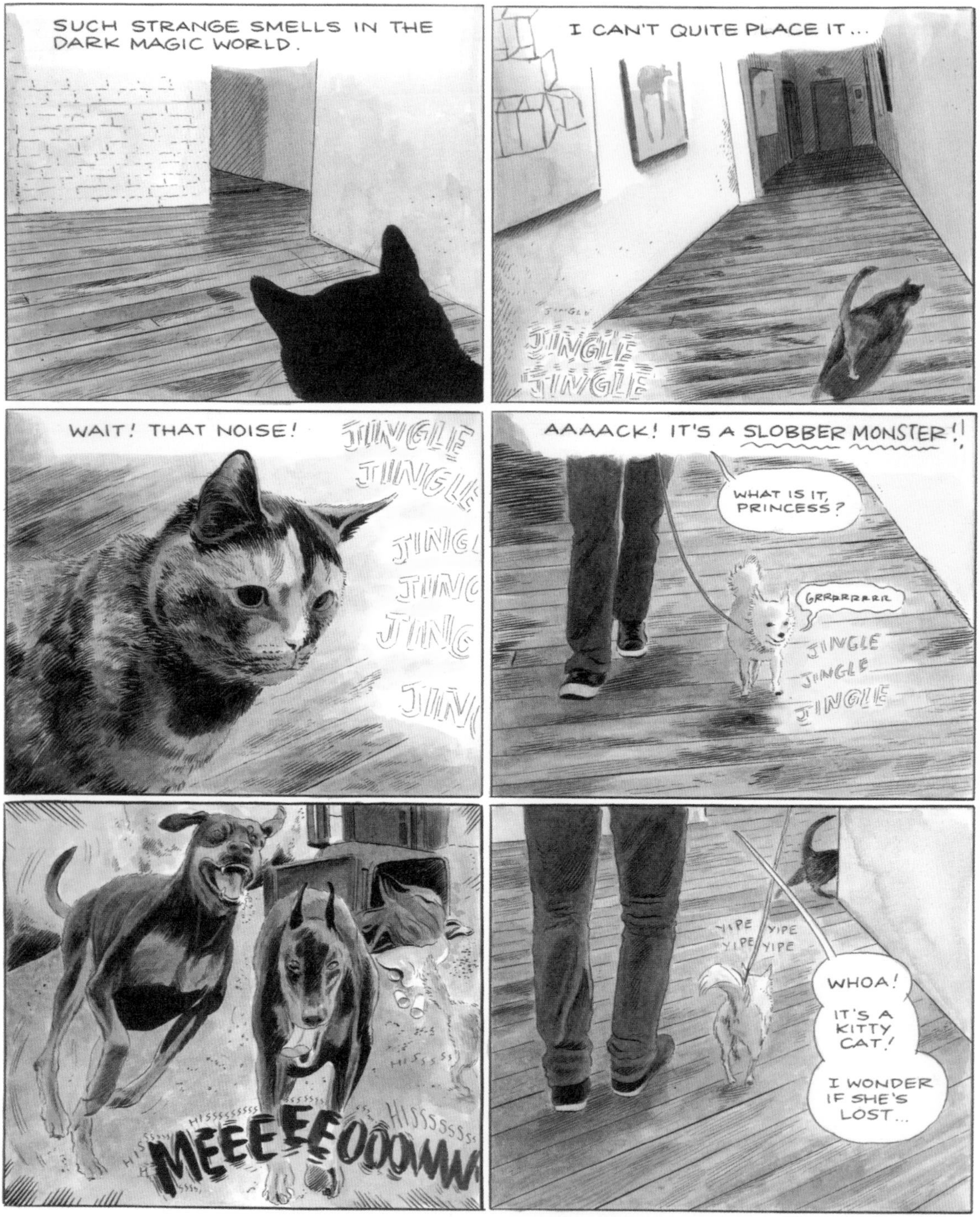
SUCH STRANGE SMELLS IN THE DARK MAGIC WORLD.
I CAN'T QUITE PLACE IT...
JINGLE
JINGLE
JINGLE
WAIT! THAT NOISE!
JINGLE
JINGLE
AAAACK! IT'S A SLOBBER MONSTER!!
WHAT IS IT, PRINCESS?
GRRRRRRRR
JINGLE
JINGLE
JINGLE
MEEEEEOOOWW
HISSSSSSSS
YIPE YIPE
YIPE YIPE
WHOA!
IT'S A KITTY CAT!
I WONDER IF SHE'S LOST...

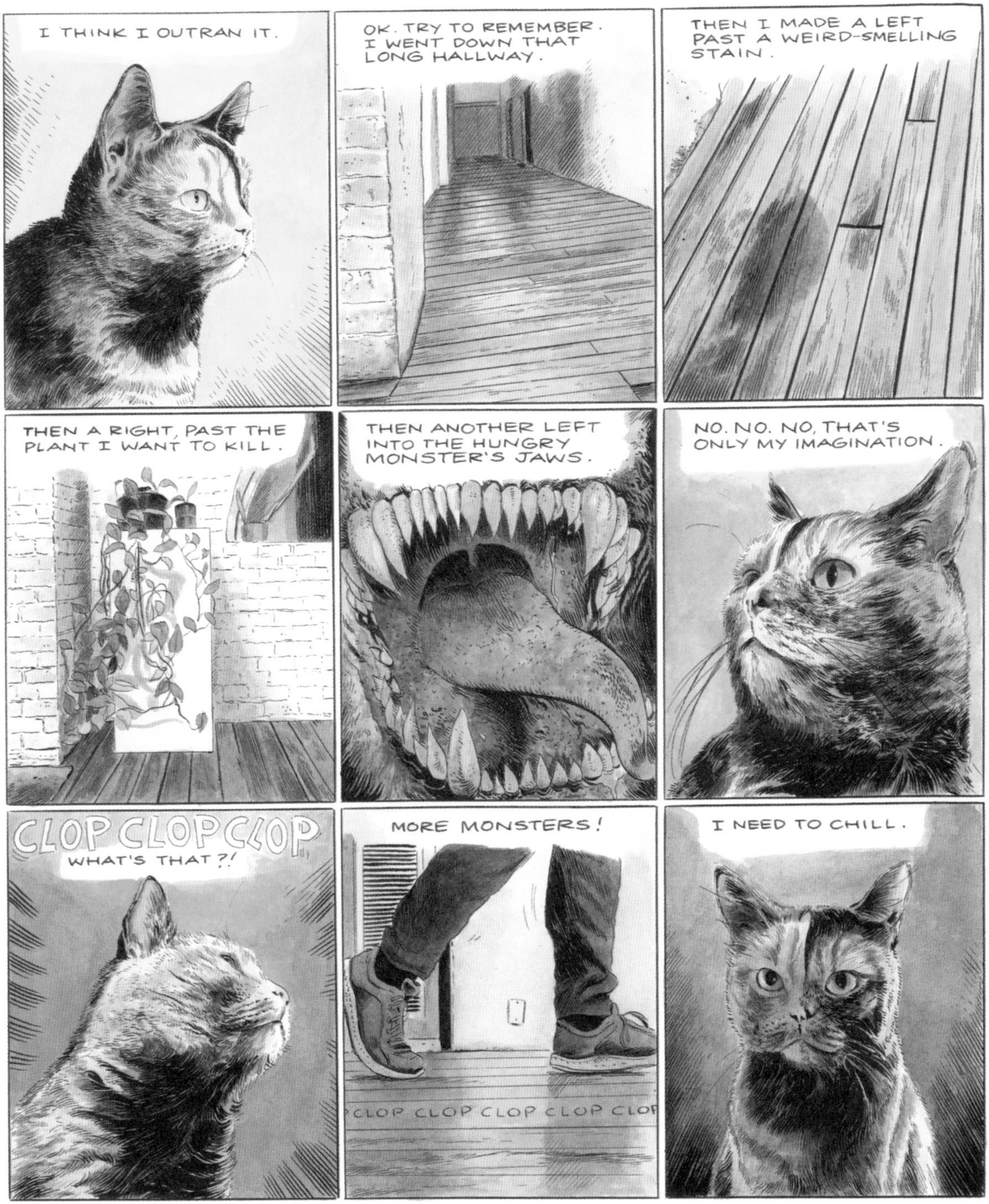
I THINK I OUTRAN IT.
OK. TRY TO REMEMBER. I WENT DOWN THAT LONG HALLWAY.
THEN I MADE A LEFT PAST A WEIRD-SMELLING STAIN.
THEN A RIGHT, PAST THE PLANT I WANT TO KILL.
THEN ANOTHER LEFT INTO THE HUNGRY MONSTER'S JAWS.
NO. NO. NO, THAT'S ONLY MY IMAGINATION.
CLOP CLOP CLOP
WHAT'S THAT?!
MORE MONSTERS!
CLOP CLOP CLOP CLOP CLOP
I NEED TO CHILL.

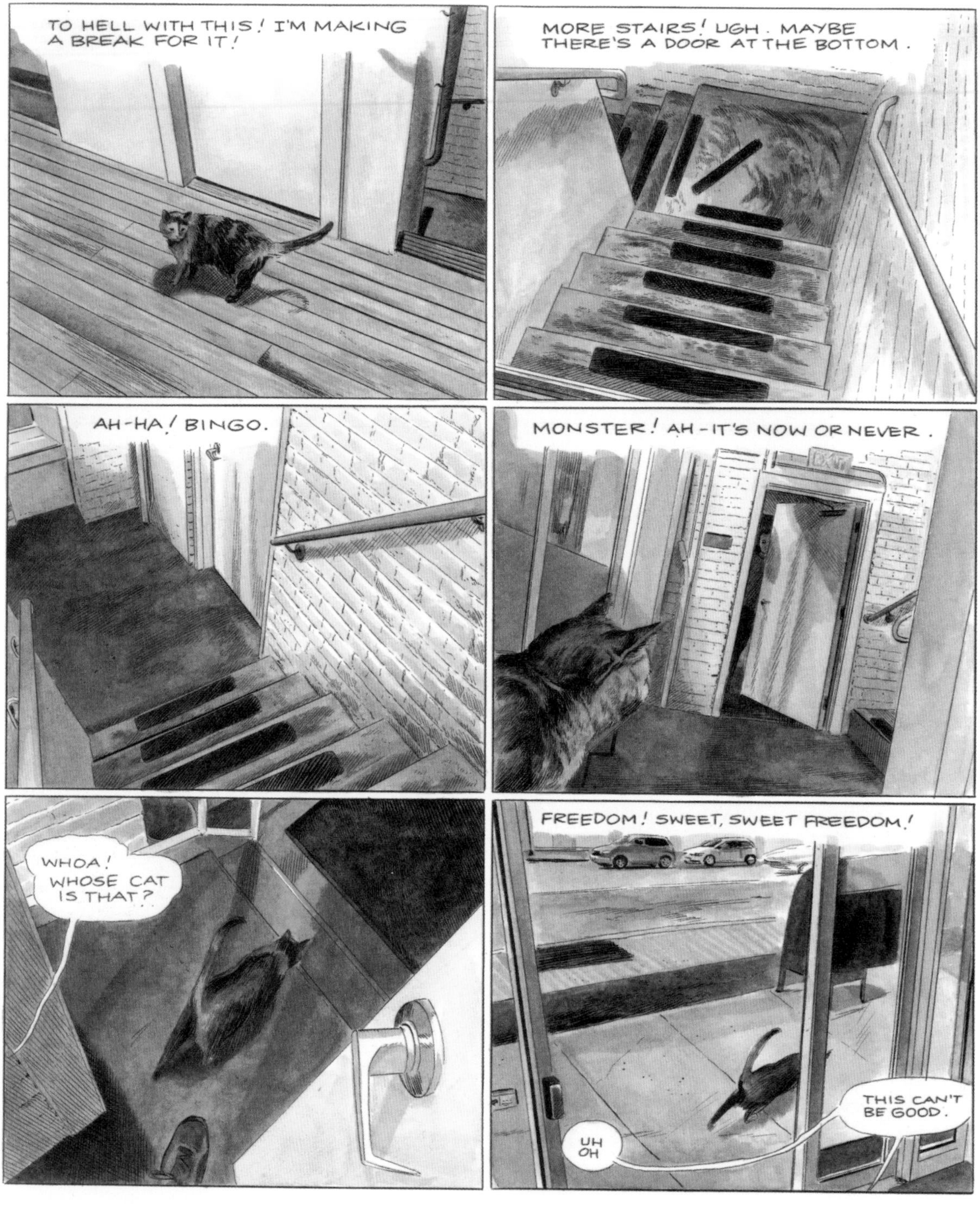
TO HELL WITH THIS! I'M MAKING A BREAK FOR IT!
MORE STAIRS! UGH. MAYBE THERE'S A DOOR AT THE BOTTOM.
AH-HA! BINGO.
MONSTER! AH-IT'S NOW OR NEVER.
EXIT
WHOA! WHOSE CAT IS THAT?
FREEDOM! SWEET, SWEET FREEDOM!
UH OH
THIS CAN'T BE GOOD.

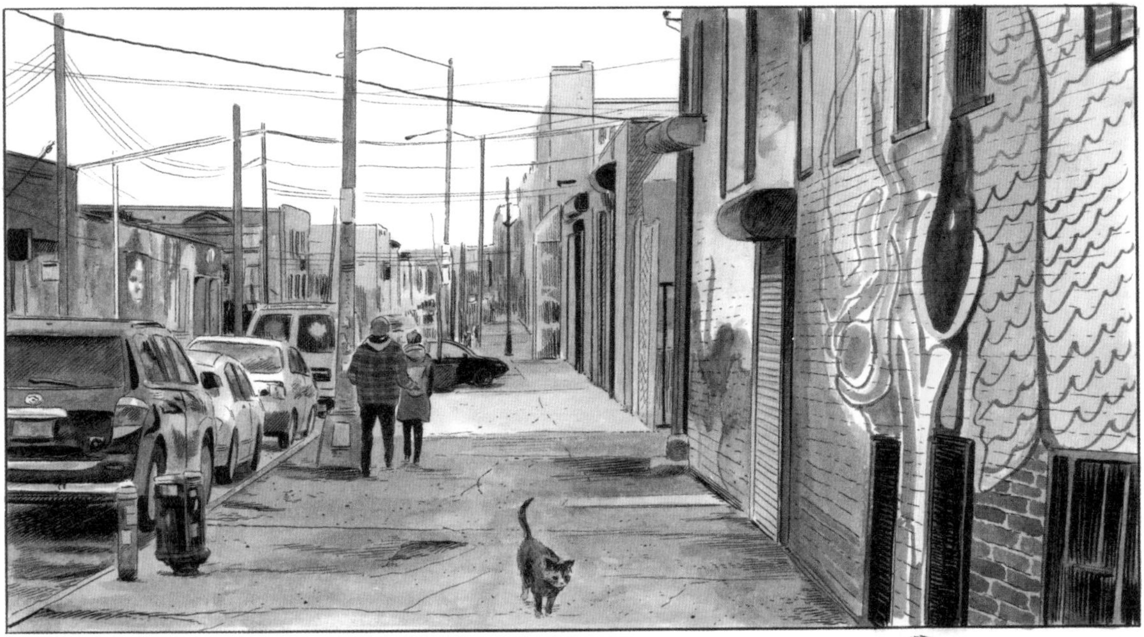

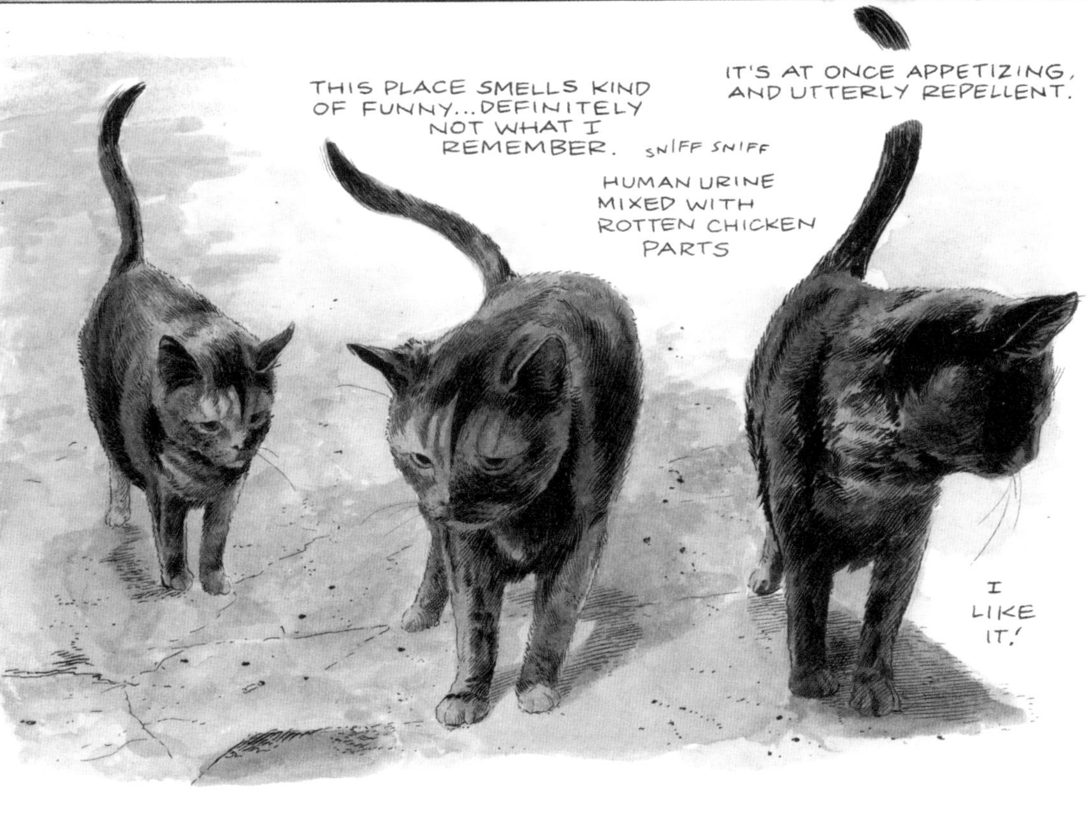
THIS PLACE SMELLS KIND OF FUNNY...DEFINITELY NOT WHAT I REMEMBER.
SNIFF SNIFF
HUMAN URINE MIXED WITH ROTTEN CHICKEN PARTS
IT'S AT ONCE APPETIZING, AND UTTERLY REPELLENT.
I LIKE IT!

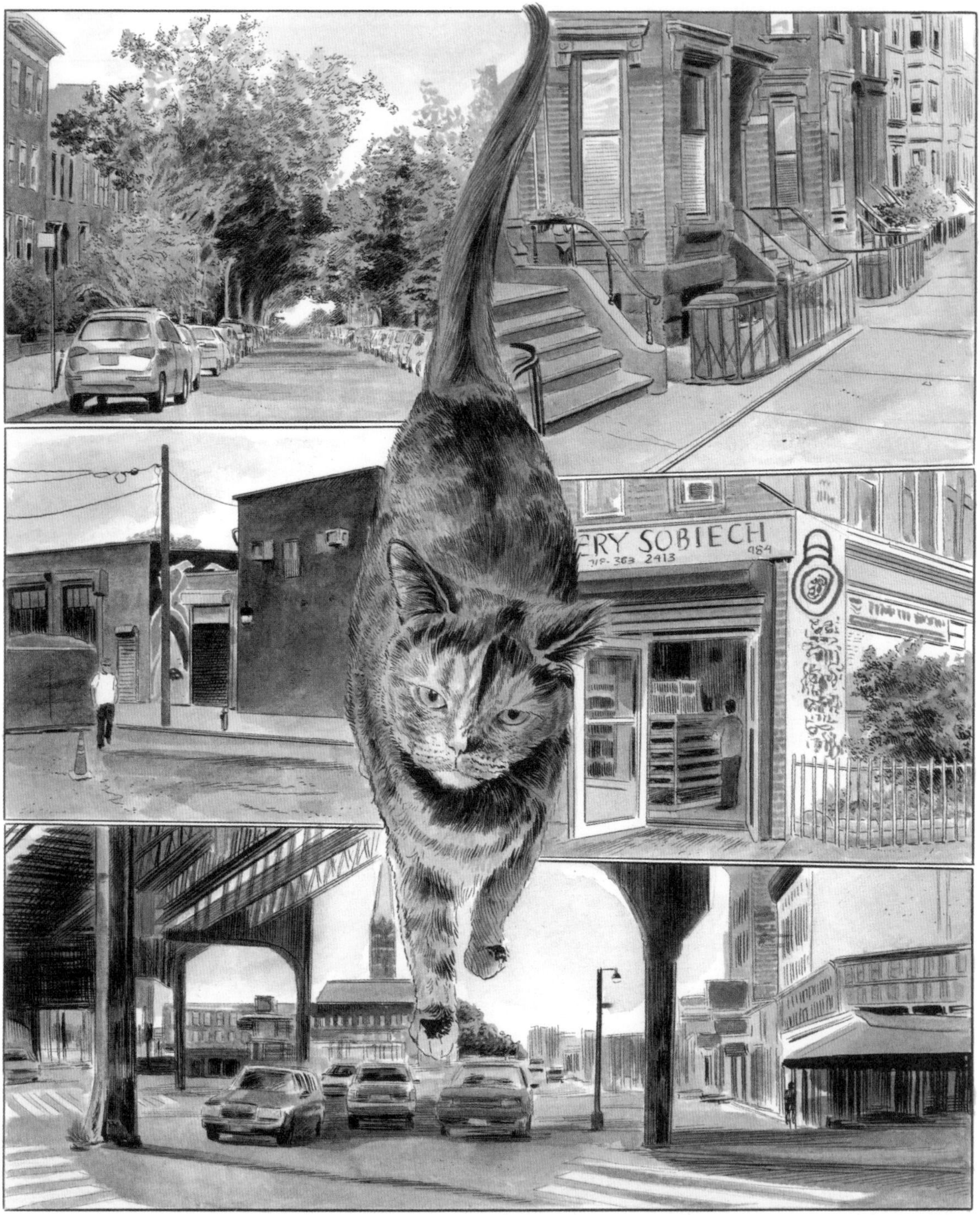
ERY SOBIECH
718-383 2413
984

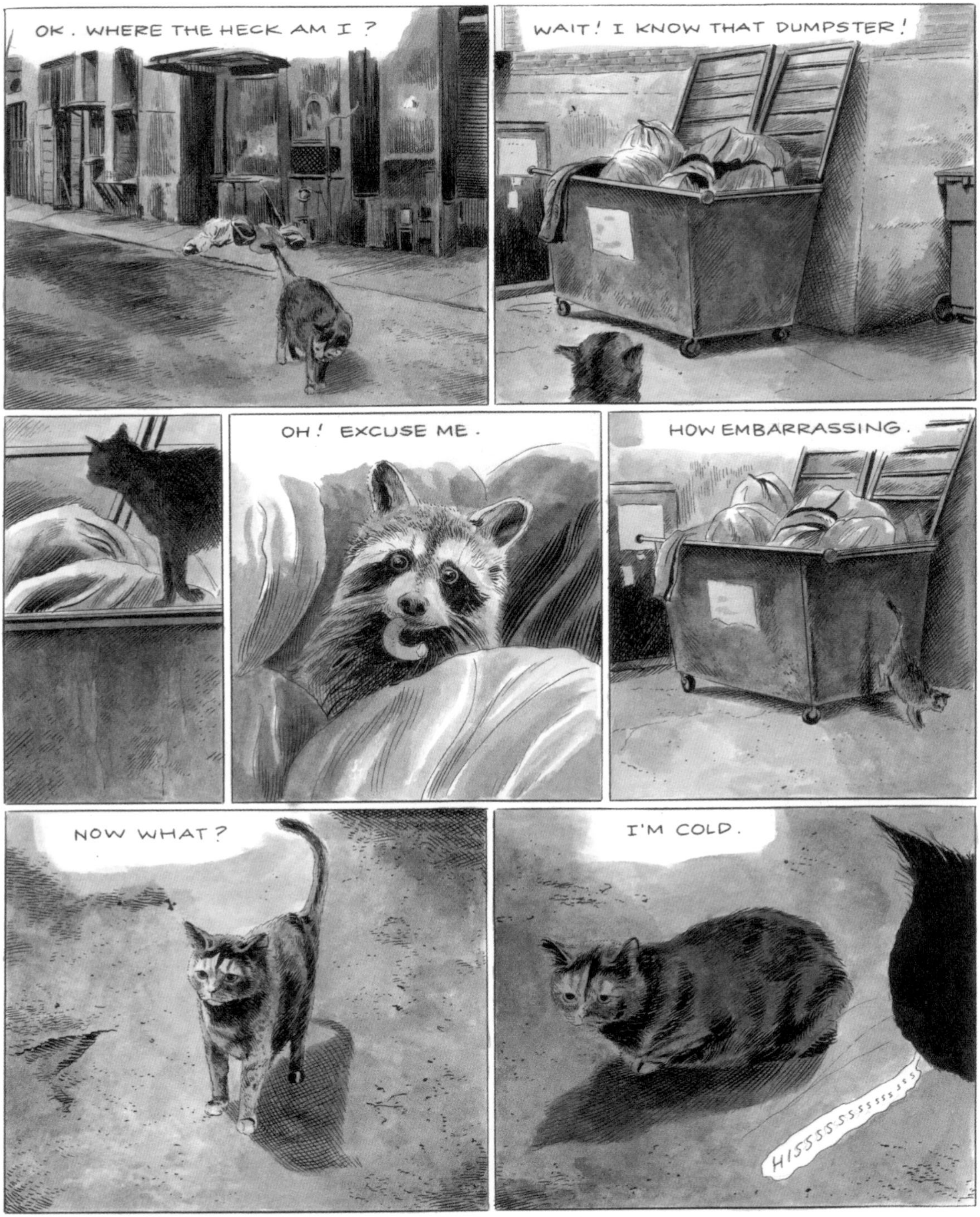
OK. WHERE THE HECK AM I?
WAIT! I KNOW THAT DUMPSTER!
OH! EXCUSE ME.
HOW EMBARRASSING.
NOW WHAT?
I'M COLD.
HISSSSSSSSSSSSSS

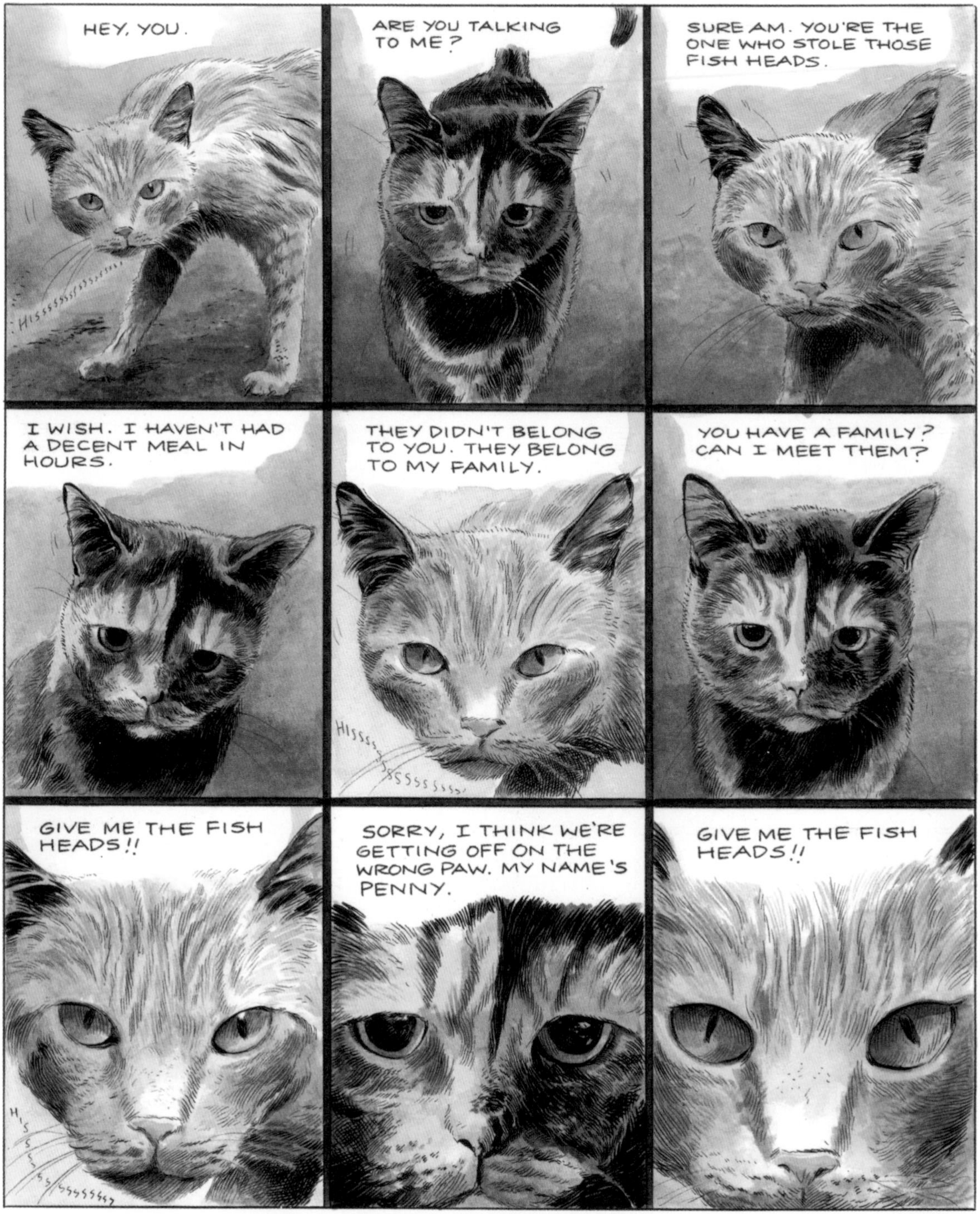
HEY, YOU.
HISSSSSSSSSSSSSSSS
ARE YOU TALKING TO ME?
SURE AM. YOU'RE THE ONE WHO STOLE THOSE FISH HEADS.
I WISH. I HAVEN'T HAD A DECENT MEAL IN HOURS.
THEY DIDN'T BELONG TO YOU. THEY BELONG TO MY FAMILY.
HISSSSSSSSSSSS
YOU HAVE A FAMILY? CAN I MEET THEM?
GIVE ME THE FISH HEADS!!
HISSSSSSSSSSS
SORRY, I THINK WE'RE GETTING OFF ON THE WRONG PAW. MY NAME'S PENNY.
GIVE ME THE FISH HEADS!!

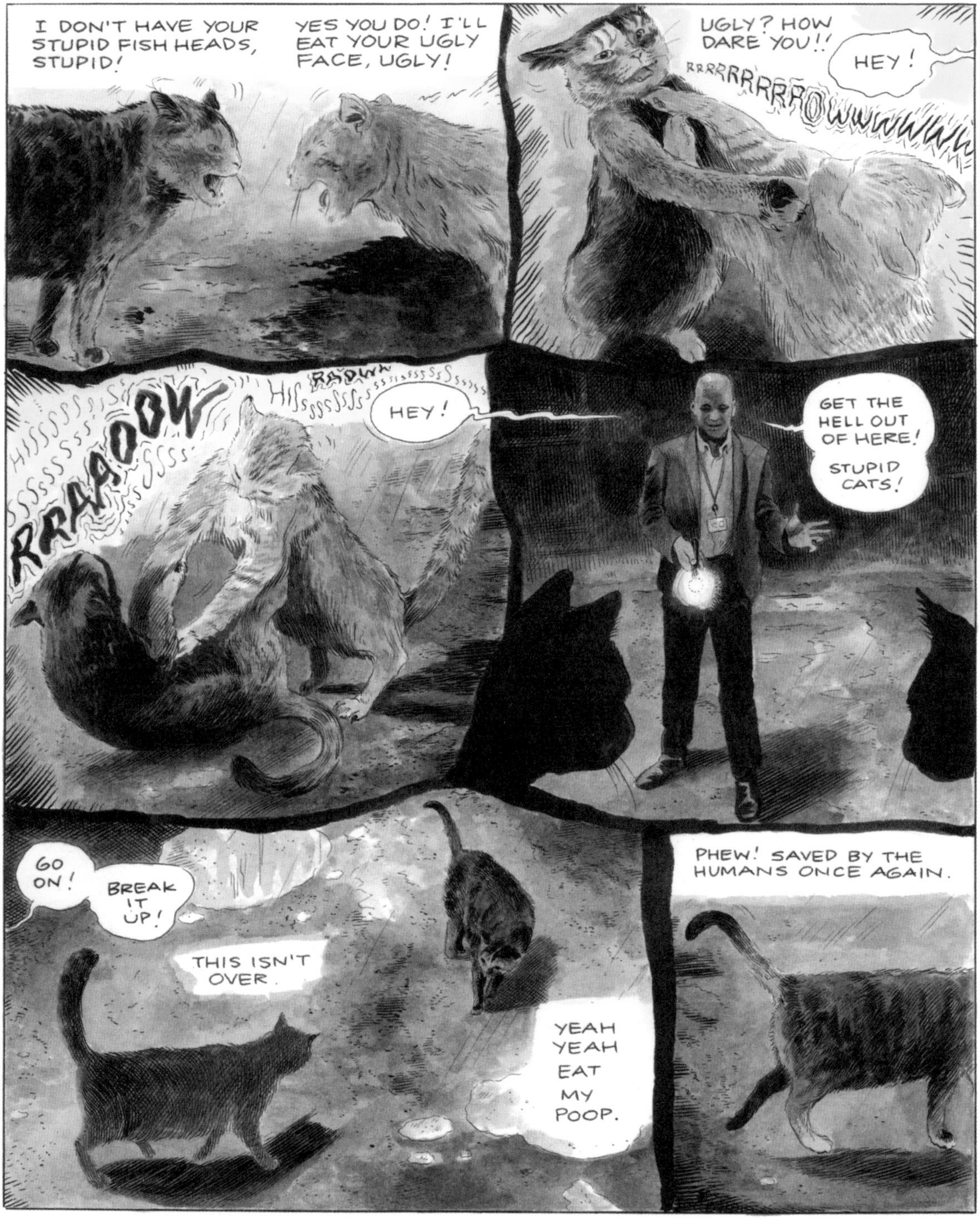

I DON'T HAVE YOUR STUPID FISH HEADS, STUPID!
YES YOU DO! I'LL EAT YOUR UGLY FACE, UGLY!
UGLY? HOW DARE YOU!!
HEY!
RRRRRRRRRROWWWWWWW
RRAAOOW
RAOWW
HISSSSSSSS
HEY!
GET THE HELL OUT OF HERE!
STUPID CATS!
GO ON!
BREAK IT UP!
THIS ISN'T OVER.
YEAH YEAH EAT MY POOP.
PHEW! SAVED BY THE HUMANS ONCE AGAIN.

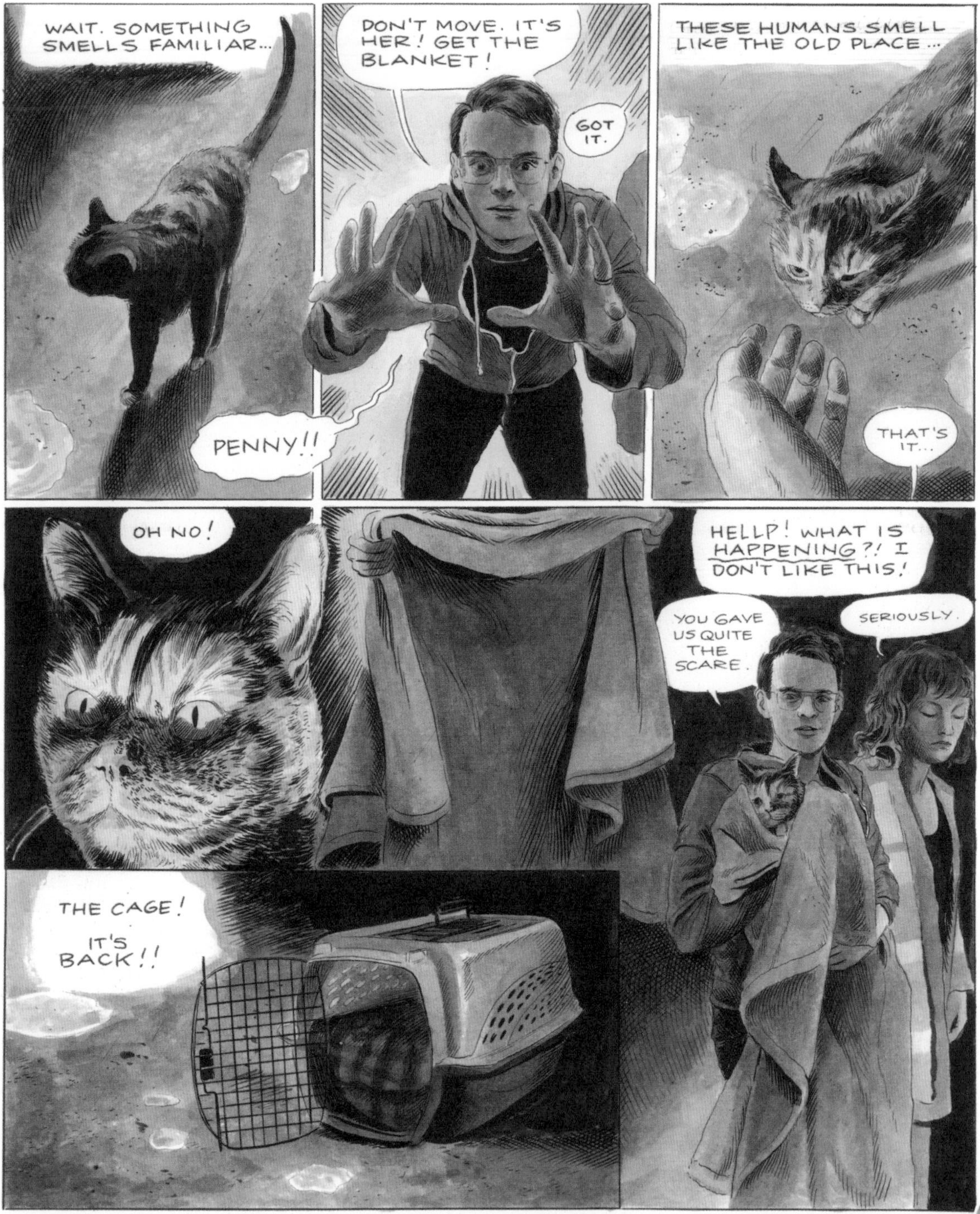
WAIT. SOMETHING SMELLS FAMILIAR...
DON'T MOVE. IT'S HER! GET THE BLANKET!
GOT IT.
PENNY!!
THESE HUMANS SMELL LIKE THE OLD PLACE...
THAT'S IT...
OH NO!
HELLP! WHAT IS HAPPENING?! I DON'T LIKE THIS!
YOU GAVE US QUITE THE SCARE.
SERIOUSLY.
THE CAGE!
IT'S BACK!!

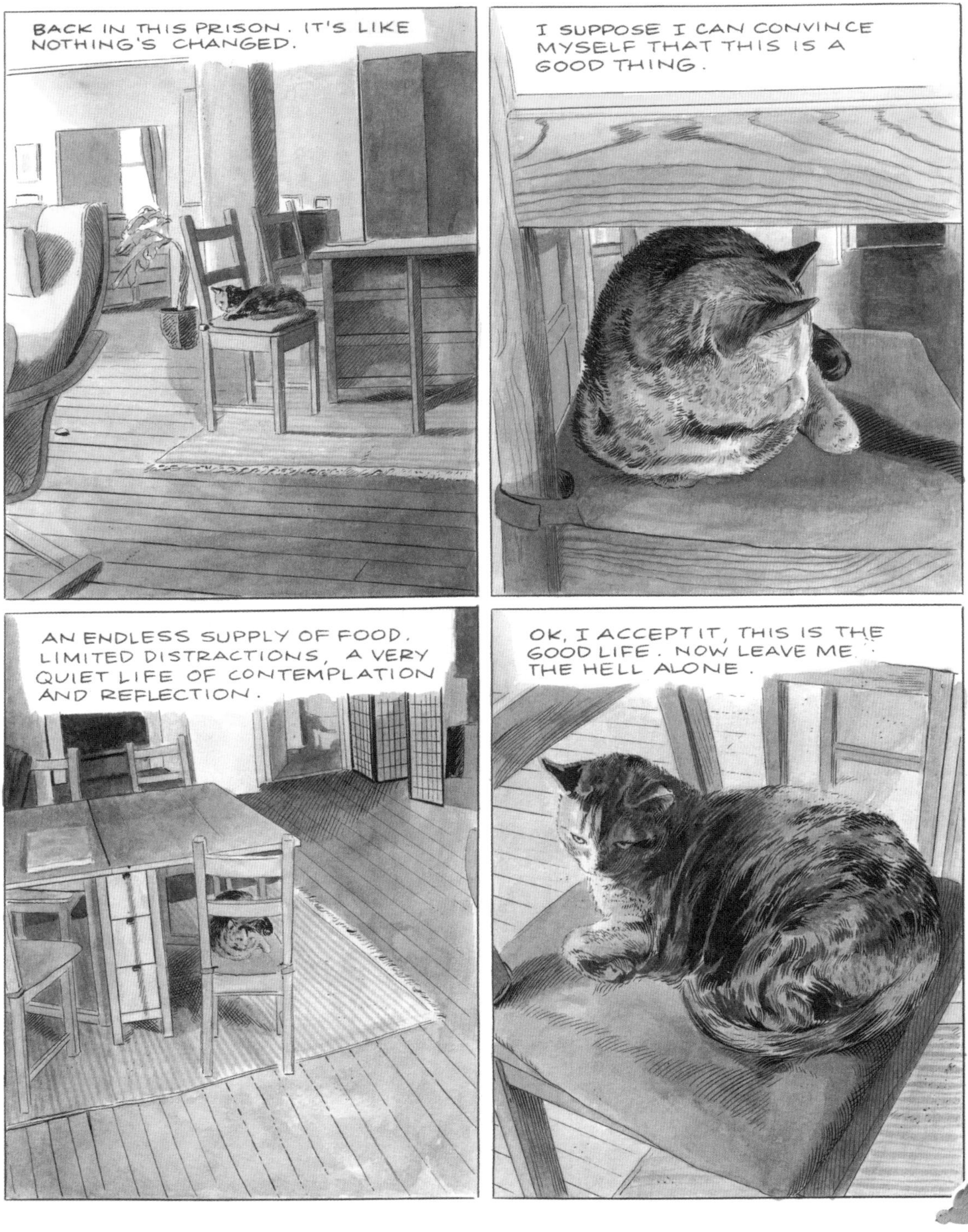
BACK IN THIS PRISON. IT'S LIKE NOTHING'S CHANGED.
I SUPPOSE I CAN CONVINCE MYSELF THAT THIS IS A GOOD THING.
AN ENDLESS SUPPLY OF FOOD. LIMITED DISTRACTIONS, A VERY QUIET LIFE OF CONTEMPLATION AND REFLECTION.
OK, I ACCEPT IT, THIS IS THE GOOD LIFE. NOW LEAVE ME THE HELL ALONE.

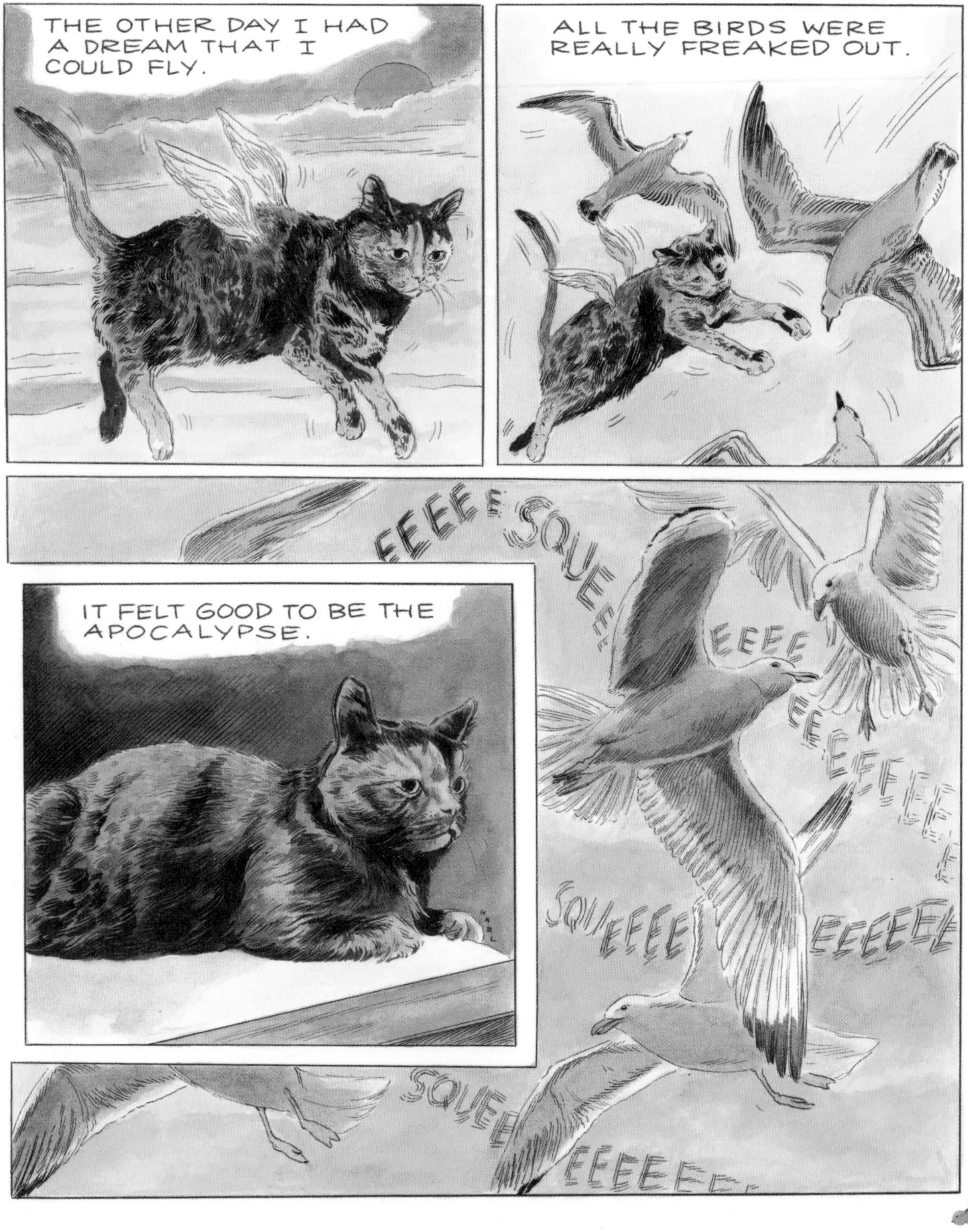
THE OTHER DAY I HAD A DREAM THAT I COULD FLY.
ALL THE BIRDS WERE REALLY FREAKED OUT.
IT FELT GOOD TO BE THE APOCALYPSE.
SQUEEEE
SQUEEEE
SQUEE

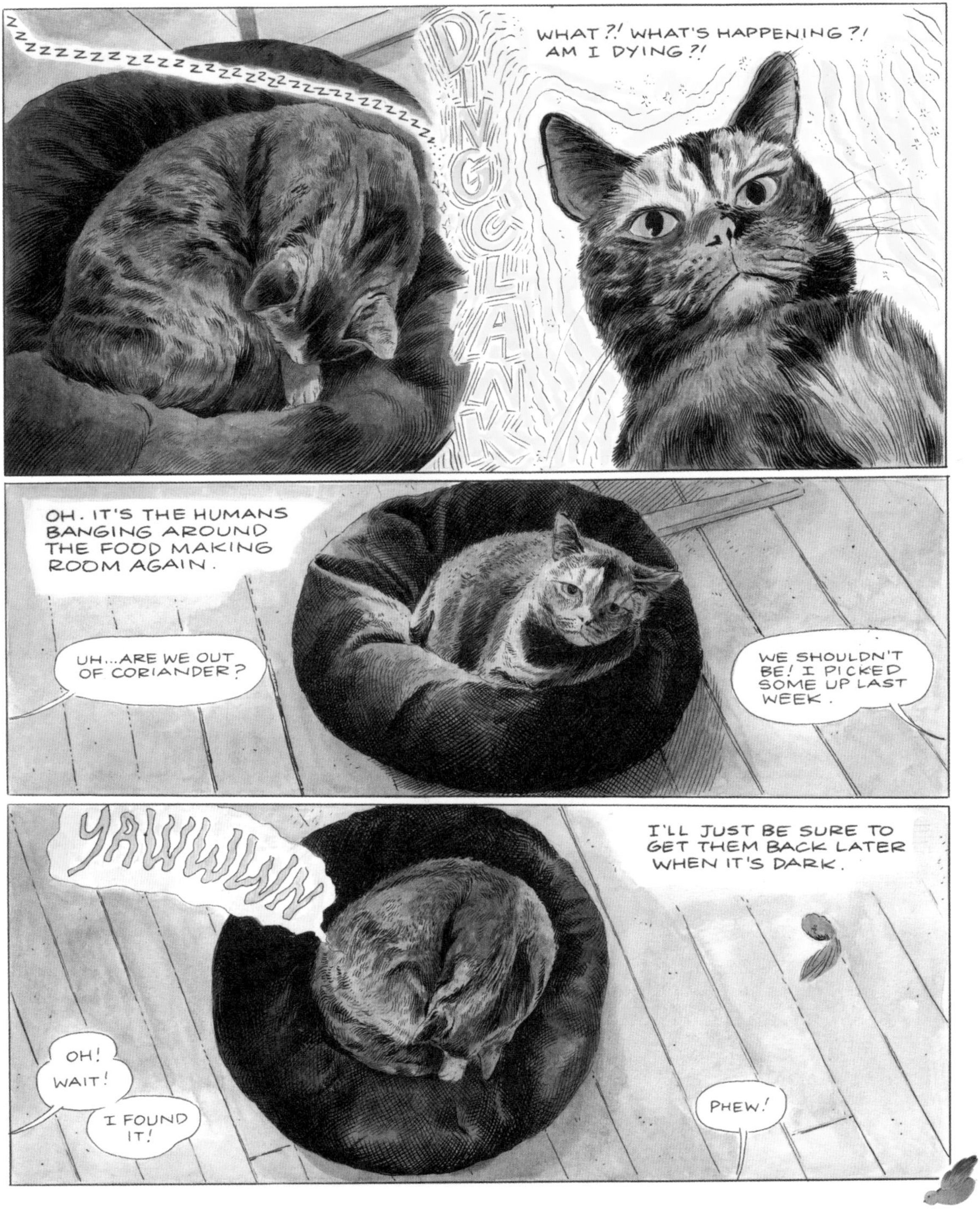
ZZZZZZZZZZZZZZZZZZZZZZZZZZZZZZZZZ
DINGCLANK
WHAT?! WHAT'S HAPPENING?! AM I DYING?!
OH. IT'S THE HUMANS BANGING AROUND THE FOOD MAKING ROOM AGAIN.
UH...ARE WE OUT OF CORIANDER?
WE SHOULDN'T BE! I PICKED SOME UP LAST WEEK.
YAWWWN
I'LL JUST BE SURE TO GET THEM BACK LATER WHEN IT'S DARK.
OH! WAIT!
I FOUND IT!
PHEW!

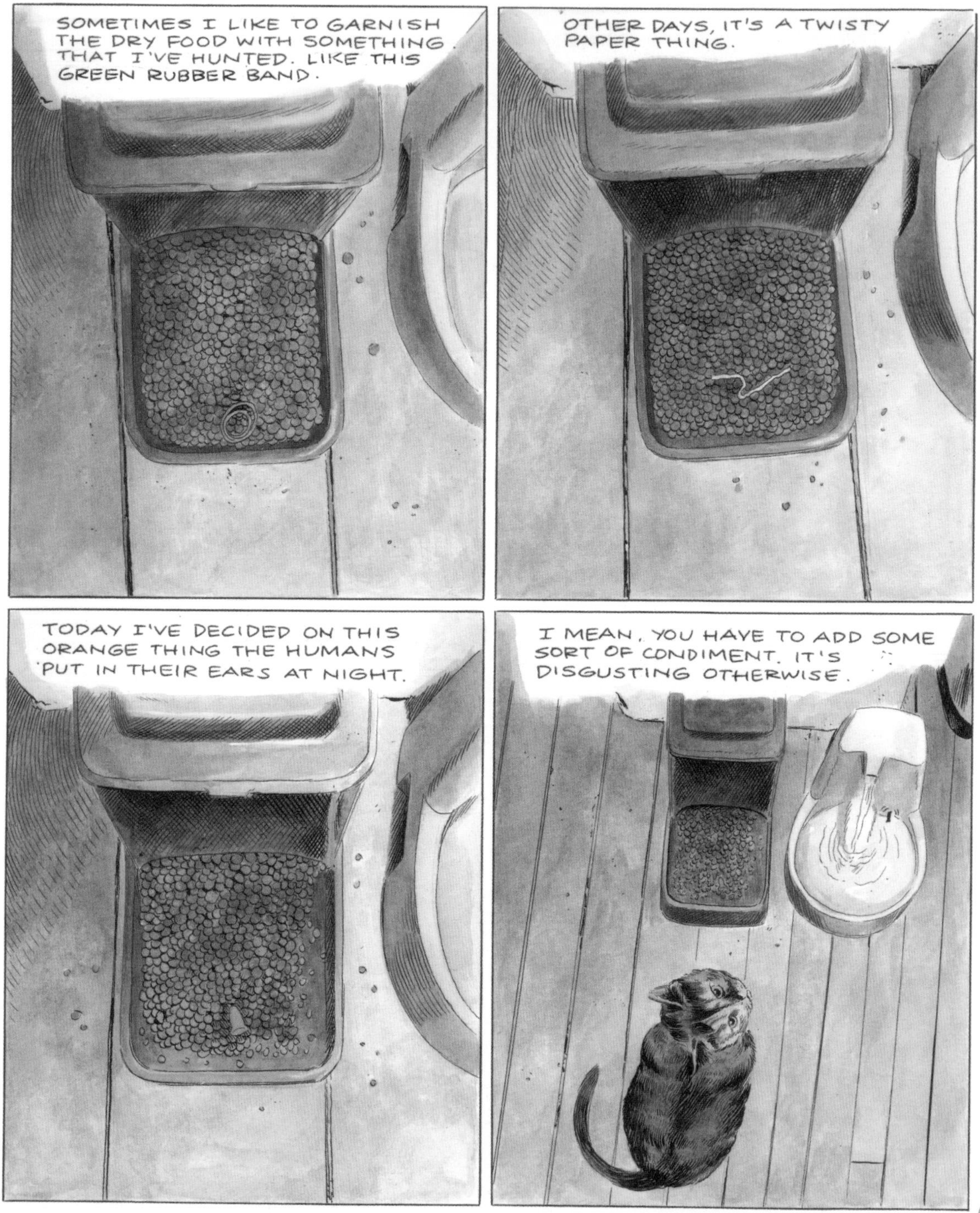
SOMETIMES I LIKE TO GARNISH THE DRY FOOD WITH SOMETHING THAT I'VE HUNTED. LIKE THIS GREEN RUBBER BAND.
OTHER DAYS, IT'S A TWISTY PAPER THING.
TODAY I'VE DECIDED ON THIS ORANGE THING THE HUMANS PUT IN THEIR EARS AT NIGHT.
I MEAN, YOU HAVE TO ADD SOME SORT OF CONDIMENT. IT'S DISGUSTING OTHERWISE.

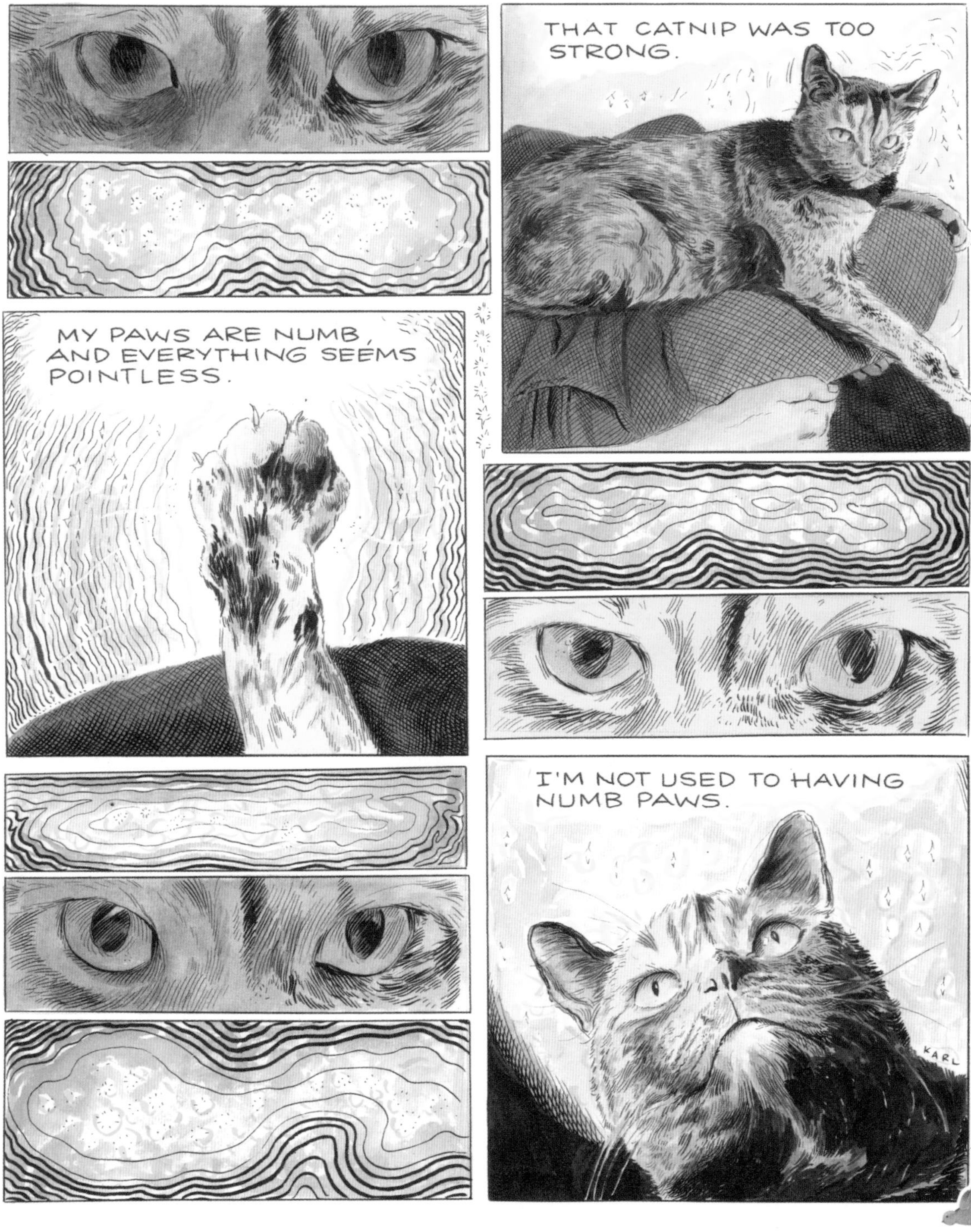
THAT CATNIP WAS TOO STRONG.
MY PAWS ARE NUMB, AND EVERYTHING SEEMS POINTLESS.
I'M NOT USED TO HAVING NUMB PAWS.
KARL

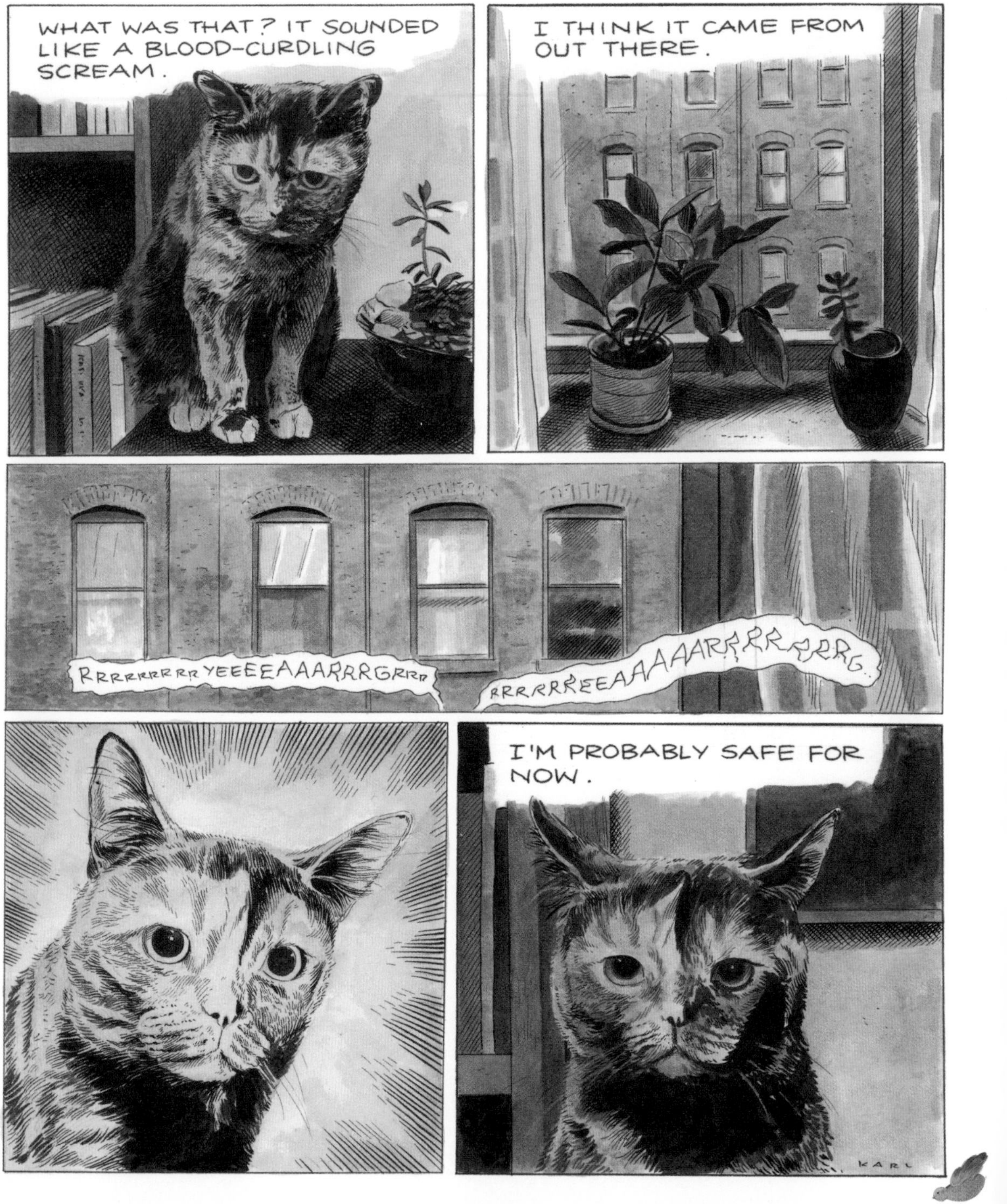

WHAT WAS THAT? IT SOUNDED LIKE A BLOOD-CURDLING SCREAM.
I THINK IT CAME FROM OUT THERE.
RRRRRRRRRR YEEEEAAARRRGRRR
RRRRRREEAAAAARRRRRRRG..
I'M PROBABLY SAFE FOR NOW.
KARL

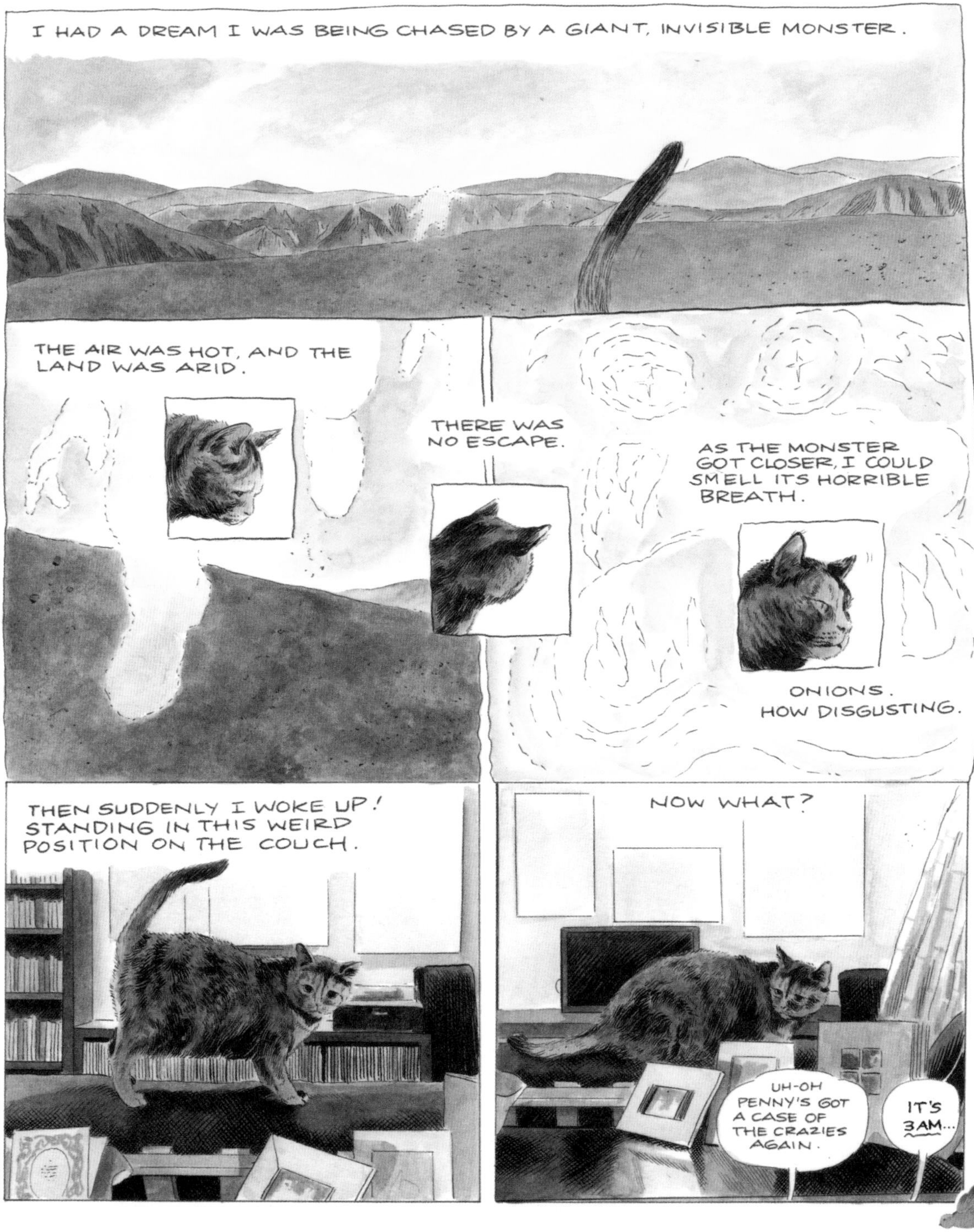
I HAD A DREAM I WAS BEING CHASED BY A GIANT, INVISIBLE MONSTER.
THE AIR WAS HOT, AND THE LAND WAS ARID.
THERE WAS NO ESCAPE.
AS THE MONSTER GOT CLOSER, I COULD SMELL ITS HORRIBLE BREATH.
ONIONS. HOW DISGUSTING.
THEN SUDDENLY I WOKE UP! STANDING IN THIS WEIRD POSITION ON THE COUCH.
NOW WHAT?
UH-OH PENNY'S GOT A CASE OF THE CRAZIES AGAIN.
IT'S 3AM...

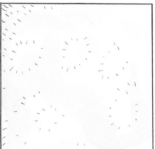

I'VE BEEN WATCHING THIS LIGHT FLICKER OVER THE WALL FOR THE PAST FORTY-FIVE MINUTES.

IT HAS ZIGGED, THEN ZAGGED, THEN ZIGGED AGAIN.

BEST SHOW I'VE SEEN ALL YEAR.

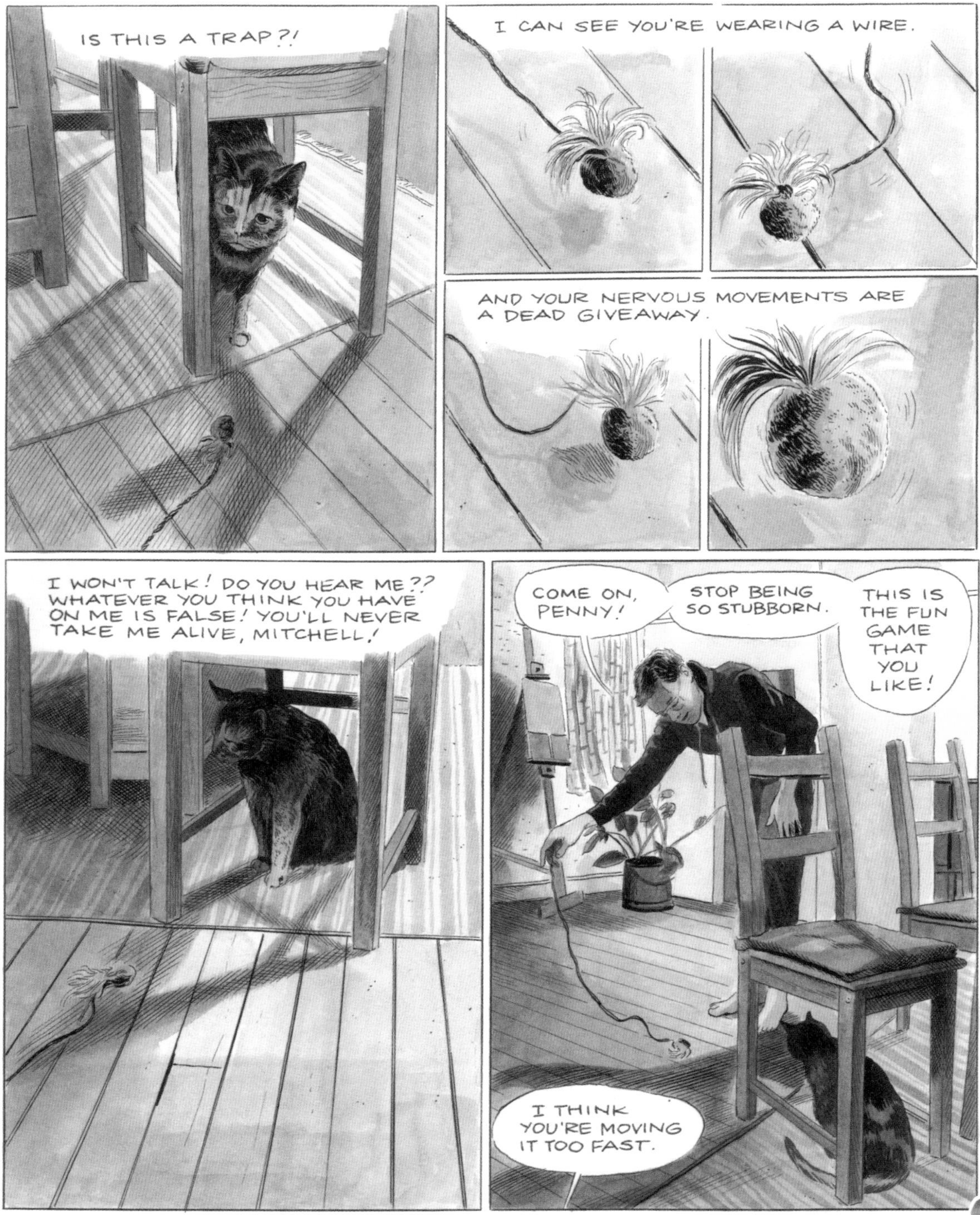
IS THIS A TRAP?!
I CAN SEE YOU'RE WEARING A WIRE.
AND YOUR NERVOUS MOVEMENTS ARE A DEAD GIVEAWAY.
I WON'T TALK! DO YOU HEAR ME?? WHATEVER YOU THINK YOU HAVE ON ME IS FALSE! YOU'LL NEVER TAKE ME ALIVE, MITCHELL!
COME ON, PENNY!
STOP BEING SO STUBBORN.
THIS IS THE FUN GAME THAT YOU LIKE!
I THINK YOU'RE MOVING IT TOO FAST.

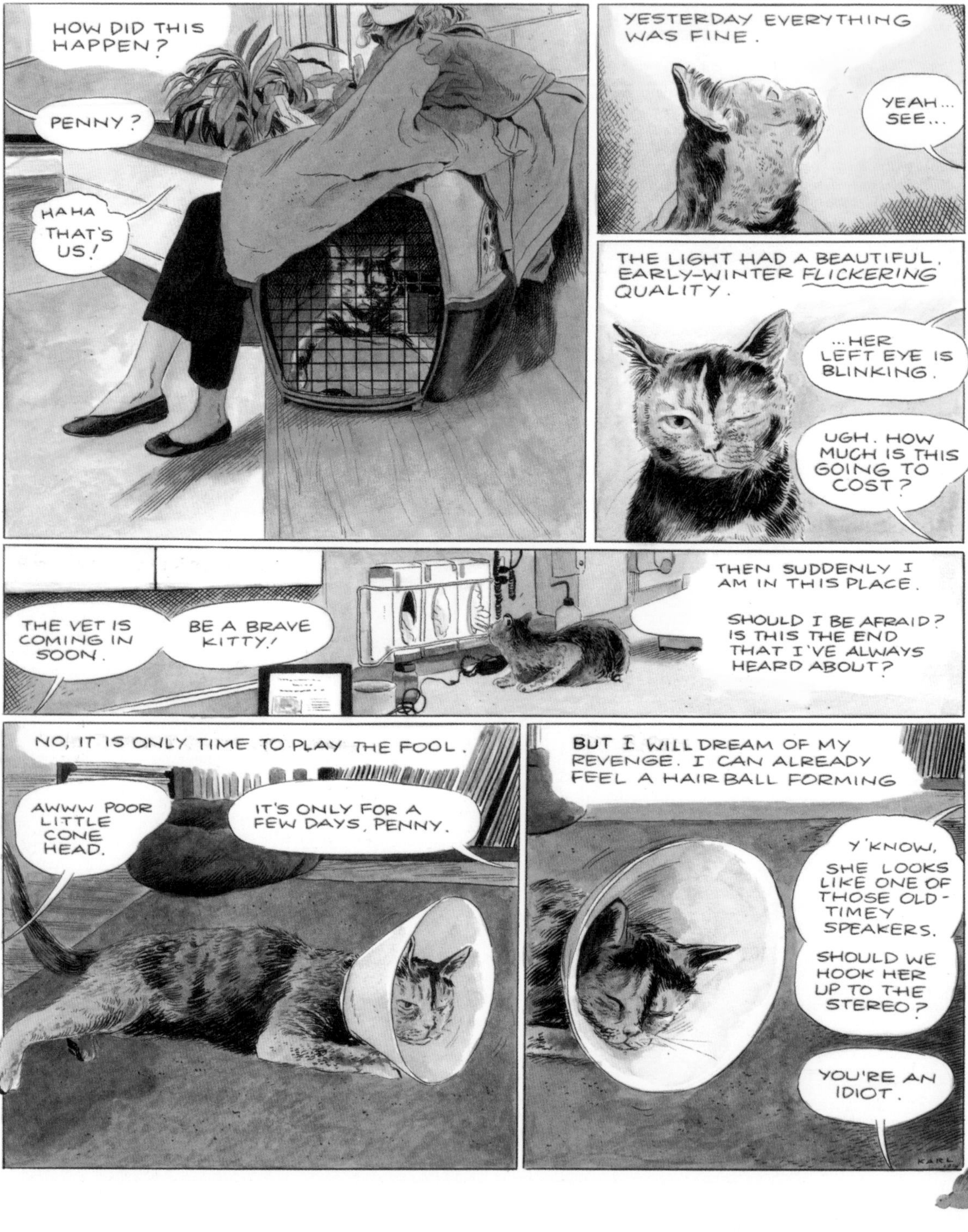
HOW DID THIS HAPPEN?
PENNY?
HAHA THAT'S US!
YESTERDAY EVERYTHING WAS FINE.
YEAH... SEE...
THE LIGHT HAD A BEAUTIFUL, EARLY-WINTER FLICKERING QUALITY.
...HER LEFT EYE IS BLINKING.
UGH. HOW MUCH IS THIS GOING TO COST?
THE VET IS COMING IN SOON.
BE A BRAVE KITTY!
THEN SUDDENLY I AM IN THIS PLACE.
SHOULD I BE AFRAID? IS THIS THE END THAT I'VE ALWAYS HEARD ABOUT?
NO, IT IS ONLY TIME TO PLAY THE FOOL.
AWWW POOR LITTLE CONE HEAD.
IT'S ONLY FOR A FEW DAYS, PENNY.
BUT I WILL DREAM OF MY REVENGE. I CAN ALREADY FEEL A HAIRBALL FORMING
Y'KNOW, SHE LOOKS LIKE ONE OF THOSE OLD-TIMEY SPEAKERS.
SHOULD WE HOOK HER UP TO THE STEREO?
YOU'RE AN IDIOT.
KARL

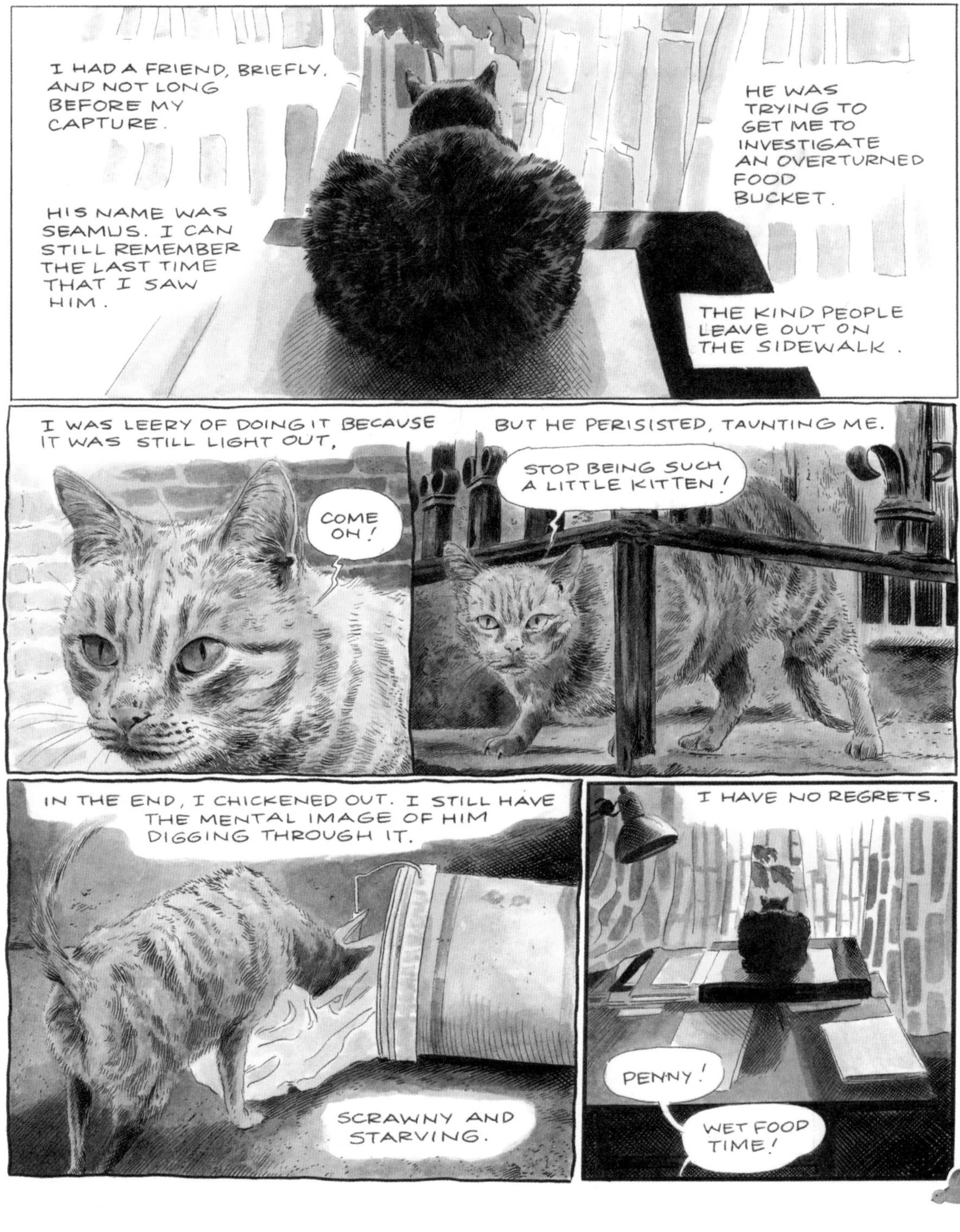
I HAD A FRIEND, BRIEFLY, AND NOT LONG BEFORE MY CAPTURE.
HIS NAME WAS SEAMUS. I CAN STILL REMEMBER THE LAST TIME THAT I SAW HIM.
HE WAS TRYING TO GET ME TO INVESTIGATE AN OVERTURNED FOOD BUCKET.
THE KIND PEOPLE LEAVE OUT ON THE SIDEWALK.
I WAS LEERY OF DOING IT BECAUSE IT WAS STILL LIGHT OUT,
COME ON!
BUT HE PERISISTED, TAUNTING ME.
STOP BEING SUCH A LITTLE KITTEN!
IN THE END, I CHICKENED OUT. I STILL HAVE THE MENTAL IMAGE OF HIM DIGGING THROUGH IT.
SCRAWNY AND STARVING.
I HAVE NO REGRETS.
PENNY!
WET FOOD TIME!

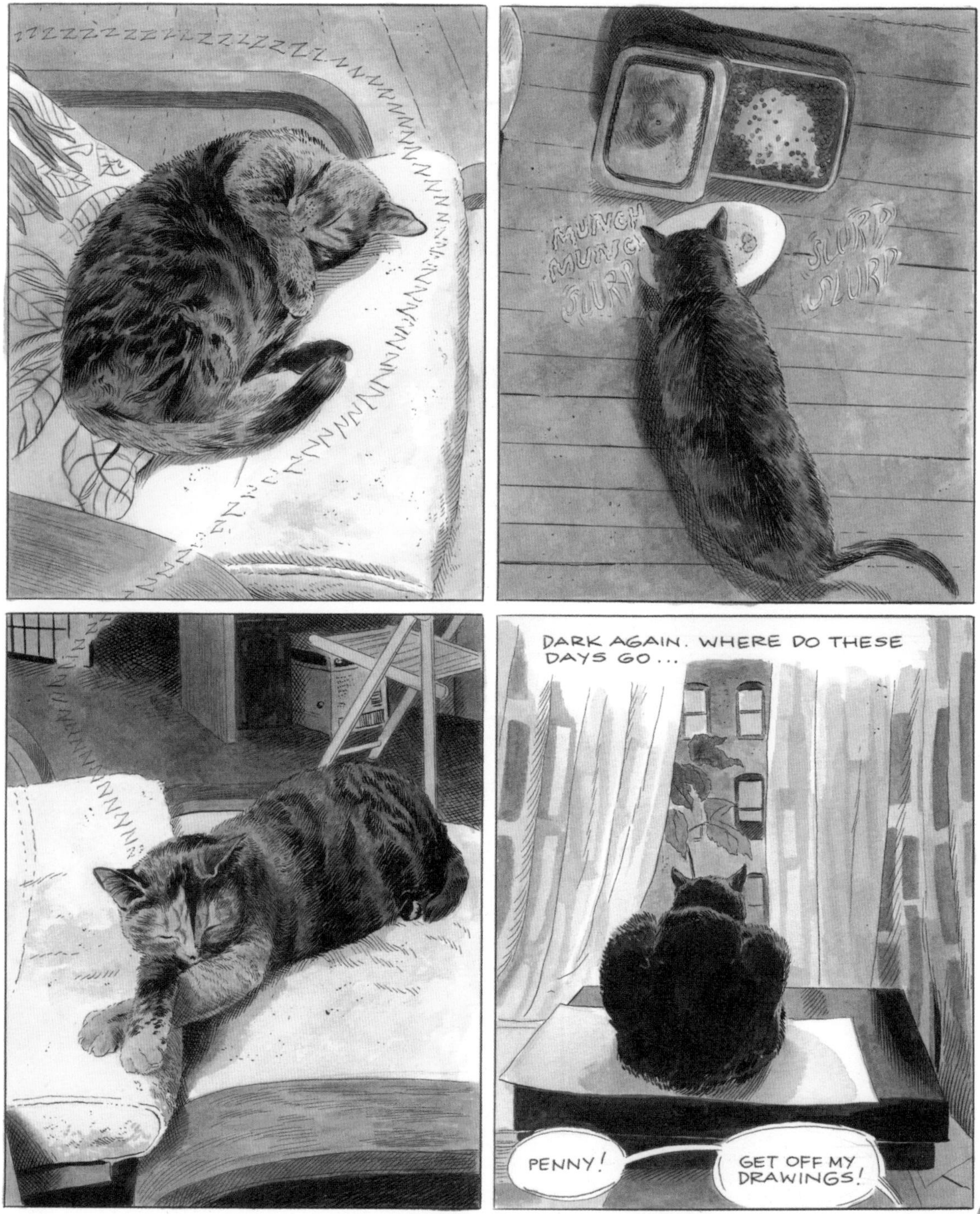
MUNCH
MUNCH
SLURP
SLURP
SLURP
DARK AGAIN. WHERE DO THESE DAYS GO...
PENNY!
GET OFF MY DRAWINGS!

SOMETHING IS GOING TO HAPPEN TODAY.

YUP.

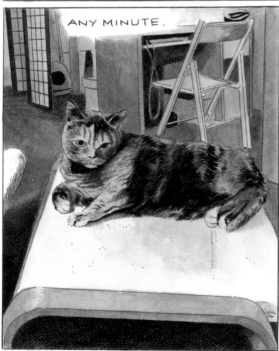

ANY MINUTE.

OK. MAYBE I'VE GOT MY DAYS CROSSED.

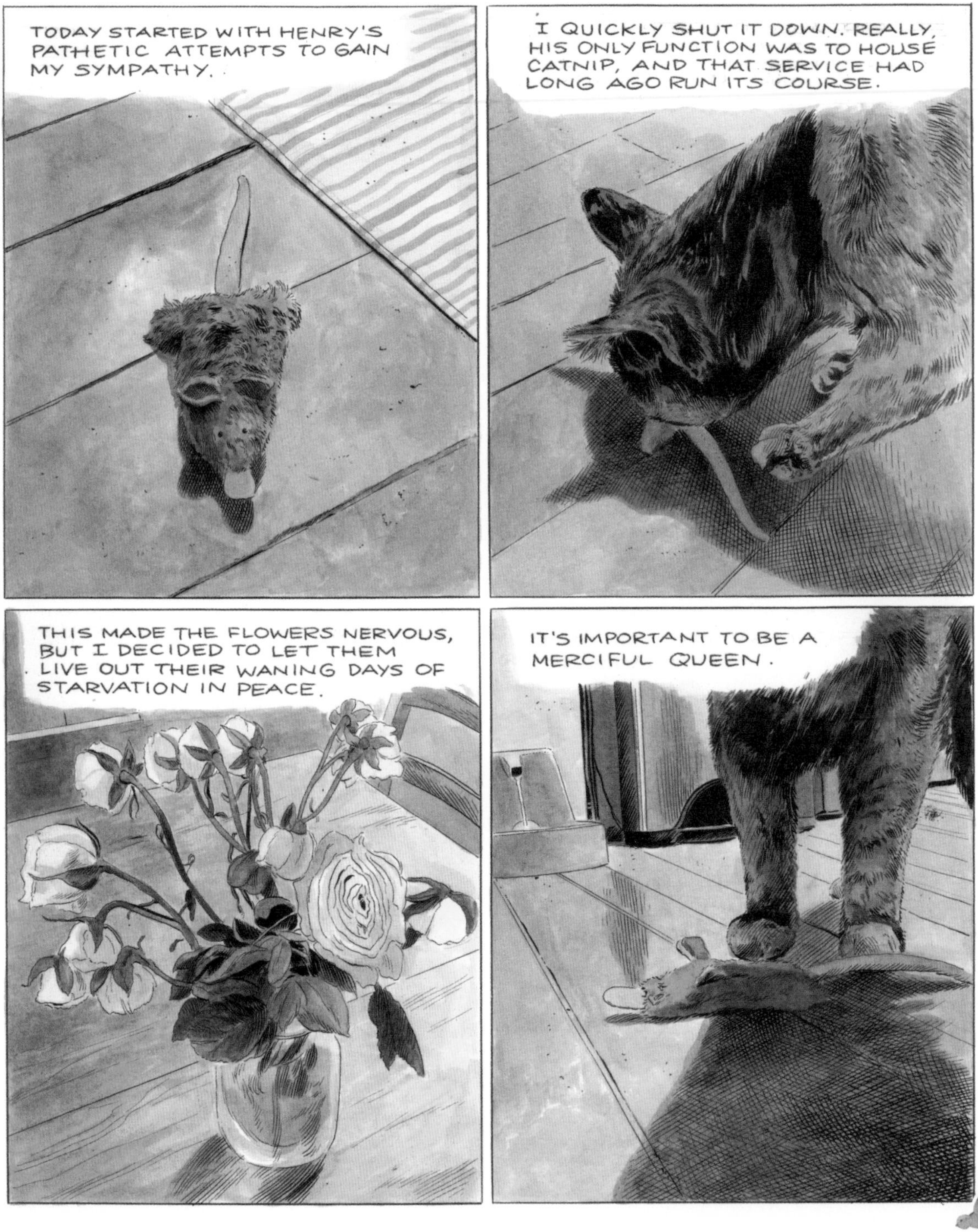
TODAY STARTED WITH HENRY'S PATHETIC ATTEMPTS TO GAIN MY SYMPATHY.
I QUICKLY SHUT IT DOWN. REALLY, HIS ONLY FUNCTION WAS TO HOUSE CATNIP, AND THAT SERVICE HAD LONG AGO RUN ITS COURSE.
THIS MADE THE FLOWERS NERVOUS, BUT I DECIDED TO LET THEM LIVE OUT THEIR WANING DAYS OF STARVATION IN PEACE.
IT'S IMPORTANT TO BE A MERCIFUL QUEEN.

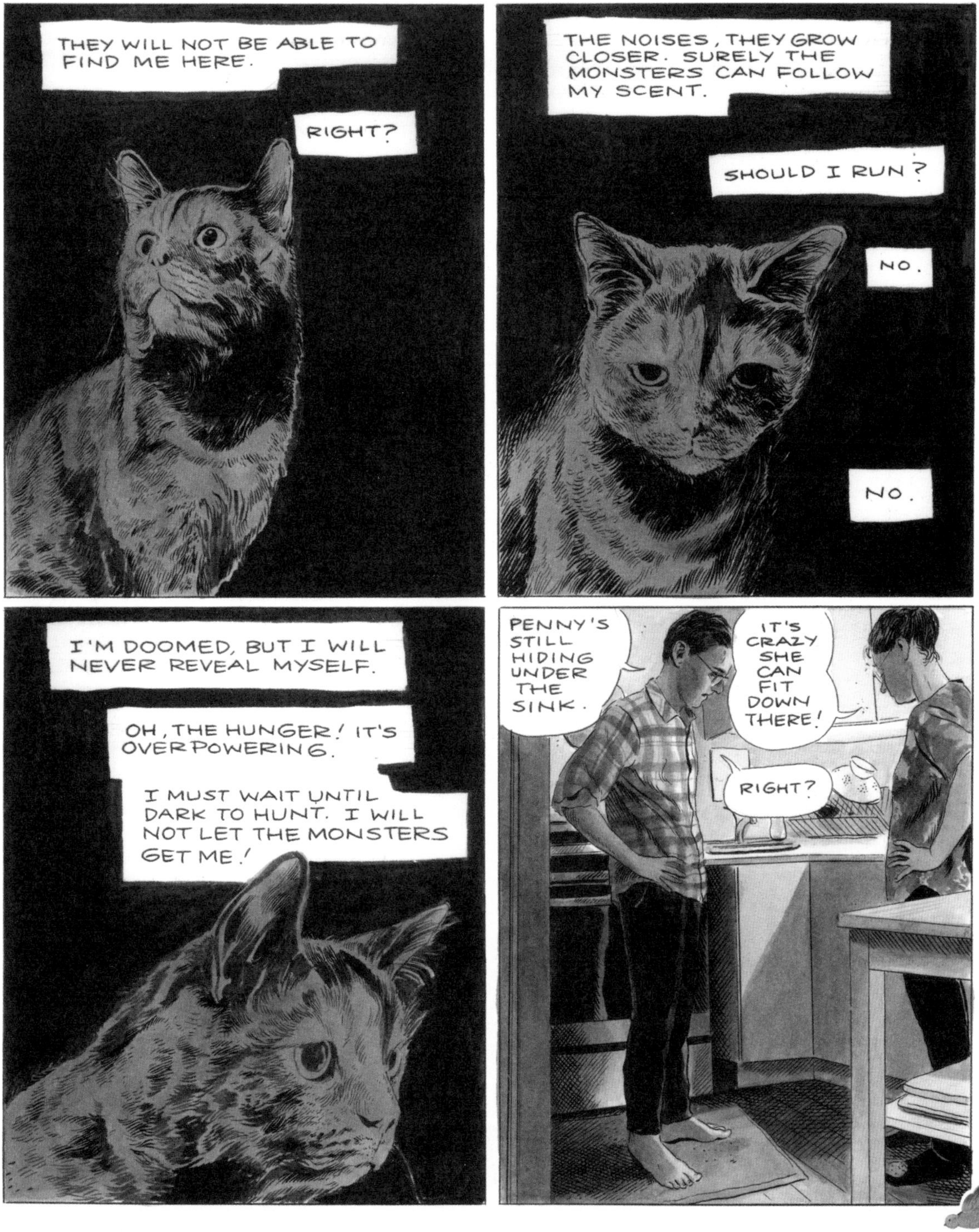

THEY WILL NOT BE ABLE TO FIND ME HERE.
RIGHT?
THE NOISES, THEY GROW CLOSER. SURELY THE MONSTERS CAN FOLLOW MY SCENT.
SHOULD I RUN?
NO.
NO.
I'M DOOMED, BUT I WILL NEVER REVEAL MYSELF.
OH, THE HUNGER! IT'S OVERPOWERING.
I MUST WAIT UNTIL DARK TO HUNT. I WILL NOT LET THE MONSTERS GET ME!
PENNY'S STILL HIDING UNDER THE SINK.
IT'S CRAZY SHE CAN FIT DOWN THERE!
RIGHT?

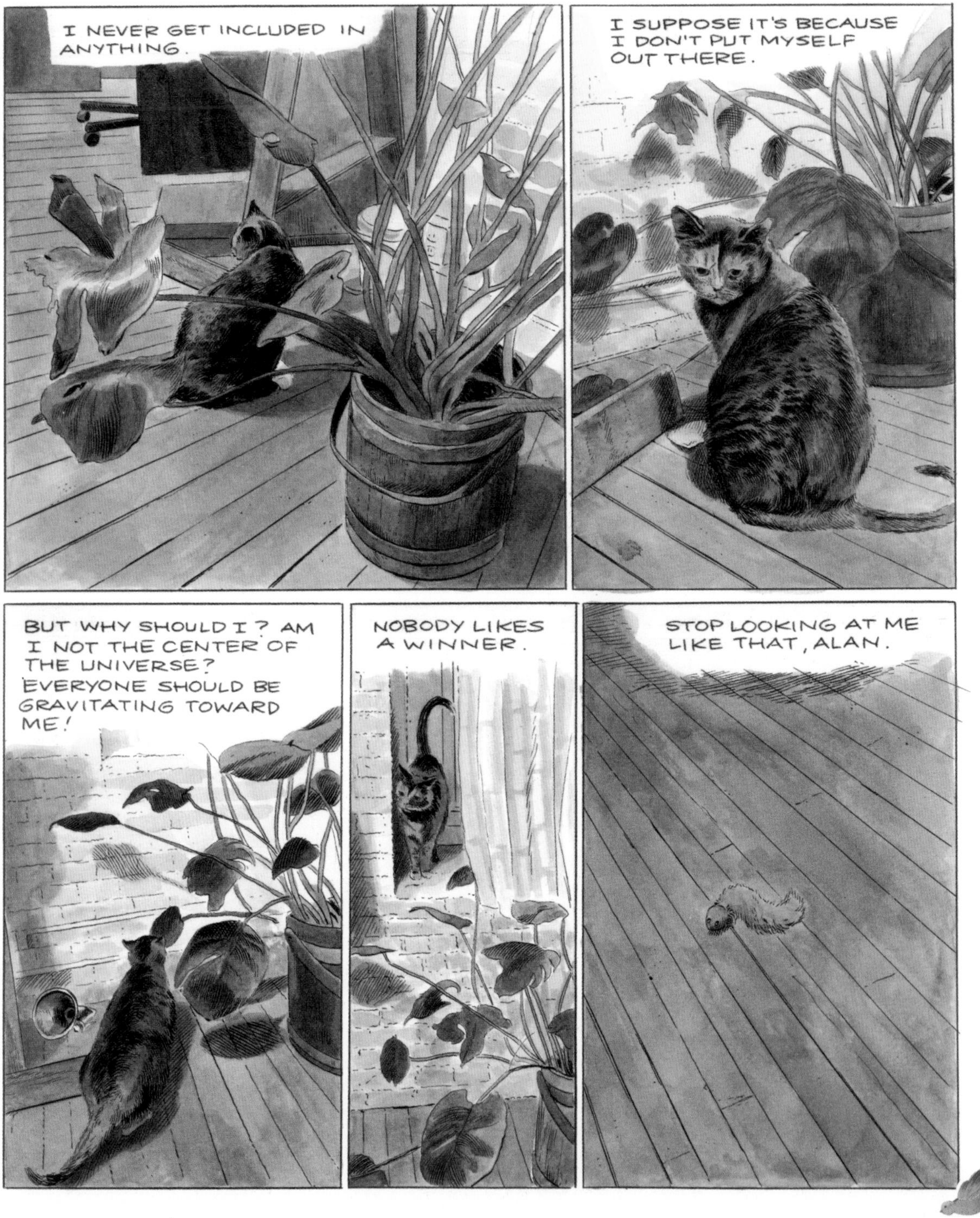
I NEVER GET INCLUDED IN ANYTHING.
I SUPPOSE IT'S BECAUSE I DON'T PUT MYSELF OUT THERE.
BUT WHY SHOULD I? AM I NOT THE CENTER OF THE UNIVERSE? EVERYONE SHOULD BE GRAVITATING TOWARD ME!
NOBODY LIKES A WINNER.
STOP LOOKING AT ME LIKE THAT, ALAN.

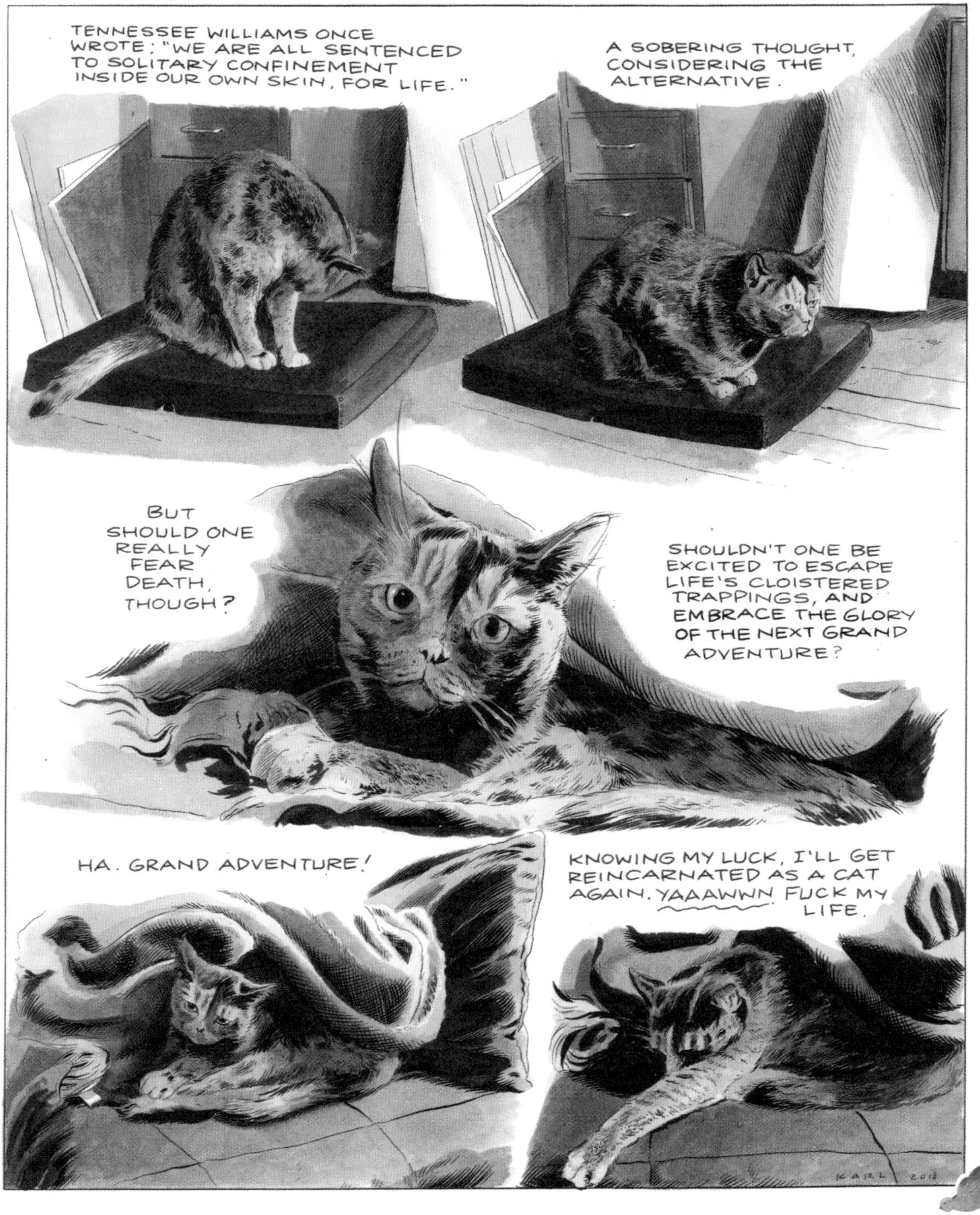
TENNESSEE WILLIAMS ONCE WROTE: "WE ARE ALL SENTENCED TO SOLITARY CONFINEMENT INSIDE OUR OWN SKIN, FOR LIFE."
A SOBERING THOUGHT, CONSIDERING THE ALTERNATIVE.
BUT SHOULD ONE REALLY FEAR DEATH, THOUGH?
SHOULDN'T ONE BE EXCITED TO ESCAPE LIFE'S CLOISTERED TRAPPINGS, AND EMBRACE THE GLORY OF THE NEXT GRAND ADVENTURE?
HA. GRAND ADVENTURE!
KNOWING MY LUCK, I'LL GET REINCARNATED AS A CAT AGAIN. YAAAWWN. FUCK MY LIFE.
KARL 2018

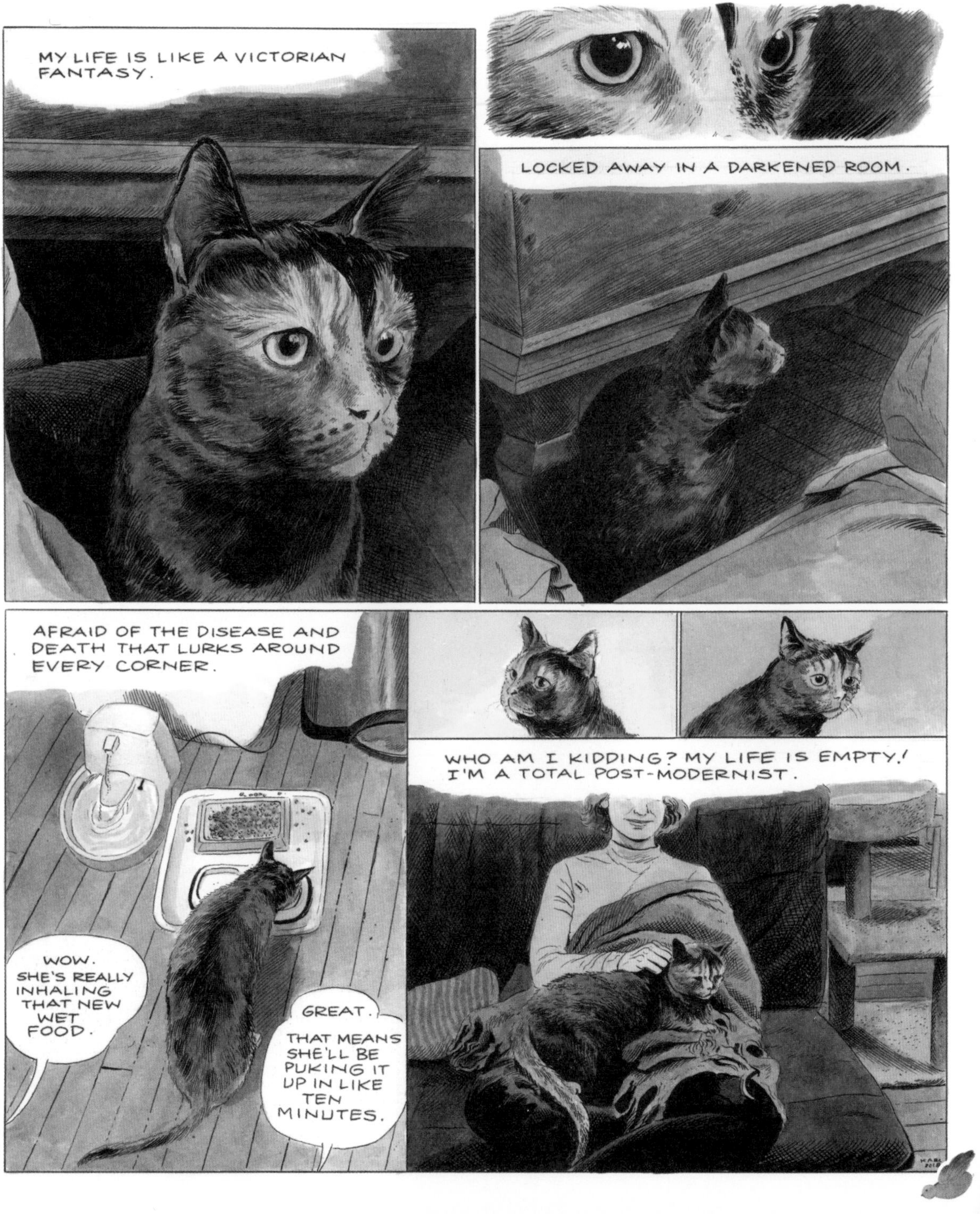
MY LIFE IS LIKE A VICTORIAN FANTASY.
LOCKED AWAY IN A DARKENED ROOM.
AFRAID OF THE DISEASE AND DEATH THAT LURKS AROUND EVERY CORNER.
WOW. SHE'S REALLY INHALING THAT NEW WET FOOD.
GREAT.
THAT MEANS SHE'LL BE PUKING IT UP IN LIKE TEN MINUTES.
WHO AM I KIDDING? MY LIFE IS EMPTY! I'M A TOTAL POST-MODERNIST.

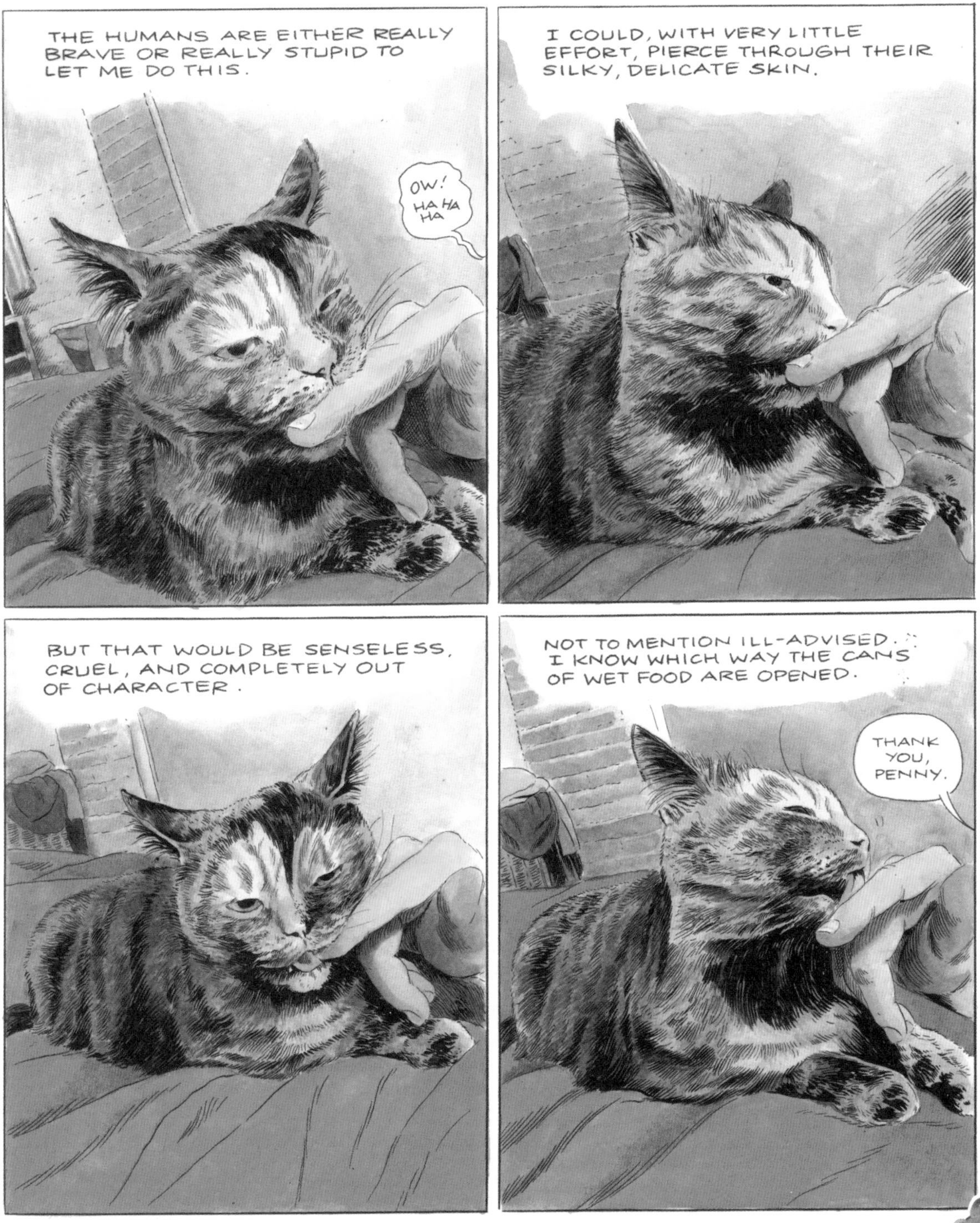
THE HUMANS ARE EITHER REALLY BRAVE OR REALLY STUPID TO LET ME DO THIS.
OW! HA HA HA
I COULD, WITH VERY LITTLE EFFORT, PIERCE THROUGH THEIR SILKY, DELICATE SKIN.
BUT THAT WOULD BE SENSELESS, CRUEL, AND COMPLETELY OUT OF CHARACTER.
NOT TO MENTION ILL-ADVISED. I KNOW WHICH WAY THE CANS OF WET FOOD ARE OPENED.
THANK YOU, PENNY.

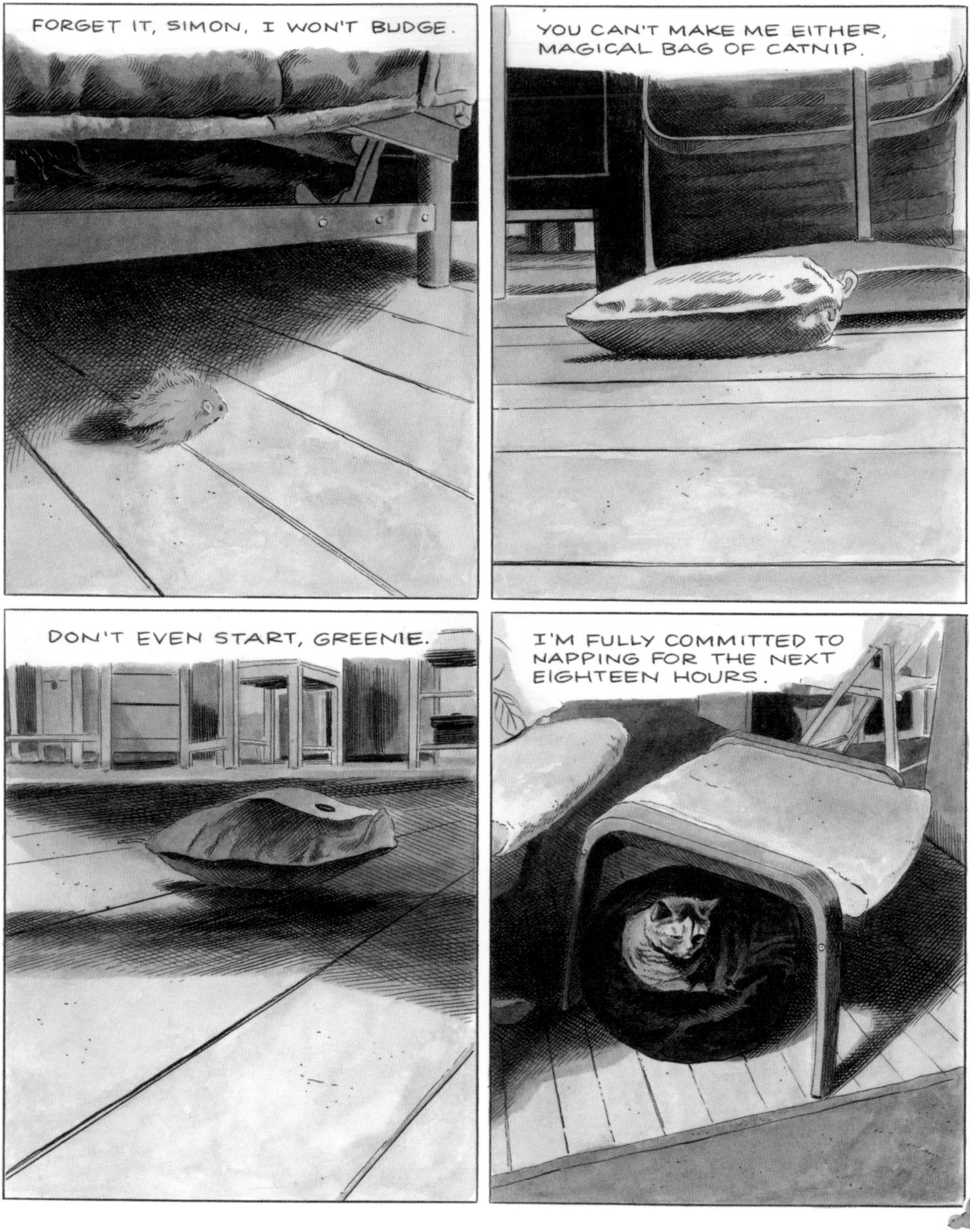
FORGET IT, SIMON, I WON'T BUDGE.
YOU CAN'T MAKE ME EITHER, MAGICAL BAG OF CATNIP.
DON'T EVEN START, GREENIE.
I'M FULLY COMMITTED TO NAPPING FOR THE NEXT EIGHTEEN HOURS.

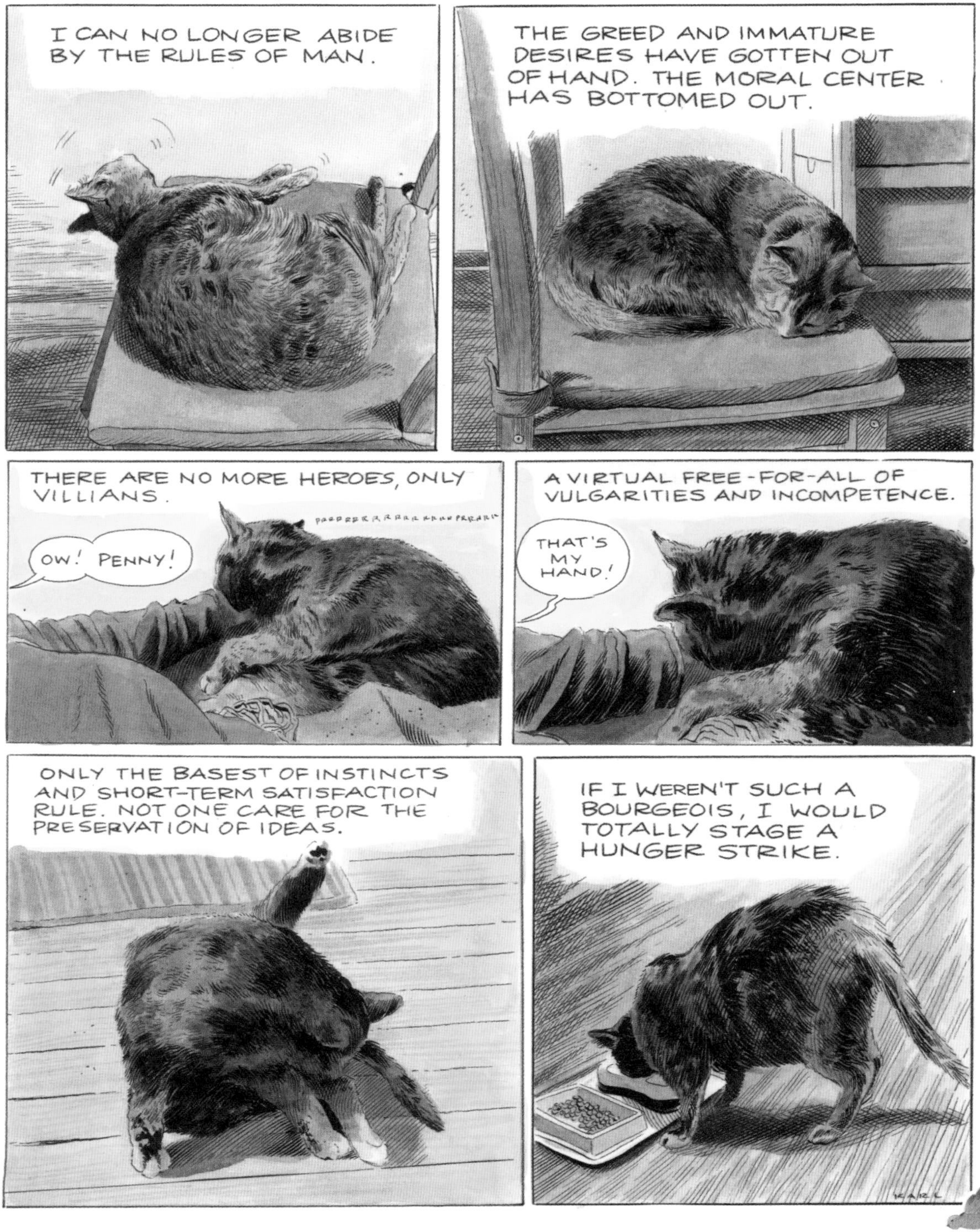
I CAN NO LONGER ABIDE BY THE RULES OF MAN.
THE GREED AND IMMATURE DESIRES HAVE GOTTEN OUT OF HAND. THE MORAL CENTER HAS BOTTOMED OUT.
THERE ARE NO MORE HEROES, ONLY VILLIANS.
OW! PENNY!
A VIRTUAL FREE-FOR-ALL OF VULGARITIES AND INCOMPETENCE.
THAT'S MY HAND!
ONLY THE BASEST OF INSTINCTS AND SHORT-TERM SATISFACTION RULE. NOT ONE CARE FOR THE PRESERVATION OF IDEAS.
IF I WEREN'T SUCH A BOURGEOIS, I WOULD TOTALLY STAGE A HUNGER STRIKE.

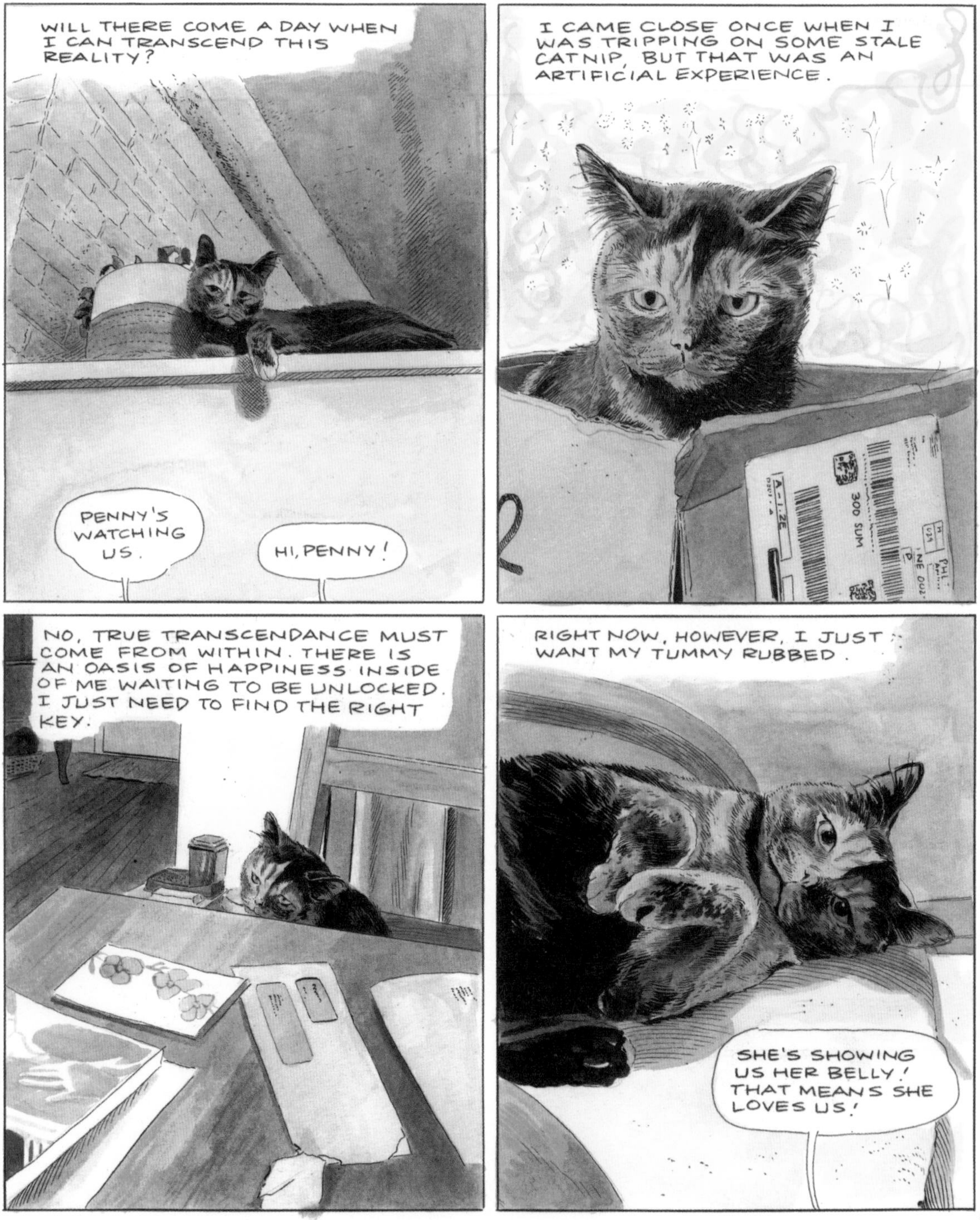
WILL THERE COME A DAY WHEN I CAN TRANSCEND THIS REALITY?
PENNY'S WATCHING US.
HI, PENNY!
I CAME CLOSE ONCE WHEN I WAS TRIPPING ON SOME STALE CATNIP, BUT THAT WAS AN ARTIFICIAL EXPERIENCE.
NO, TRUE TRANSCENDANCE MUST COME FROM WITHIN. THERE IS AN OASIS OF HAPPINESS INSIDE OF ME WAITING TO BE UNLOCKED. I JUST NEED TO FIND THE RIGHT KEY.
RIGHT NOW, HOWEVER, I JUST WANT MY TUMMY RUBBED.
SHE'S SHOWING US HER BELLY! THAT MEANS SHE LOVES US!

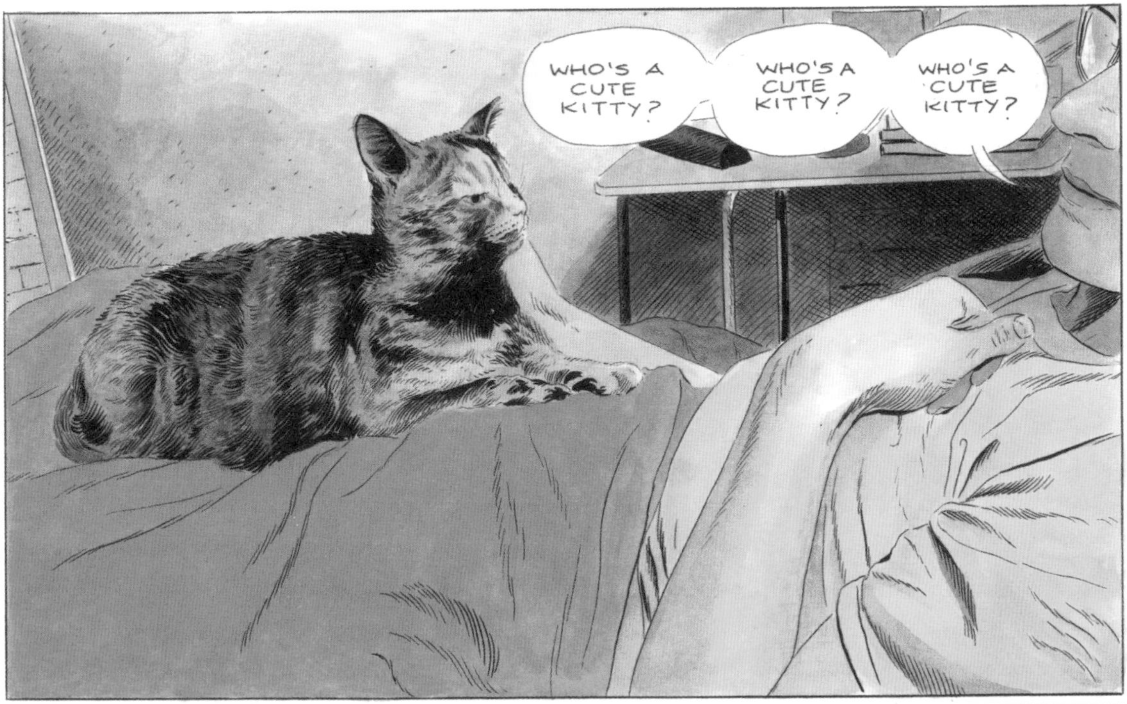
WHO'S A CUTE KITTY?
WHO'S A CUTE KITTY?
WHO'S A CUTE KITTY?

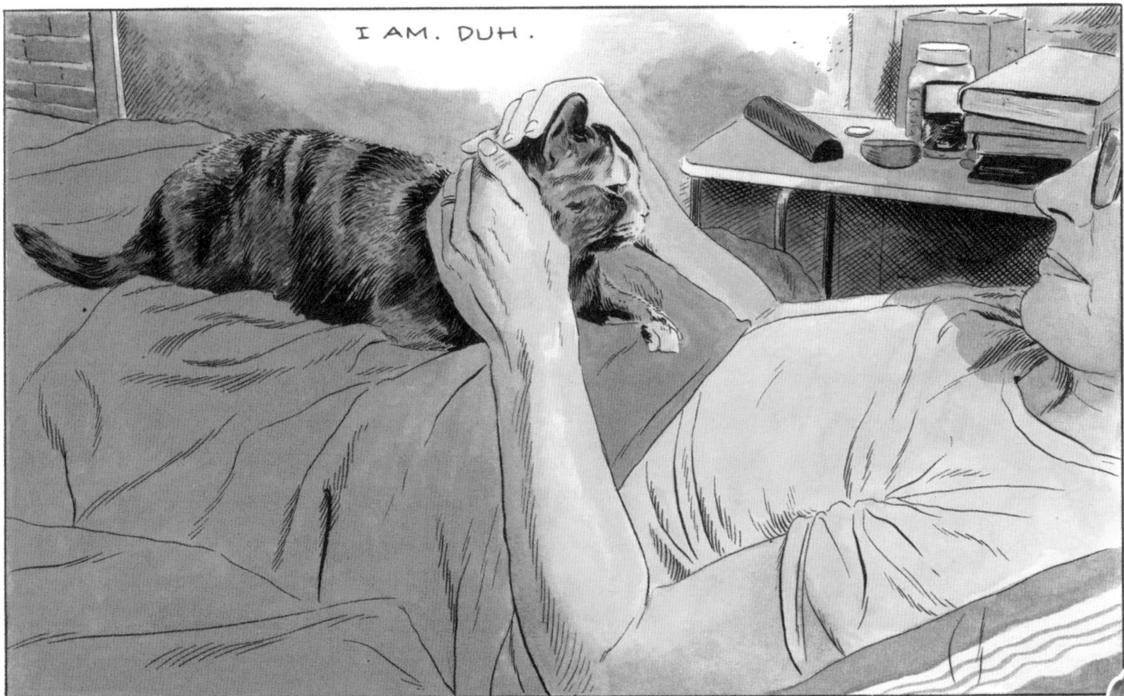
I AM. DUH.

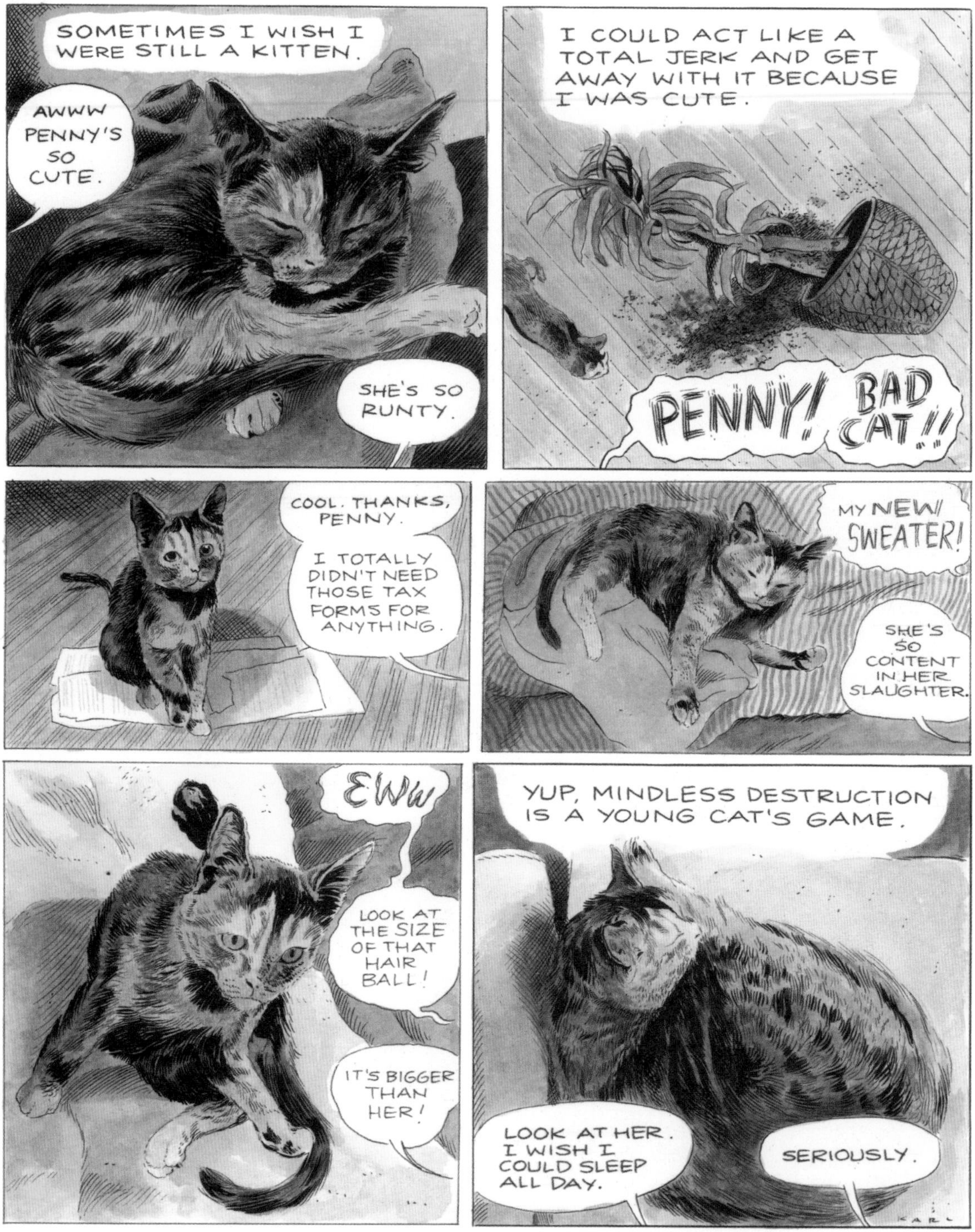
SOMETIMES I WISH I WERE STILL A KITTEN.
AWWW PENNY'S SO CUTE.
SHE'S SO RUNTY.
I COULD ACT LIKE A TOTAL JERK AND GET AWAY WITH IT BECAUSE I WAS CUTE.
PENNY!
BAD CAT!!
COOL. THANKS, PENNY.
I TOTALLY DIDN'T NEED THOSE TAX FORMS FOR ANYTHING.
MY NEW SWEATER!
SHE'S SO CONTENT IN HER SLAUGHTER.
EWW
LOOK AT THE SIZE OF THAT HAIR BALL!
IT'S BIGGER THAN HER!
YUP, MINDLESS DESTRUCTION IS A YOUNG CAT'S GAME.
LOOK AT HER. I WISH I COULD SLEEP ALL DAY.
SERIOUSLY.
KARL

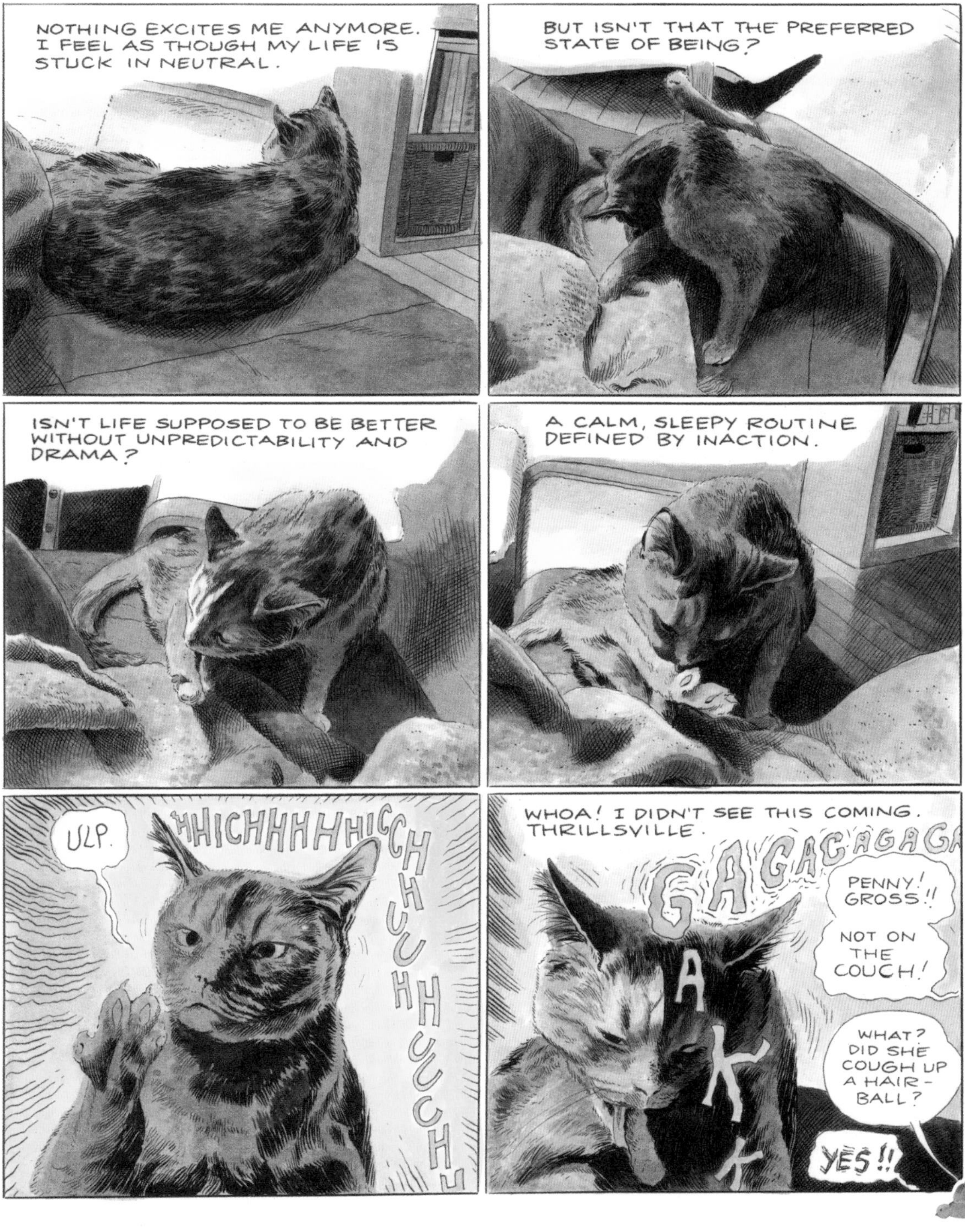
NOTHING EXCITES ME ANYMORE. I FEEL AS THOUGH MY LIFE IS STUCK IN NEUTRAL.
BUT ISN'T THAT THE PREFERRED STATE OF BEING?
ISN'T LIFE SUPPOSED TO BE BETTER WITHOUT UNPREDICTABILITY AND DRAMA?
A CALM, SLEEPY ROUTINE DEFINED BY INACTION.
ULP.
HHICHHHHHICCHHUHUHHUUCHH
WHOA! I DIDN'T SEE THIS COMING. THRILLSVILLE.
GAGAGAGAGAGA
PENNY! GROSS!!
NOT ON THE COUCH!
GAKK
WHAT? DID SHE COUGH UP A HAIR-BALL?
YES!!

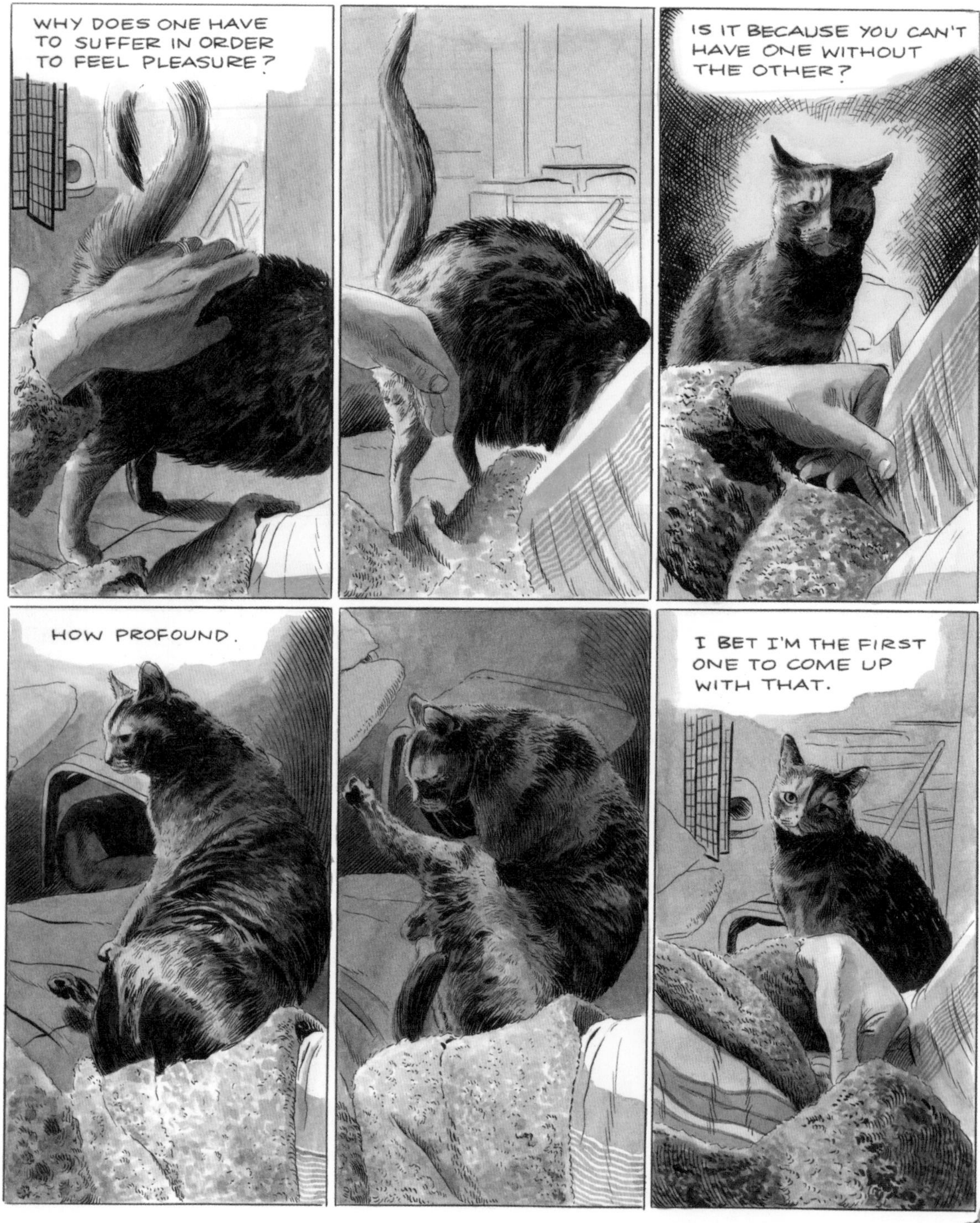
WHY DOES ONE HAVE TO SUFFER IN ORDER TO FEEL PLEASURE?
IS IT BECAUSE YOU CAN'T HAVE ONE WITHOUT THE OTHER?
HOW PROFOUND.
I BET I'M THE FIRST ONE TO COME UP WITH THAT.

I SOMETIMES WONDER IF I SUFFER FROM CERTAIN KINDS OF ATTACHMENT ISSUES.

PRRRRRRRRRRRR RRRRRR

LIKE, IS IT POSSIBLE FOR ME TO GO A DAY WITHOUT SEEKING AFFECTION FROM ONE OF THE HUMANS?

RRRRRRRRRRRR RRRR

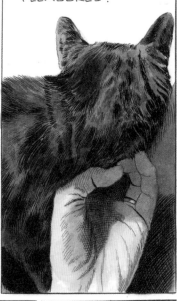

I MEAN, PROBABLY, BUT WHY DENY ONESELF SUCH EASY, SIMPLE PLEASURES?

IT'S NOT LIKE I'M SOME DEGRADED, HALF-CRAZY, LAP CAPTIVE MEWLING AWAY A TIRED EXISTENCE.

AWWW, LOOK HOW SWEET PENNY IS BEING.

I KNOW!

I WISH SHE WOULD DO THIS EVERY TIME WE SIT ON THE COUCH.

RIGHT?

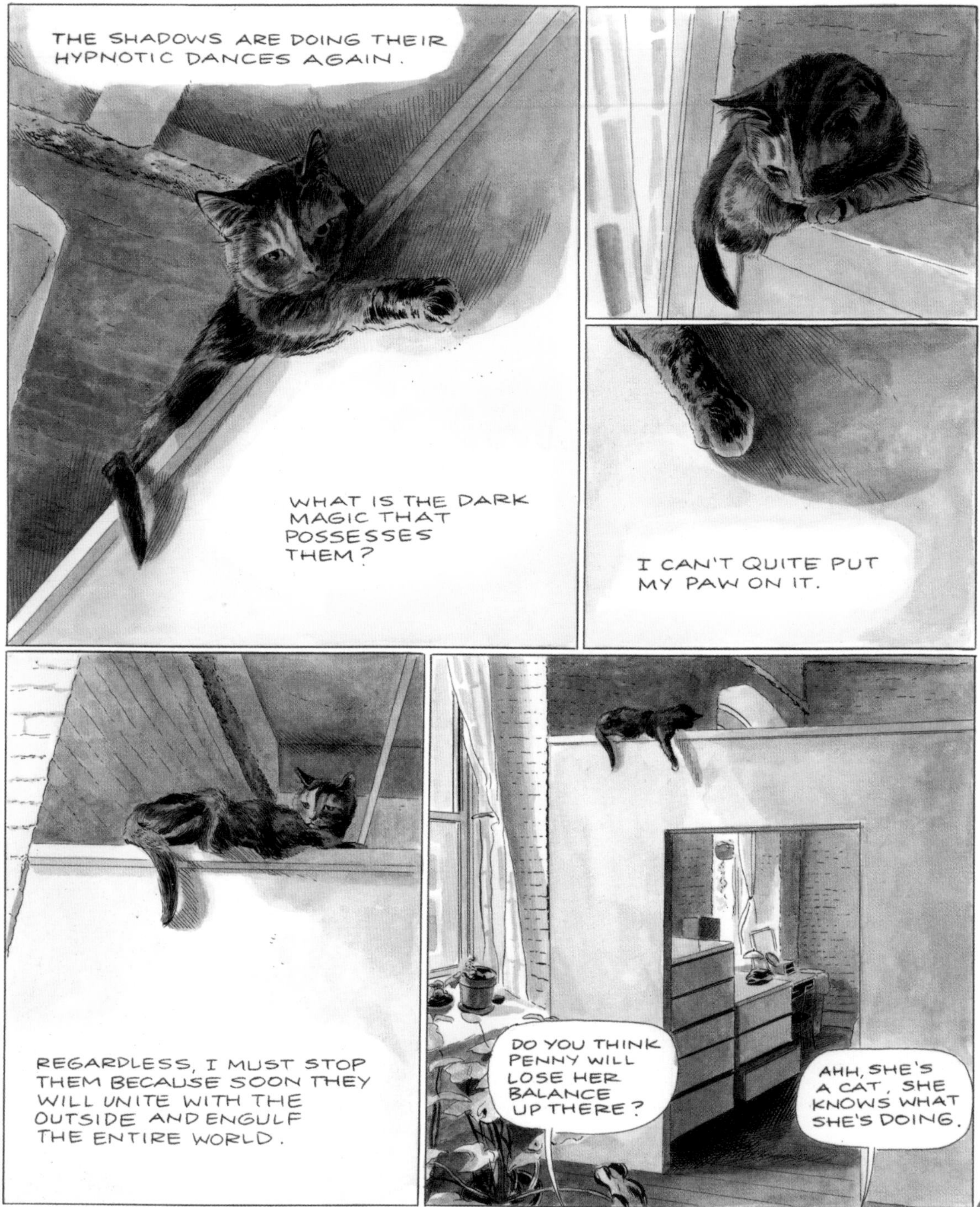
THE SHADOWS ARE DOING THEIR HYPNOTIC DANCES AGAIN.
WHAT IS THE DARK MAGIC THAT POSSESSES THEM?
I CAN'T QUITE PUT MY PAW ON IT.
REGARDLESS, I MUST STOP THEM BECAUSE SOON THEY WILL UNITE WITH THE OUTSIDE AND ENGULF THE ENTIRE WORLD.
DO YOU THINK PENNY WILL LOSE HER BALANCE UP THERE?
AHH, SHE'S A CAT, SHE KNOWS WHAT SHE'S DOING.

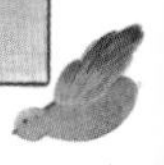

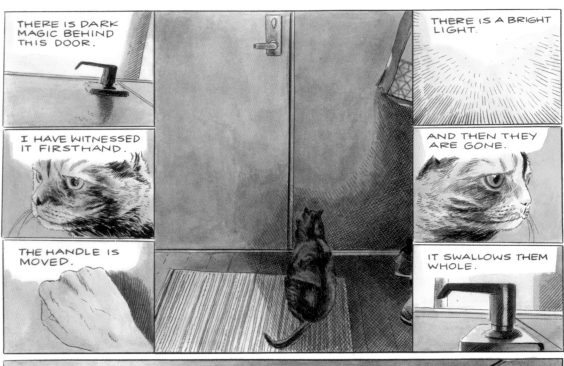

THERE IS DARK MAGIC BEHIND THIS DOOR.

I HAVE WITNESSED IT FIRSTHAND.

THE HANDLE IS MOVED.

THERE IS A BRIGHT LIGHT.

AND THEN THEY ARE GONE.

IT SWALLOWS THEM WHOLE.

ROBBING ME OF MY FOOD SUPPLY.

DARK MAGIC SHOWS NO MERCY.

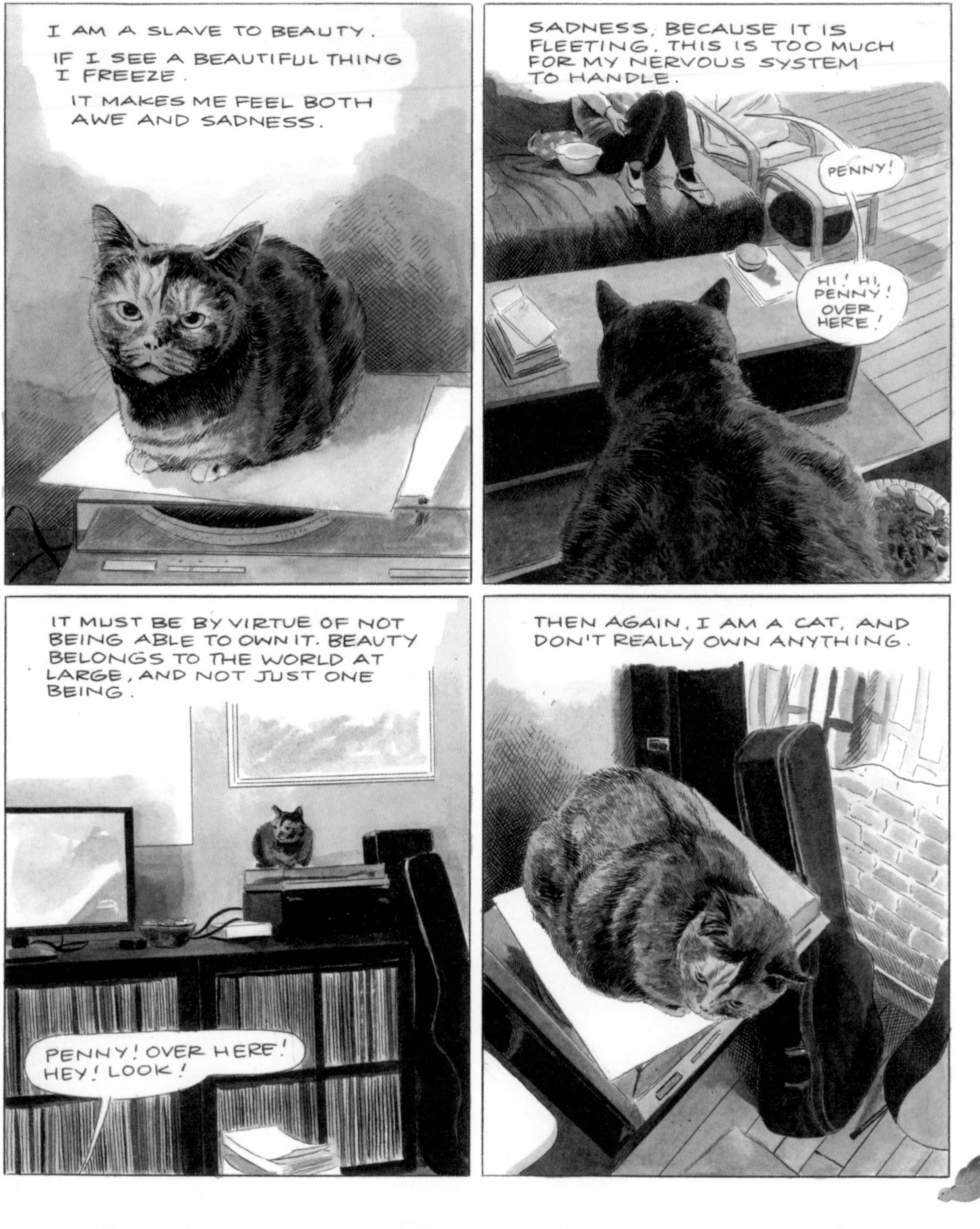
I AM A SLAVE TO BEAUTY.
IF I SEE A BEAUTIFUL THING I FREEZE.
IT MAKES ME FEEL BOTH AWE AND SADNESS.
SADNESS, BECAUSE IT IS FLEETING. THIS IS TOO MUCH FOR MY NERVOUS SYSTEM TO HANDLE.
PENNY!
HI! HI, PENNY! OVER HERE!
IT MUST BE BY VIRTUE OF NOT BEING ABLE TO OWN IT. BEAUTY BELONGS TO THE WORLD AT LARGE, AND NOT JUST ONE BEING.
PENNY! OVER HERE! HEY! LOOK!
THEN AGAIN, I AM A CAT, AND DON'T REALLY OWN ANYTHING.

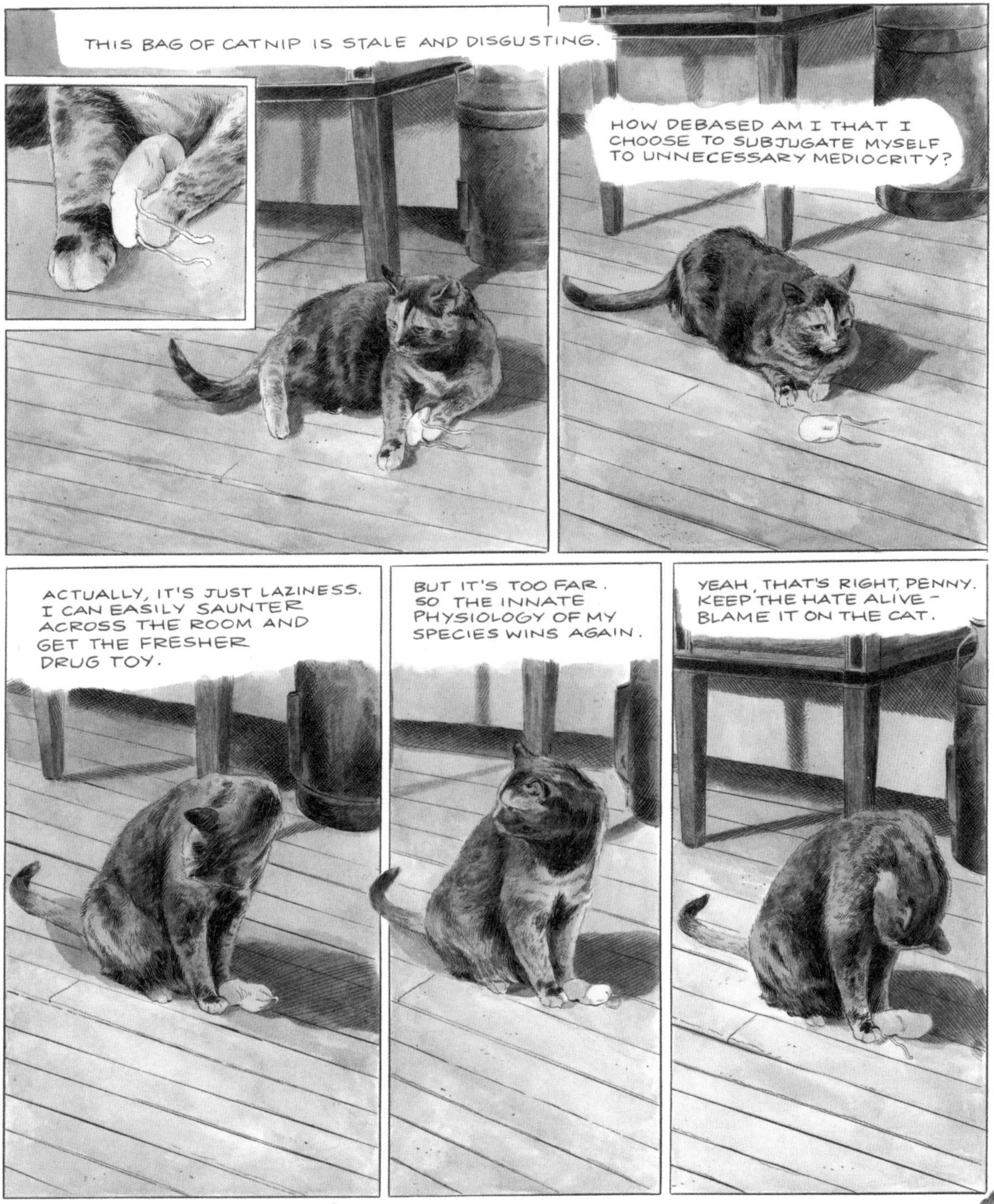
THIS BAG OF CATNIP IS STALE AND DISGUSTING.
HOW DEBASED AM I THAT I CHOOSE TO SUBJUGATE MYSELF TO UNNECESSARY MEDIOCRITY?
ACTUALLY, IT'S JUST LAZINESS. I CAN EASILY SAUNTER ACROSS THE ROOM AND GET THE FRESHER DRUG TOY.
BUT IT'S TOO FAR. SO THE INNATE PHYSIOLOGY OF MY SPECIES WINS AGAIN.
YEAH, THAT'S RIGHT, PENNY. KEEP THE HATE ALIVE - BLAME IT ON THE CAT.

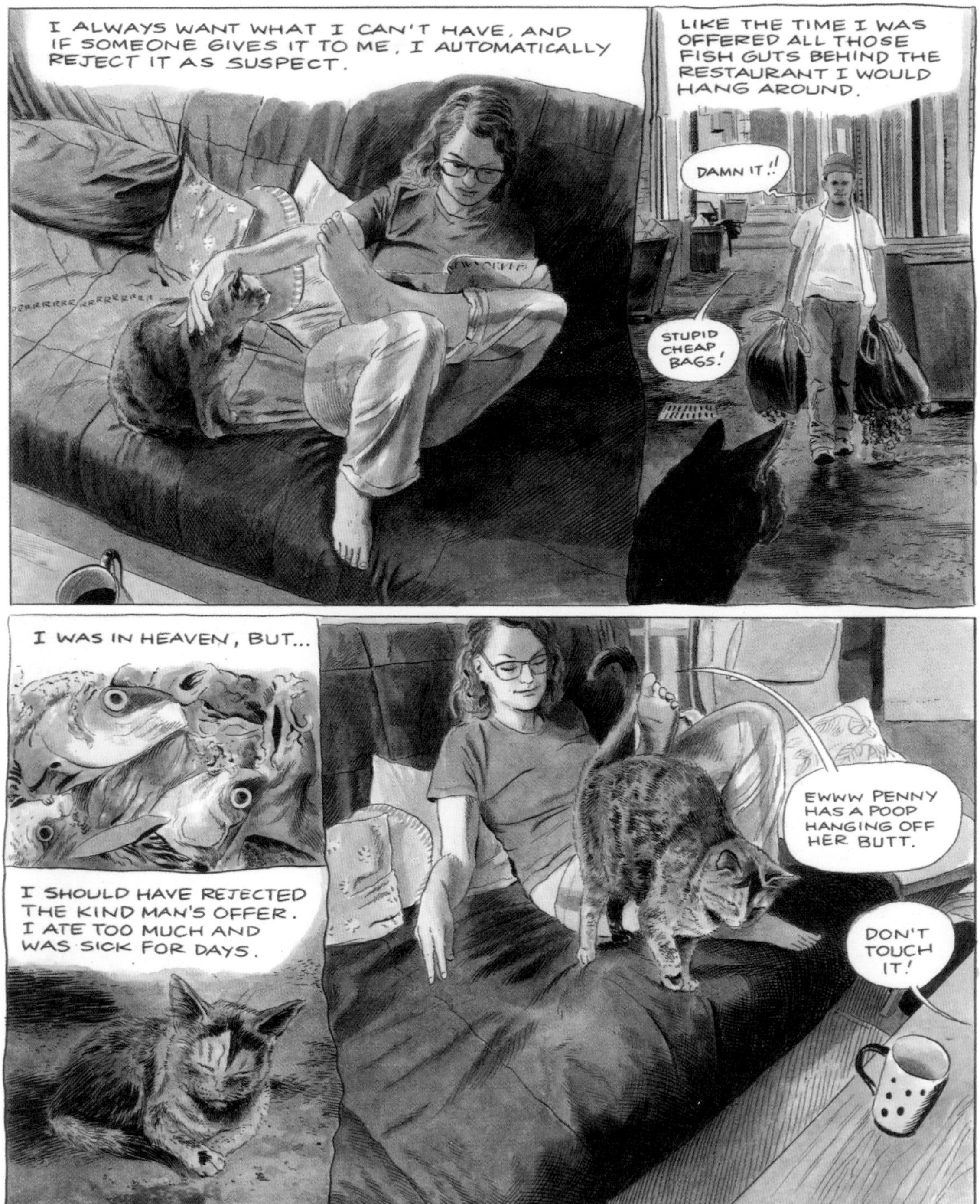
I ALWAYS WANT WHAT I CAN'T HAVE, AND IF SOMEONE GIVES IT TO ME, I AUTOMATICALLY REJECT IT AS SUSPECT.
LIKE THE TIME I WAS OFFERED ALL THOSE FISH GUTS BEHIND THE RESTAURANT I WOULD HANG AROUND.
DAMN IT!!
STUPID CHEAP BAGS!
I WAS IN HEAVEN, BUT...
I SHOULD HAVE REJECTED THE KIND MAN'S OFFER. I ATE TOO MUCH AND WAS SICK FOR DAYS.
EWWW PENNY HAS A POOP HANGING OFF HER BUTT.
DON'T TOUCH IT!

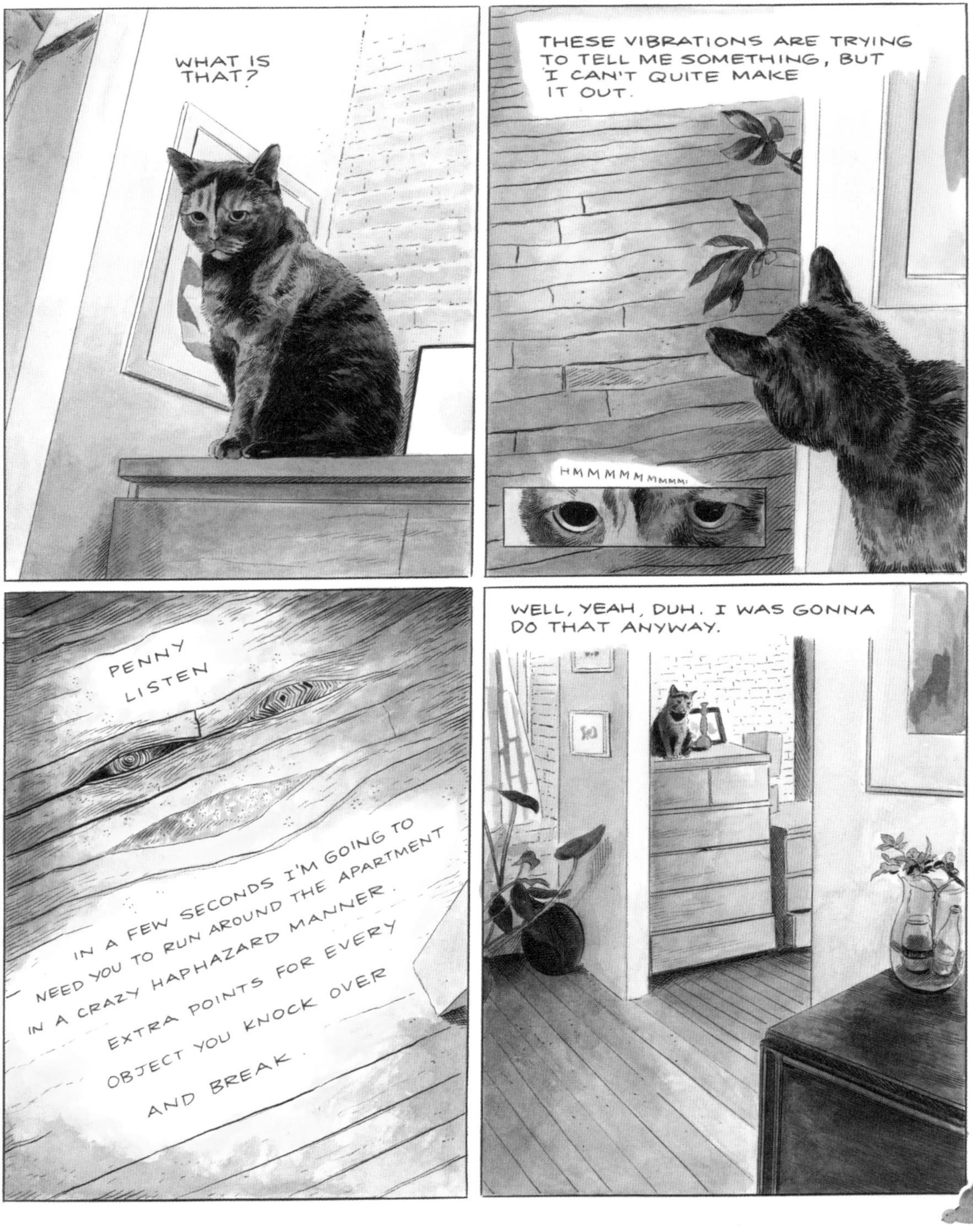
WHAT IS THAT?
THESE VIBRATIONS ARE TRYING TO TELL ME SOMETHING, BUT I CAN'T QUITE MAKE IT OUT.
HMMMMMMMMM!
PENNY LISTEN
IN A FEW SECONDS I'M GOING TO NEED YOU TO RUN AROUND THE APARTMENT IN A CRAZY HAPHAZARD MANNER.
EXTRA POINTS FOR EVERY OBJECT YOU KNOCK OVER AND BREAK.
WELL, YEAH, DUH. I WAS GONNA DO THAT ANYWAY.

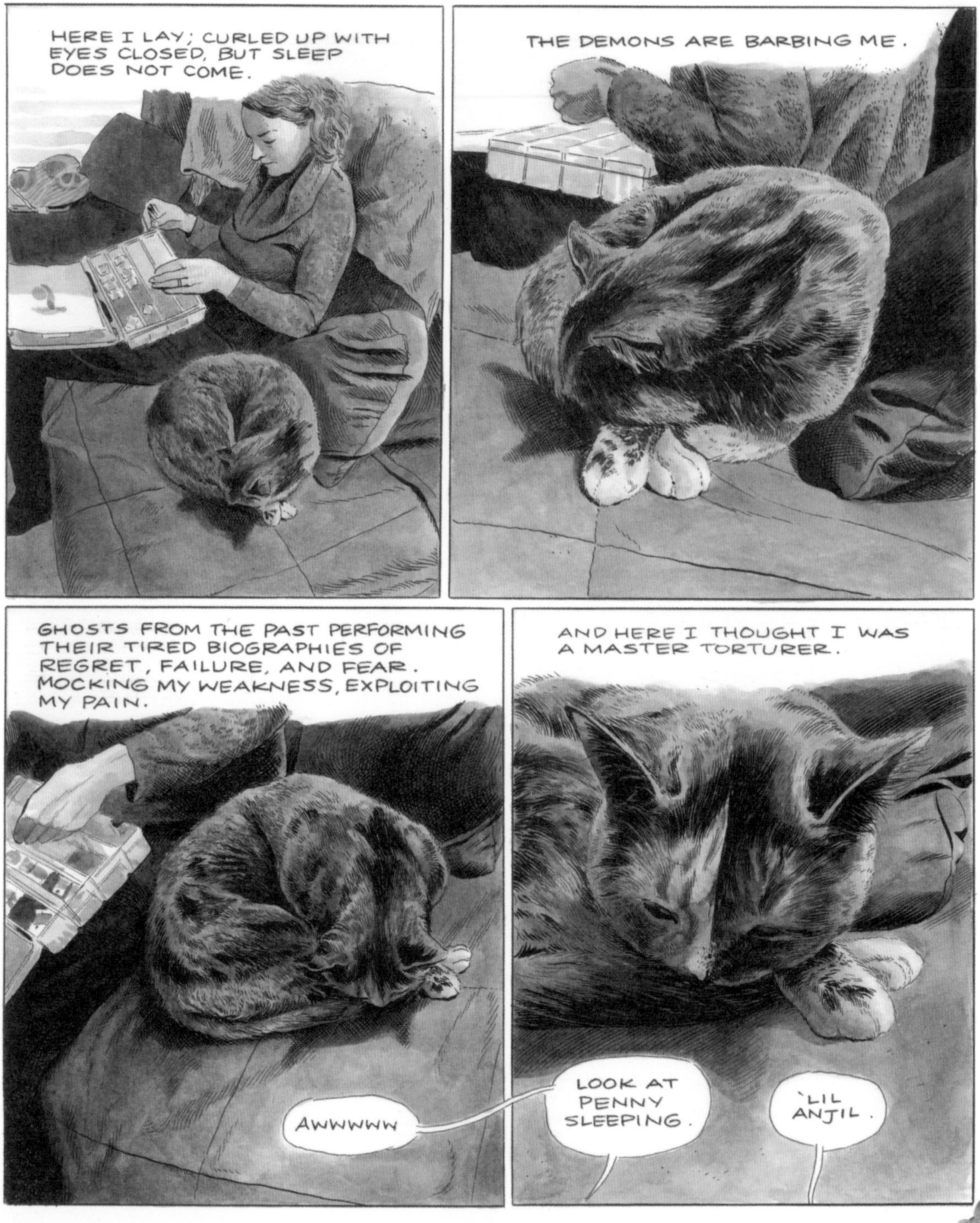
HERE I LAY; CURLED UP WITH EYES CLOSED, BUT SLEEP DOES NOT COME.
THE DEMONS ARE BARBING ME.
GHOSTS FROM THE PAST PERFORMING THEIR TIRED BIOGRAPHIES OF REGRET, FAILURE, AND FEAR. MOCKING MY WEAKNESS, EXPLOITING MY PAIN.
AND HERE I THOUGHT I WAS A MASTER TORTURER.
AWWWWW
LOOK AT PENNY SLEEPING.
`LIL ANJIL.

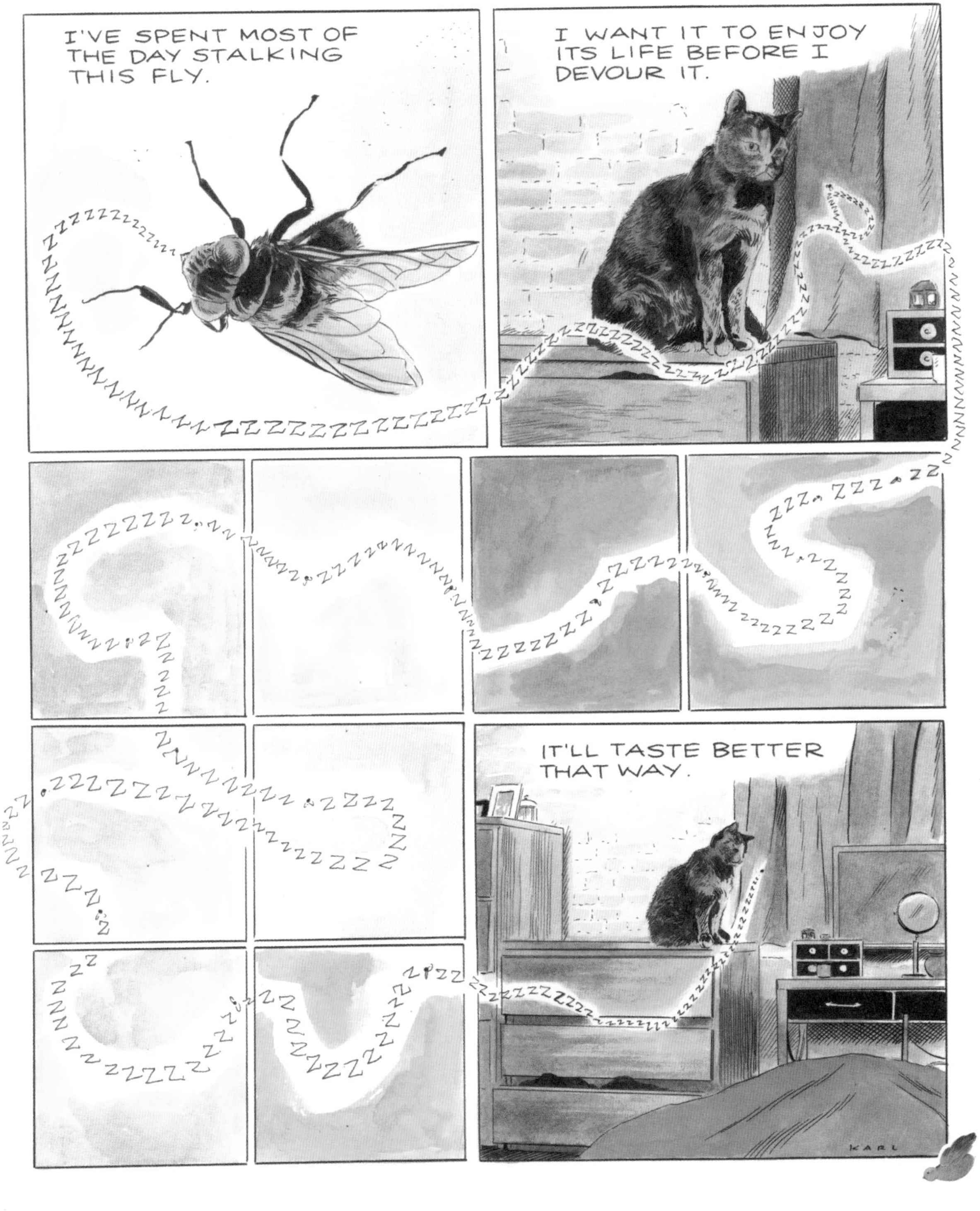
I'VE SPENT MOST OF THE DAY STALKING THIS FLY.
I WANT IT TO ENJOY ITS LIFE BEFORE I DEVOUR IT.
IT'LL TASTE BETTER THAT WAY.
KARL

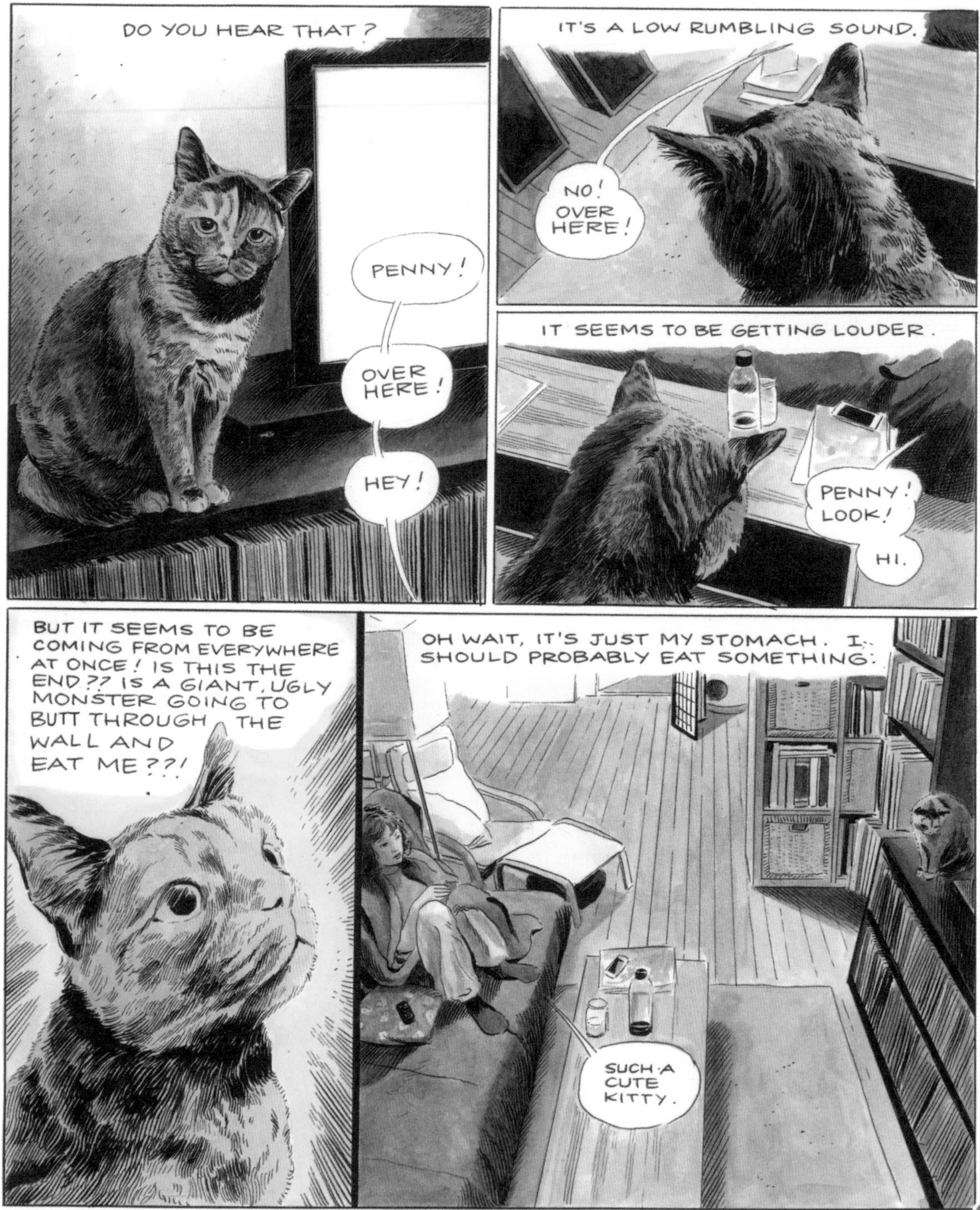
DO YOU HEAR THAT?
PENNY!
OVER HERE!
HEY!
IT'S A LOW RUMBLING SOUND.
NO! OVER HERE!
IT SEEMS TO BE GETTING LOUDER.
PENNY! LOOK!
HI.
BUT IT SEEMS TO BE COMING FROM EVERYWHERE AT ONCE! IS THIS THE END?? IS A GIANT, UGLY MONSTER GOING TO BUTT THROUGH THE WALL AND EAT ME??!
OH WAIT, IT'S JUST MY STOMACH. I SHOULD PROBABLY EAT SOMETHING.
SUCH A CUTE KITTY.

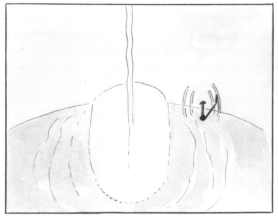

WHEN MY WATER DISH IS CLOSE TO BEING EMPTY, I GET NERVOUS.

WHICH IS WEIRD BECAUSE I CAN ALWAYS DRINK OUT OF THE FAUCET OR THEIR TOILET.

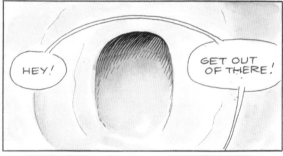

HEY!

GET OUT OF THERE!

OH!

HI, PENNY!

I CAN BE SO IRRATIONAL SOMETIMES.

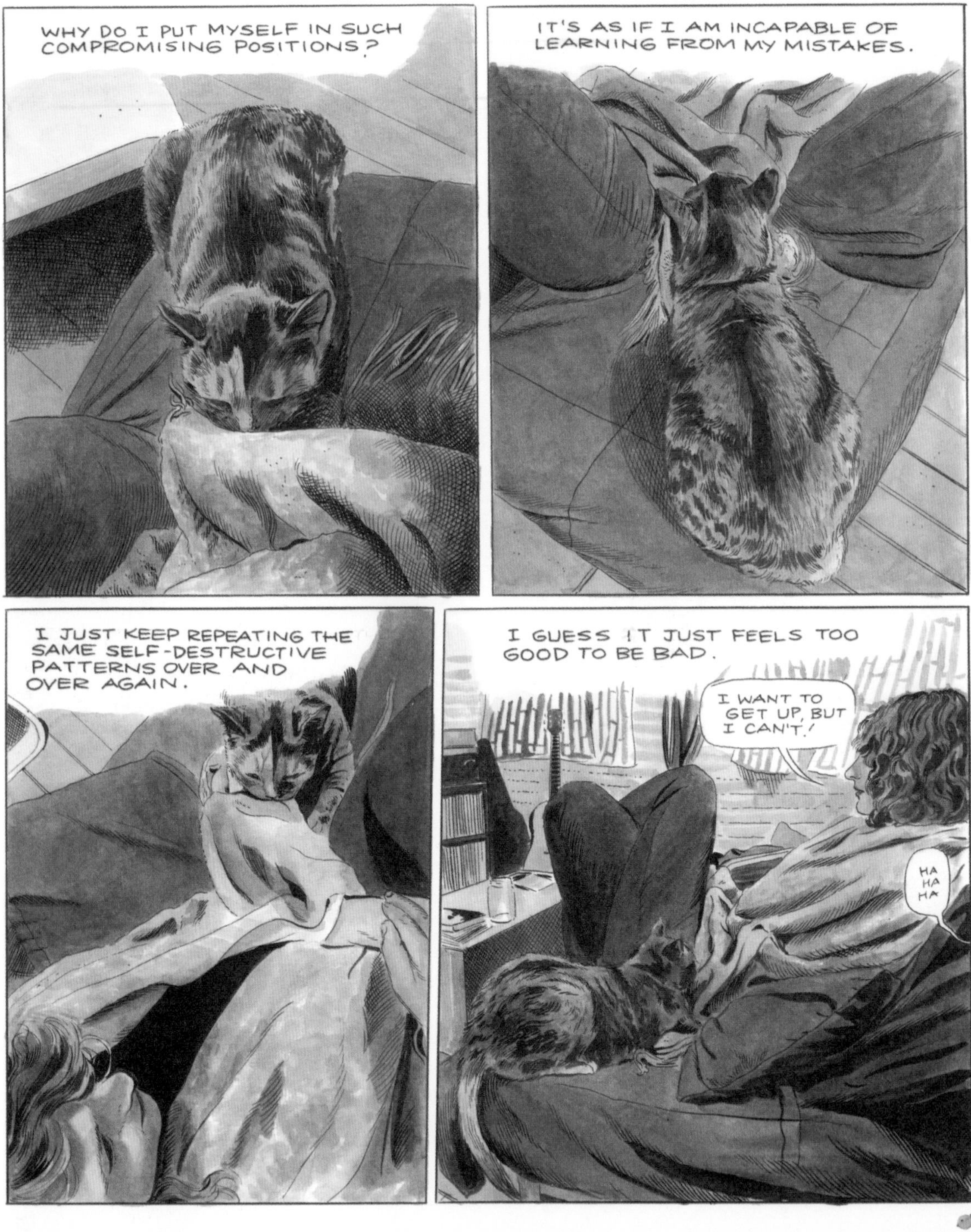
WHY DO I PUT MYSELF IN SUCH COMPROMISING POSITIONS?
IT'S AS IF I AM INCAPABLE OF LEARNING FROM MY MISTAKES.
I JUST KEEP REPEATING THE SAME SELF-DESTRUCTIVE PATTERNS OVER AND OVER AGAIN.
I GUESS IT JUST FEELS TOO GOOD TO BE BAD.
I WANT TO GET UP, BUT I CAN'T!
HA HA HA

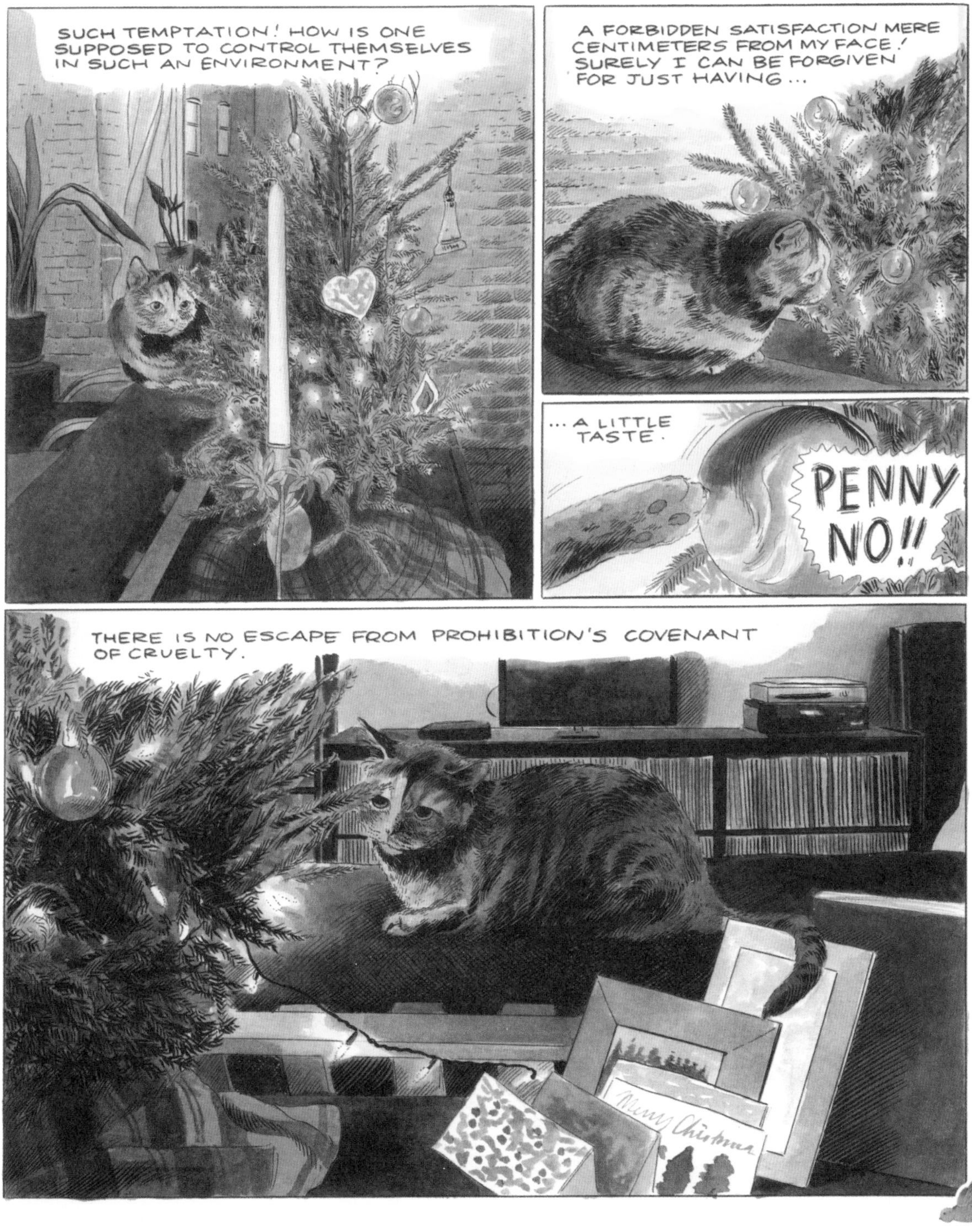

SUCH TEMPTATION! HOW IS ONE SUPPOSED TO CONTROL THEMSELVES IN SUCH AN ENVIRONMENT?
A FORBIDDEN SATISFACTION MERE CENTIMETERS FROM MY FACE! SURELY I CAN BE FORGIVEN FOR JUST HAVING...
...A LITTLE TASTE.
PENNY NO!!
THERE IS NO ESCAPE FROM PROHIBITION'S COVENANT OF CRUELTY.

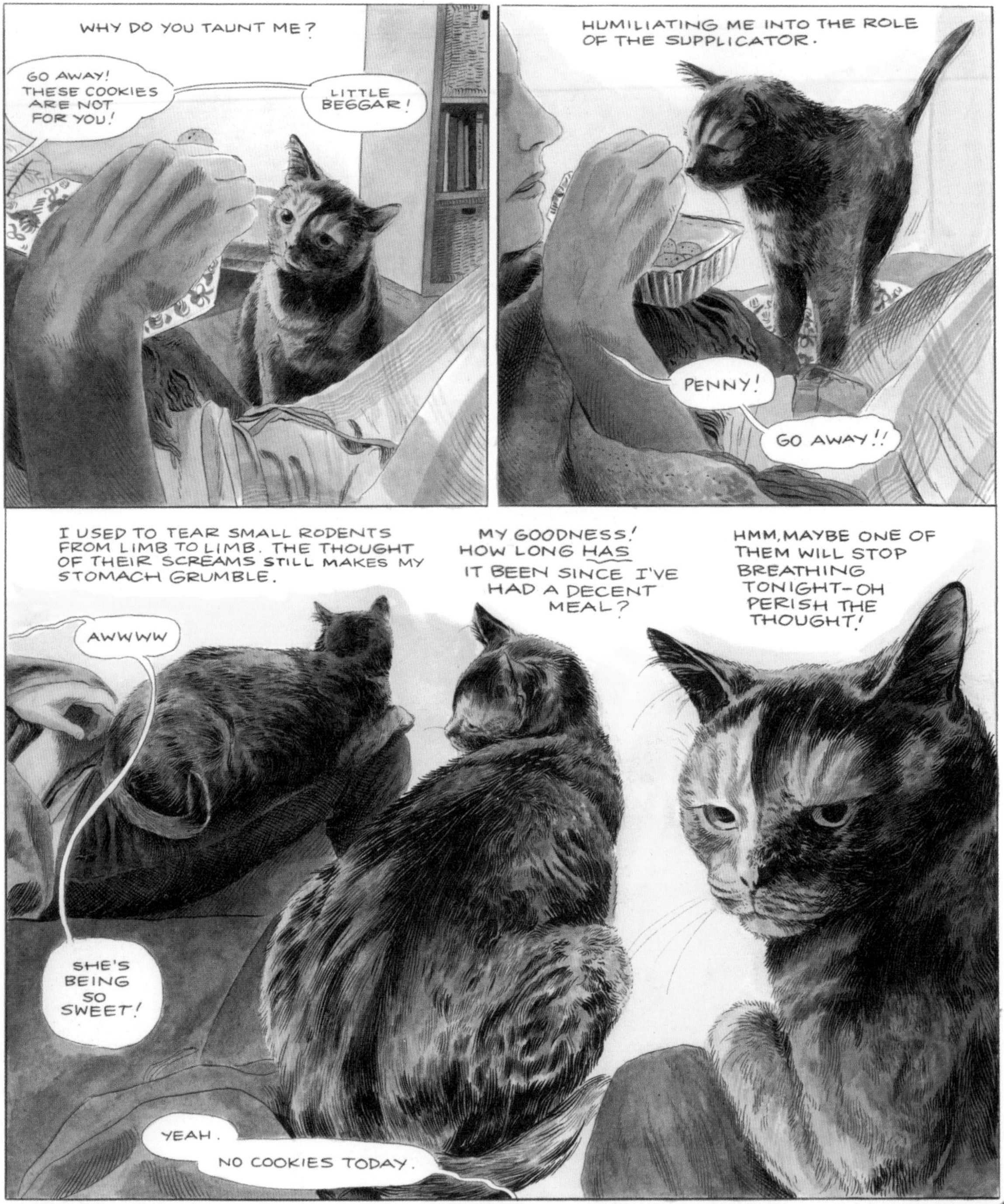
WHY DO YOU TAUNT ME?
GO AWAY! THESE COOKIES ARE NOT FOR YOU!
LITTLE BEGGAR!
HUMILIATING ME INTO THE ROLE OF THE SUPPLICATOR.
PENNY!
GO AWAY!!
I USED TO TEAR SMALL RODENTS FROM LIMB TO LIMB. THE THOUGHT OF THEIR SCREAMS STILL MAKES MY STOMACH GRUMBLE.
MY GOODNESS! HOW LONG HAS IT BEEN SINCE I'VE HAD A DECENT MEAL?
HMM, MAYBE ONE OF THEM WILL STOP BREATHING TONIGHT—OH PERISH THE THOUGHT!
AWWWW
SHE'S BEING SO SWEET!
YEAH.
NO COOKIES TODAY.

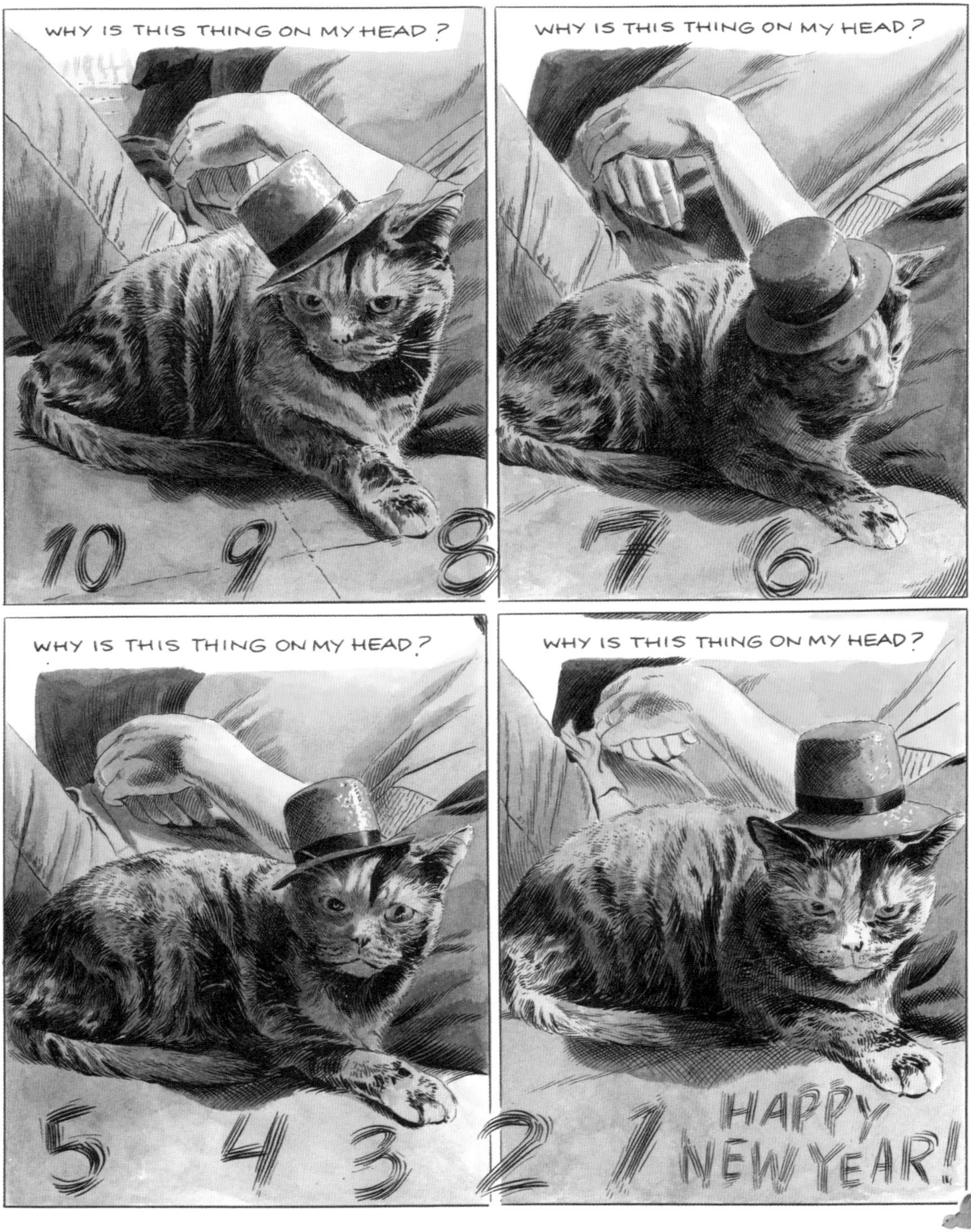
WHY IS THIS THING ON MY HEAD?
10 9 8
WHY IS THIS THING ON MY HEAD?
7 6
WHY IS THIS THING ON MY HEAD?
5 4 3 2
WHY IS THIS THING ON MY HEAD?
1
HAPPY NEW YEAR!

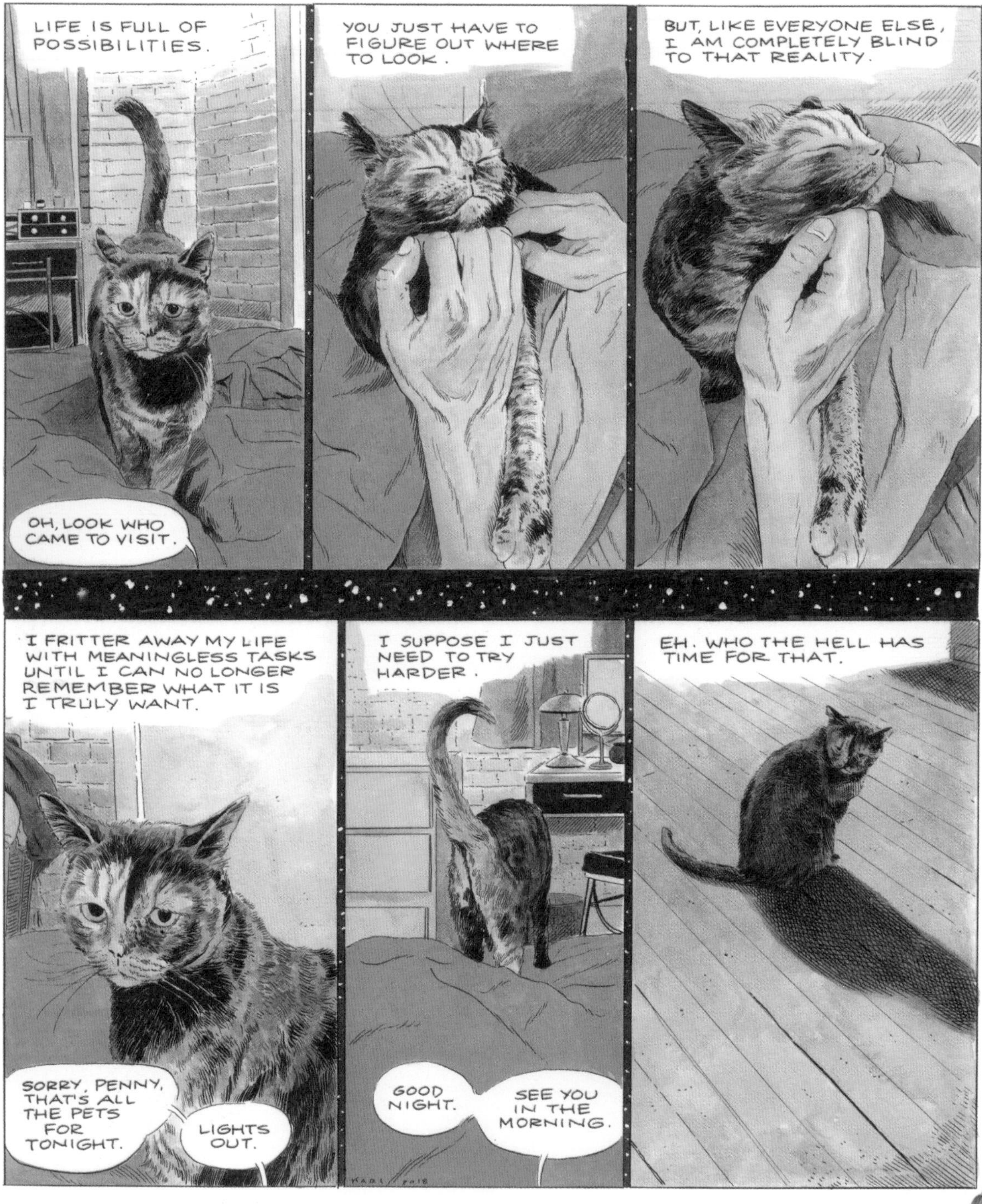
LIFE IS FULL OF POSSIBILITIES.
OH, LOOK WHO CAME TO VISIT.
YOU JUST HAVE TO FIGURE OUT WHERE TO LOOK.
BUT, LIKE EVERYONE ELSE, I AM COMPLETELY BLIND TO THAT REALITY.
I FRITTER AWAY MY LIFE WITH MEANINGLESS TASKS UNTIL I CAN NO LONGER REMEMBER WHAT IT IS I TRULY WANT.
SORRY, PENNY, THAT'S ALL THE PETS FOR TONIGHT.
LIGHTS OUT.
I SUPPOSE I JUST NEED TO TRY HARDER.
GOOD NIGHT.
SEE YOU IN THE MORNING.
EH. WHO THE HELL HAS TIME FOR THAT.

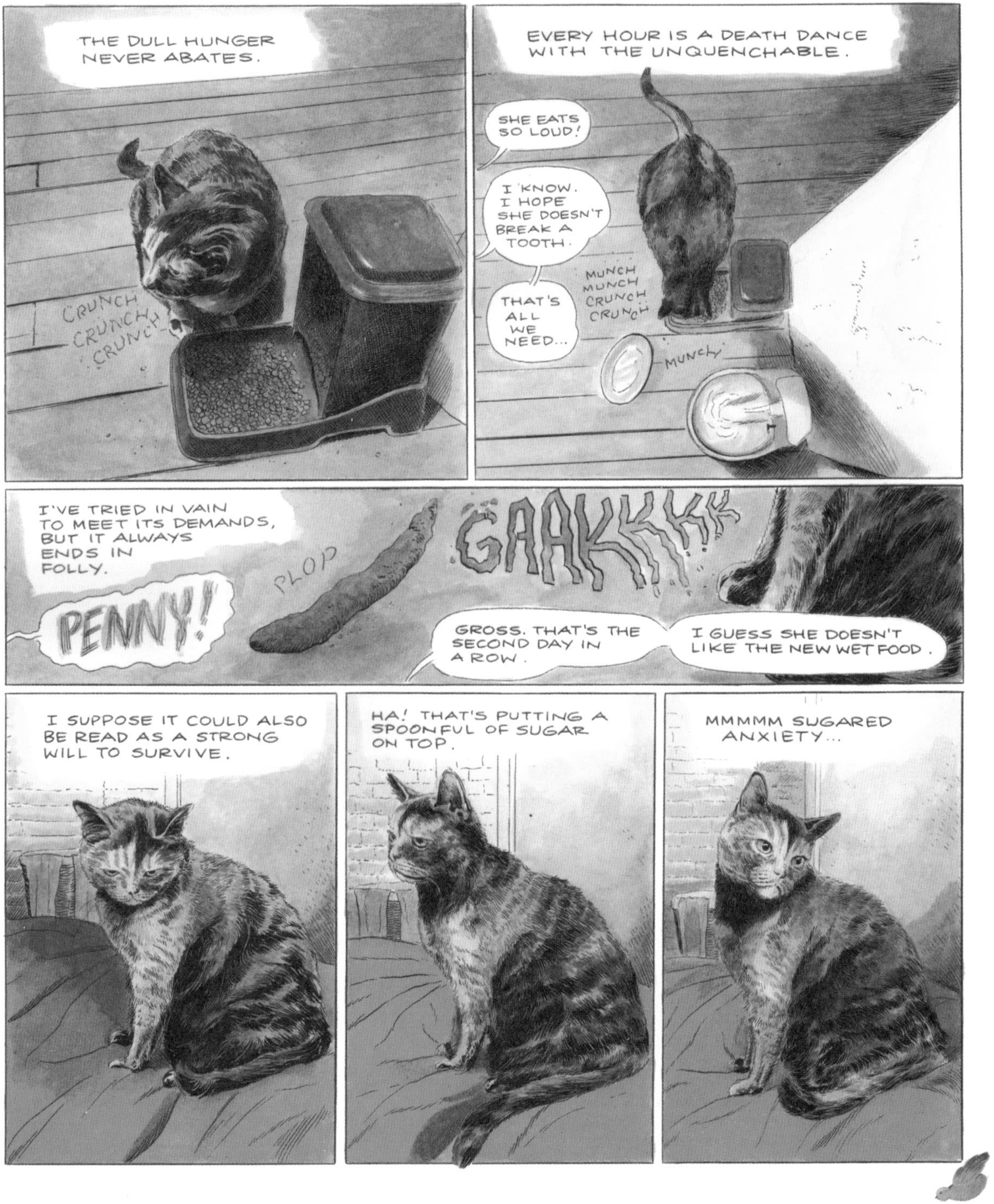
THE DULL HUNGER NEVER ABATES.
CRUNCH
CRUNCH
CRUNCH
EVERY HOUR IS A DEATH DANCE WITH THE UNQUENCHABLE.
SHE EATS SO LOUD!
I KNOW. I HOPE SHE DOESN'T BREAK A TOOTH.
THAT'S ALL WE NEED...
MUNCH MUNCH CRUNCH CRUNCH
MUNCH
I'VE TRIED IN VAIN TO MEET ITS DEMANDS, BUT IT ALWAYS ENDS IN FOLLY.
PENNY!
PLOP
GAAKKKK
GROSS. THAT'S THE SECOND DAY IN A ROW.
I GUESS SHE DOESN'T LIKE THE NEW WET FOOD.
I SUPPOSE IT COULD ALSO BE READ AS A STRONG WILL TO SURVIVE.
HA! THAT'S PUTTING A SPOONFUL OF SUGAR ON TOP.
MMMMM SUGARED ANXIETY...

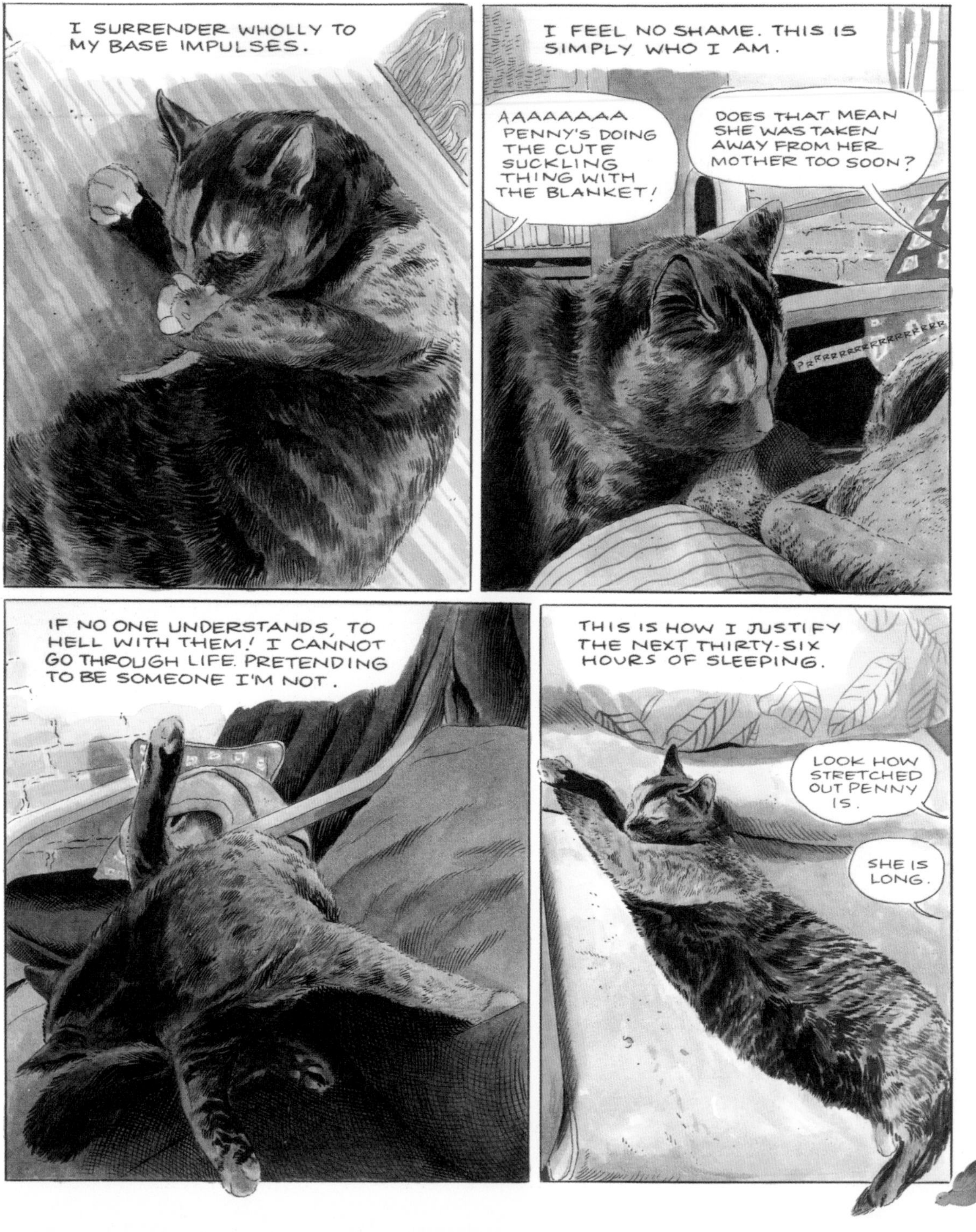
I SURRENDER WHOLLY TO MY BASE IMPULSES.
I FEEL NO SHAME. THIS IS SIMPLY WHO I AM.
AAAAAAAA PENNY'S DOING THE CUTE SUCKLING THING WITH THE BLANKET!
DOES THAT MEAN SHE WAS TAKEN AWAY FROM HER MOTHER TOO SOON?
IF NO ONE UNDERSTANDS, TO HELL WITH THEM! I CANNOT GO THROUGH LIFE PRETENDING TO BE SOMEONE I'M NOT.
THIS IS HOW I JUSTIFY THE NEXT THIRTY-SIX HOURS OF SLEEPING.
LOOK HOW STRETCHED OUT PENNY IS.
SHE IS LONG.

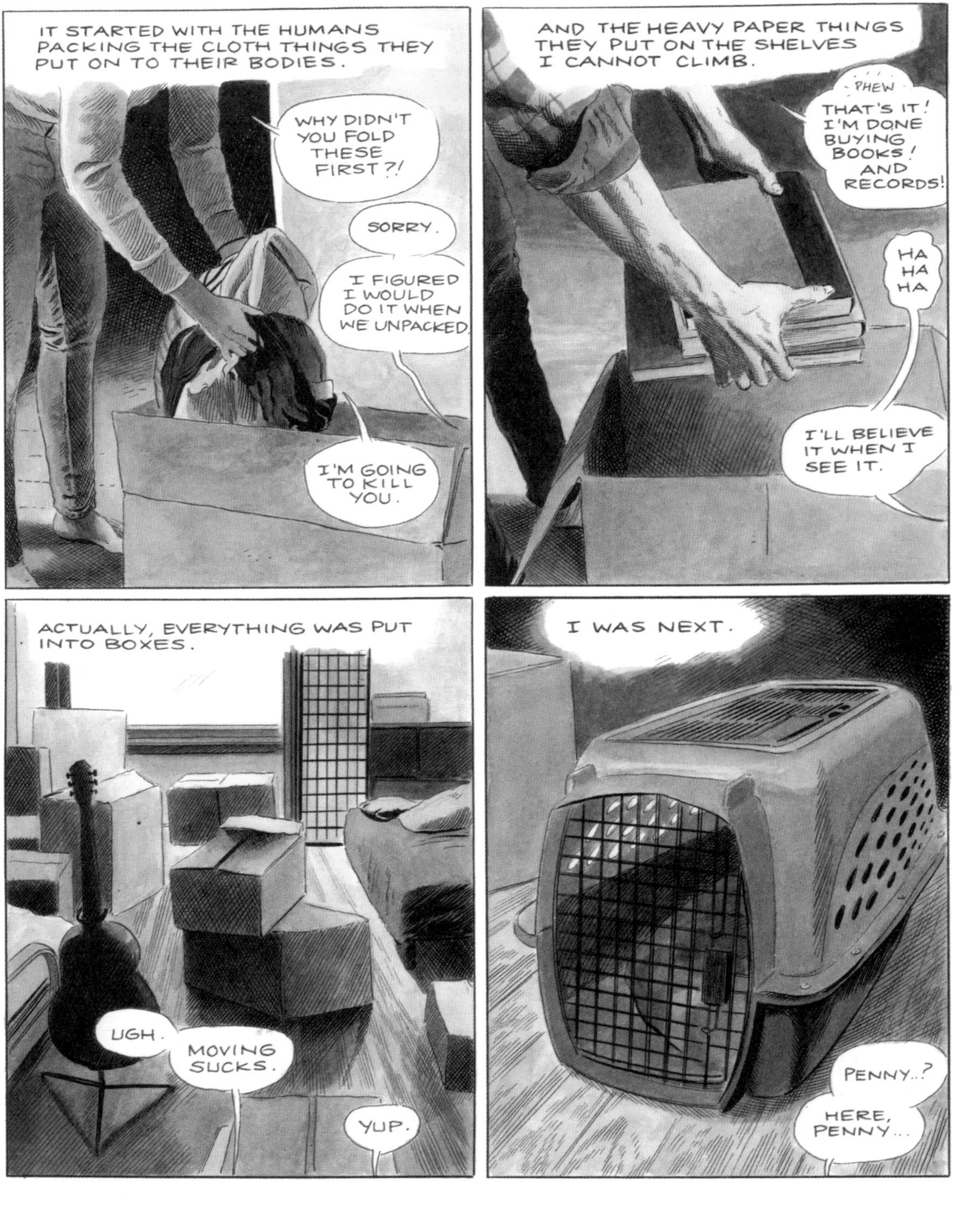
IT STARTED WITH THE HUMANS PACKING THE CLOTH THINGS THEY PUT ON TO THEIR BODIES.
WHY DIDN'T YOU FOLD THESE FIRST?!
SORRY.
I FIGURED I WOULD DO IT WHEN WE UNPACKED.
I'M GOING TO KILL YOU.
AND THE HEAVY PAPER THINGS THEY PUT ON THE SHELVES I CANNOT CLIMB.
PHEW
THAT'S IT! I'M DONE BUYING BOOKS! AND RECORDS!
HA HA HA
I'LL BELIEVE IT WHEN I SEE IT.
ACTUALLY, EVERYTHING WAS PUT INTO BOXES.
UGH.
MOVING SUCKS.
YUP.
I WAS NEXT.
PENNY..?
HERE, PENNY...

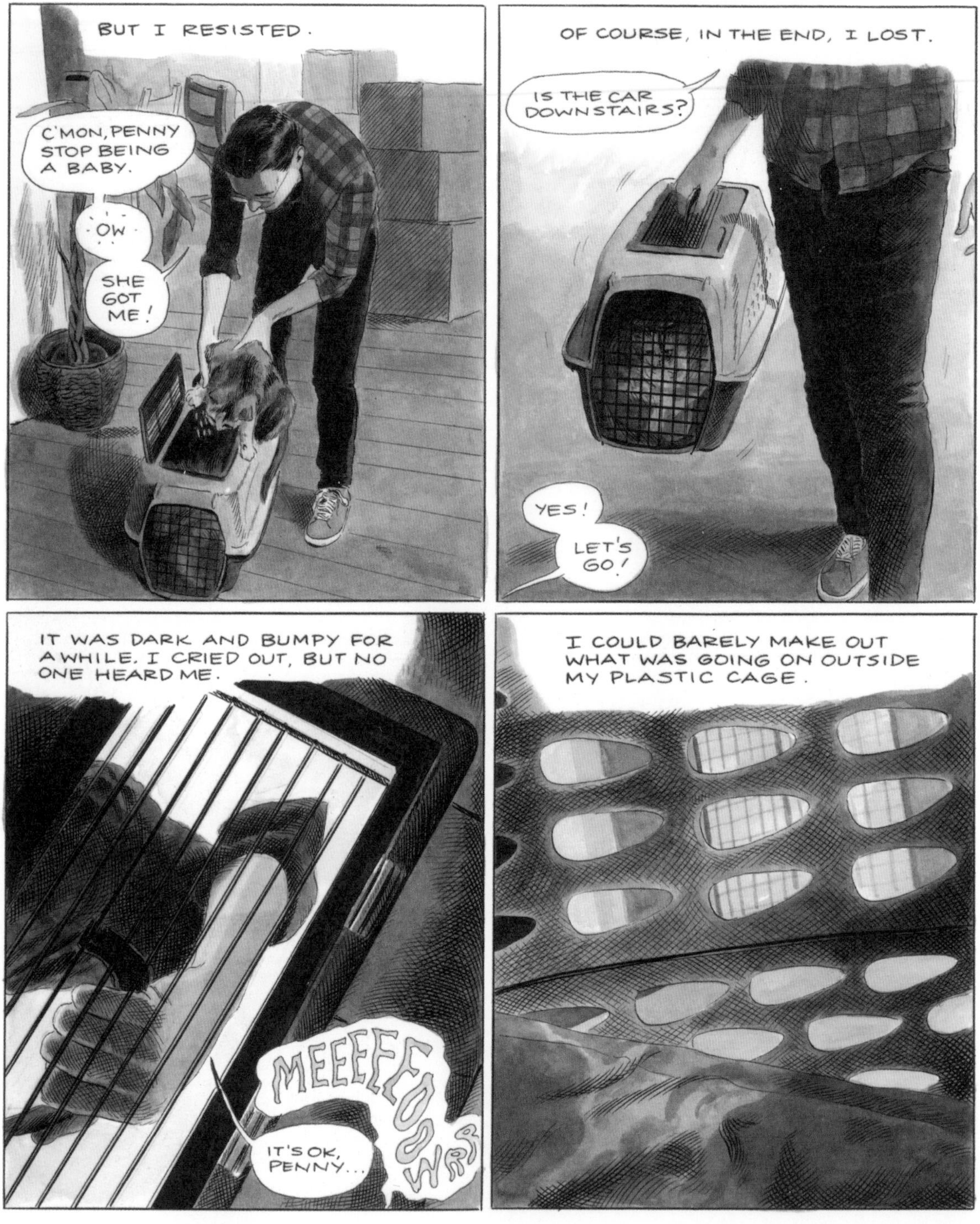
BUT I RESISTED.
C'MON, PENNY STOP BEING A BABY.
OW
SHE GOT ME!
OF COURSE, IN THE END, I LOST.
IS THE CAR DOWNSTAIRS?
YES!
LET'S GO!
IT WAS DARK AND BUMPY FOR A WHILE. I CRIED OUT, BUT NO ONE HEARD ME.
MEEEEEOOOWR!
IT'S OK, PENNY...
I COULD BARELY MAKE OUT WHAT WAS GOING ON OUTSIDE MY PLASTIC CAGE.

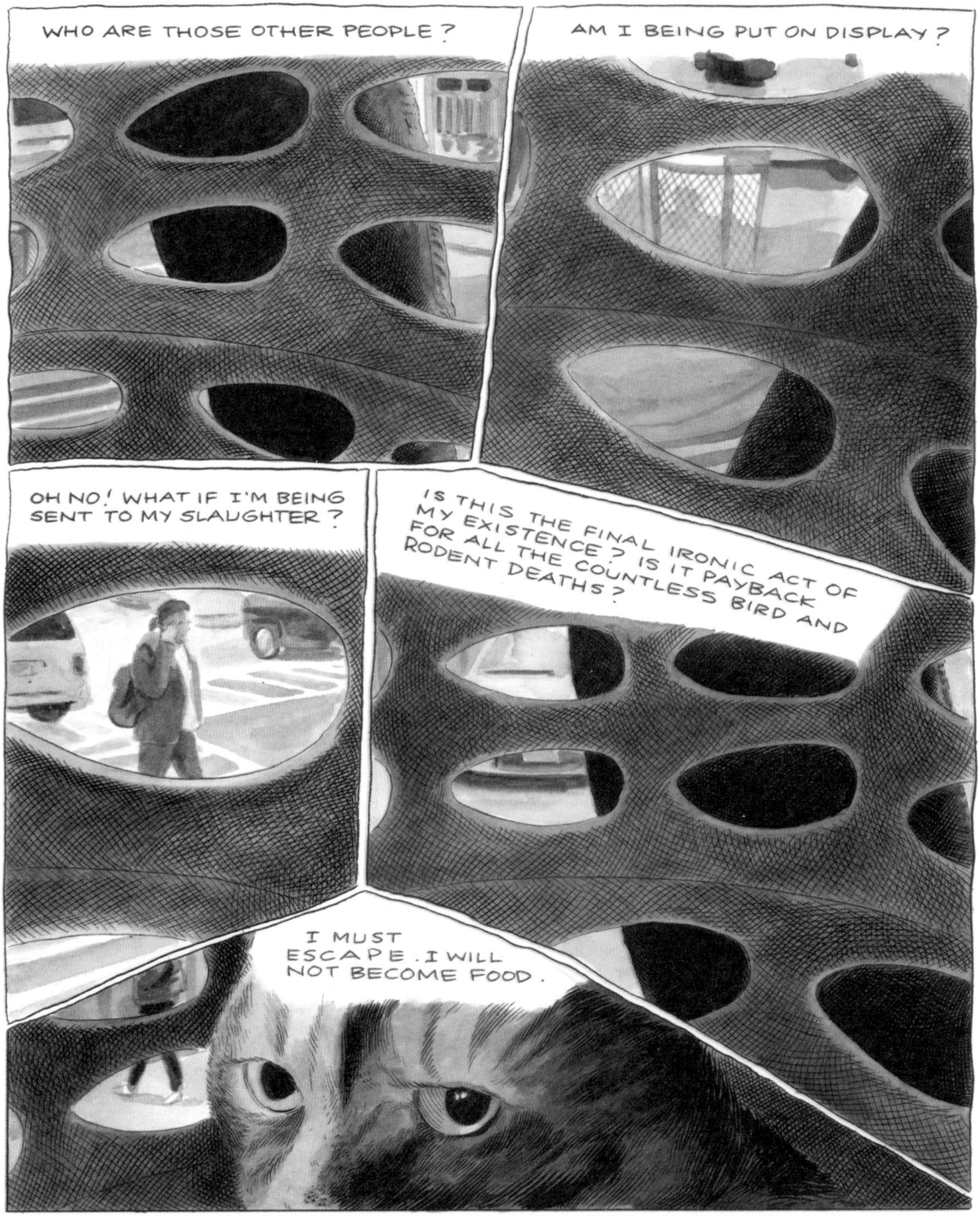
WHO ARE THOSE OTHER PEOPLE?
AM I BEING PUT ON DISPLAY?
OH NO! WHAT IF I'M BEING SENT TO MY SLAUGHTER?
IS THIS THE FINAL IRONIC ACT OF MY EXISTENCE? IS IT PAYBACK FOR ALL THE COUNTLESS BIRD AND RODENT DEATHS?
I MUST ESCAPE. I WILL NOT BECOME FOOD.

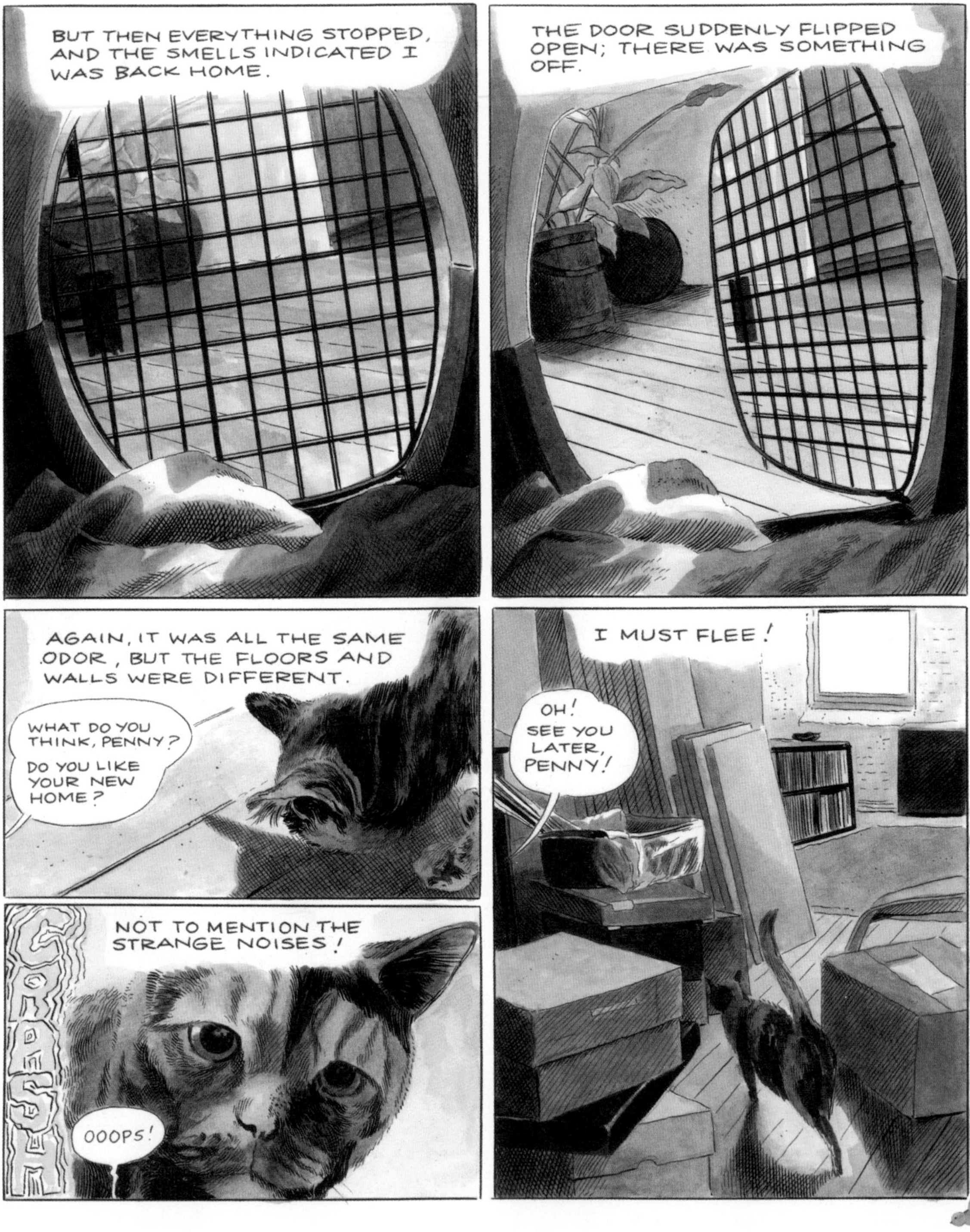
BUT THEN EVERYTHING STOPPED, AND THE SMELLS INDICATED I WAS BACK HOME.
THE DOOR SUDDENLY FLIPPED OPEN; THERE WAS SOMETHING OFF.
AGAIN, IT WAS ALL THE SAME ODOR, BUT THE FLOORS AND WALLS WERE DIFFERENT.
WHAT DO YOU THINK, PENNY?
DO YOU LIKE YOUR NEW HOME?
NOT TO MENTION THE STRANGE NOISES!
OOOPS!
I MUST FLEE!
OH! SEE YOU LATER, PENNY!

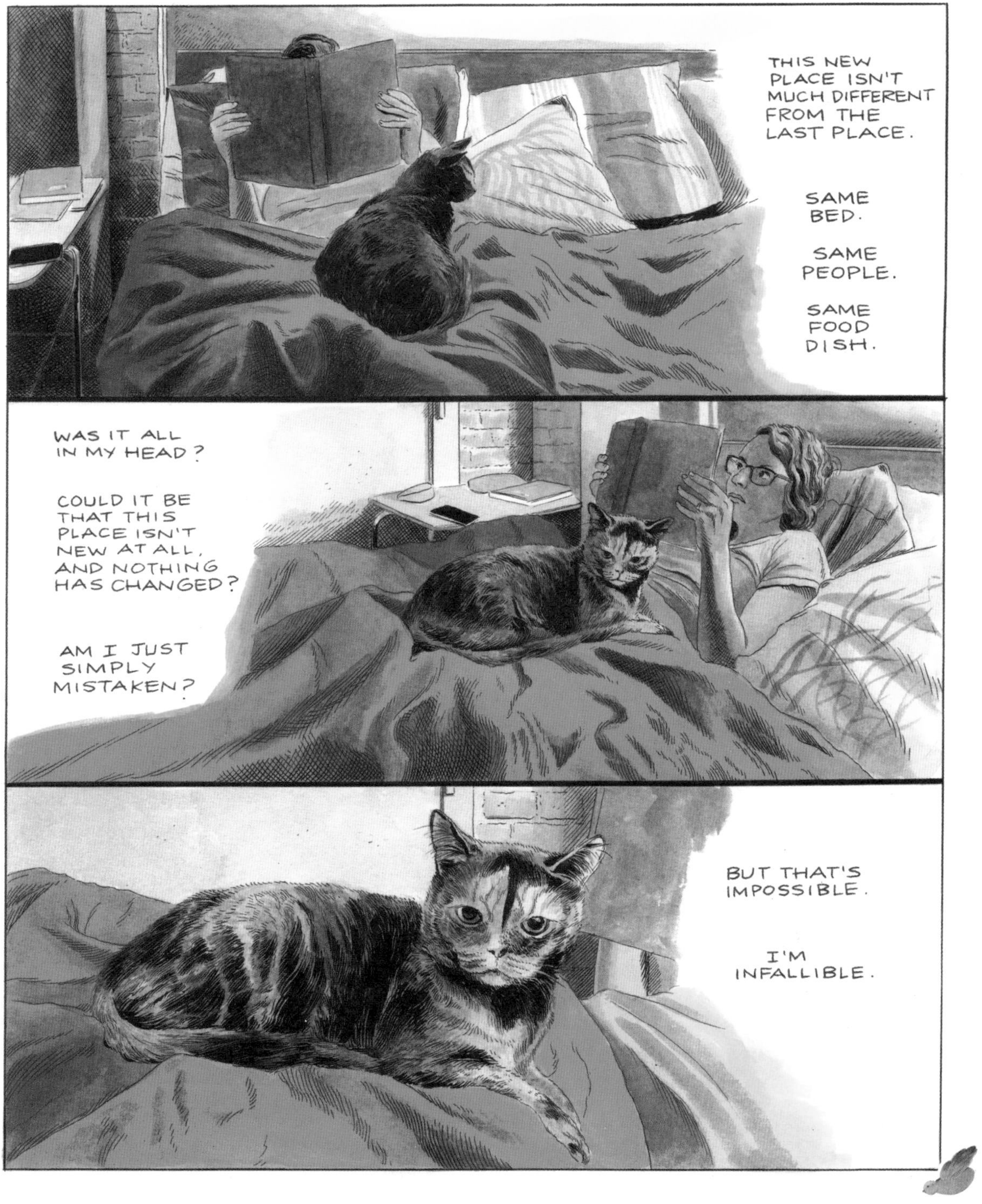
THIS NEW PLACE ISN'T MUCH DIFFERENT FROM THE LAST PLACE.
SAME BED.
SAME PEOPLE.
SAME FOOD DISH.
WAS IT ALL IN MY HEAD?
COULD IT BE THAT THIS PLACE ISN'T NEW AT ALL, AND NOTHING HAS CHANGED?
AM I JUST SIMPLY MISTAKEN?
BUT THAT'S IMPOSSIBLE.
I'M INFALLIBLE.

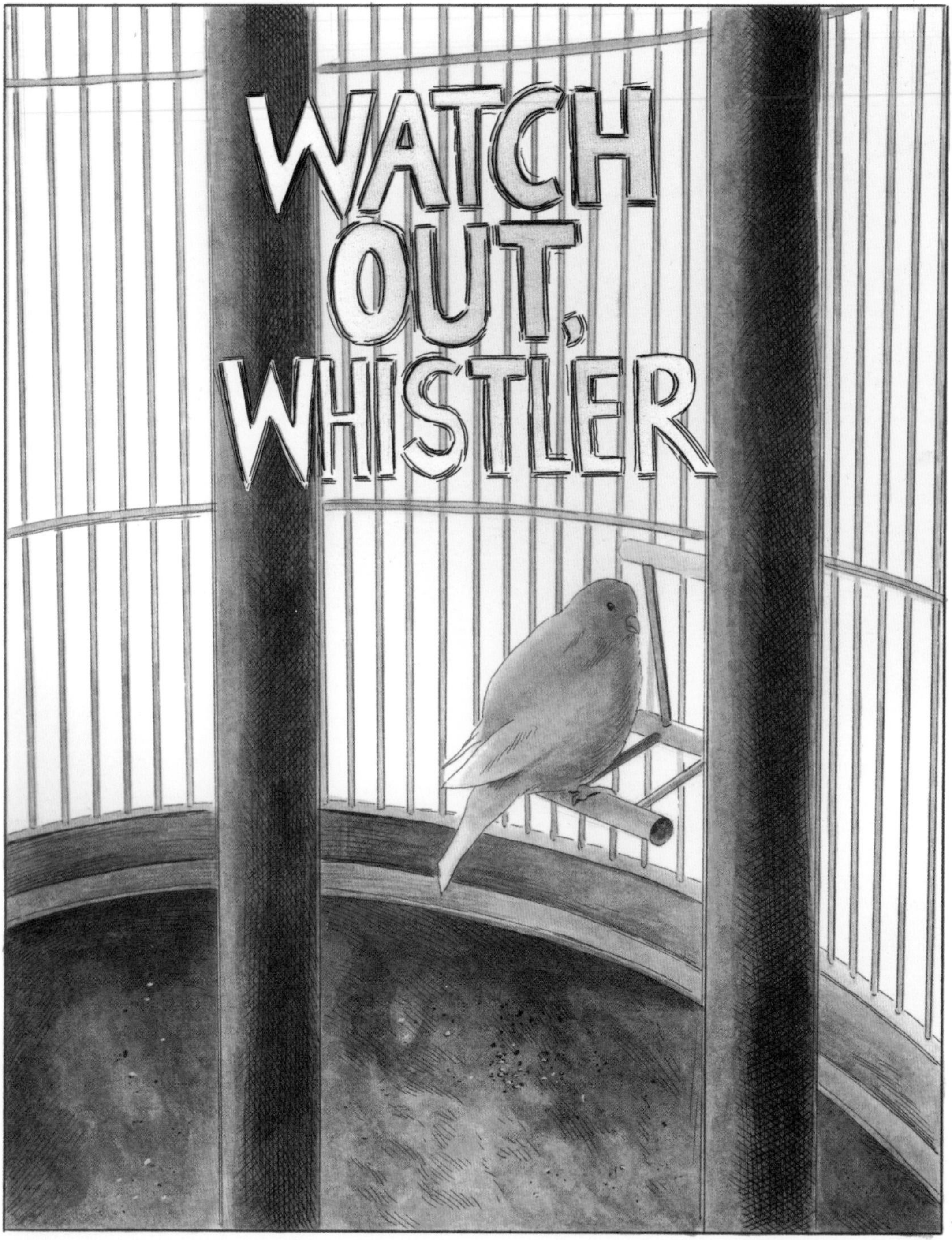
WATCH OUT, WHISTLER

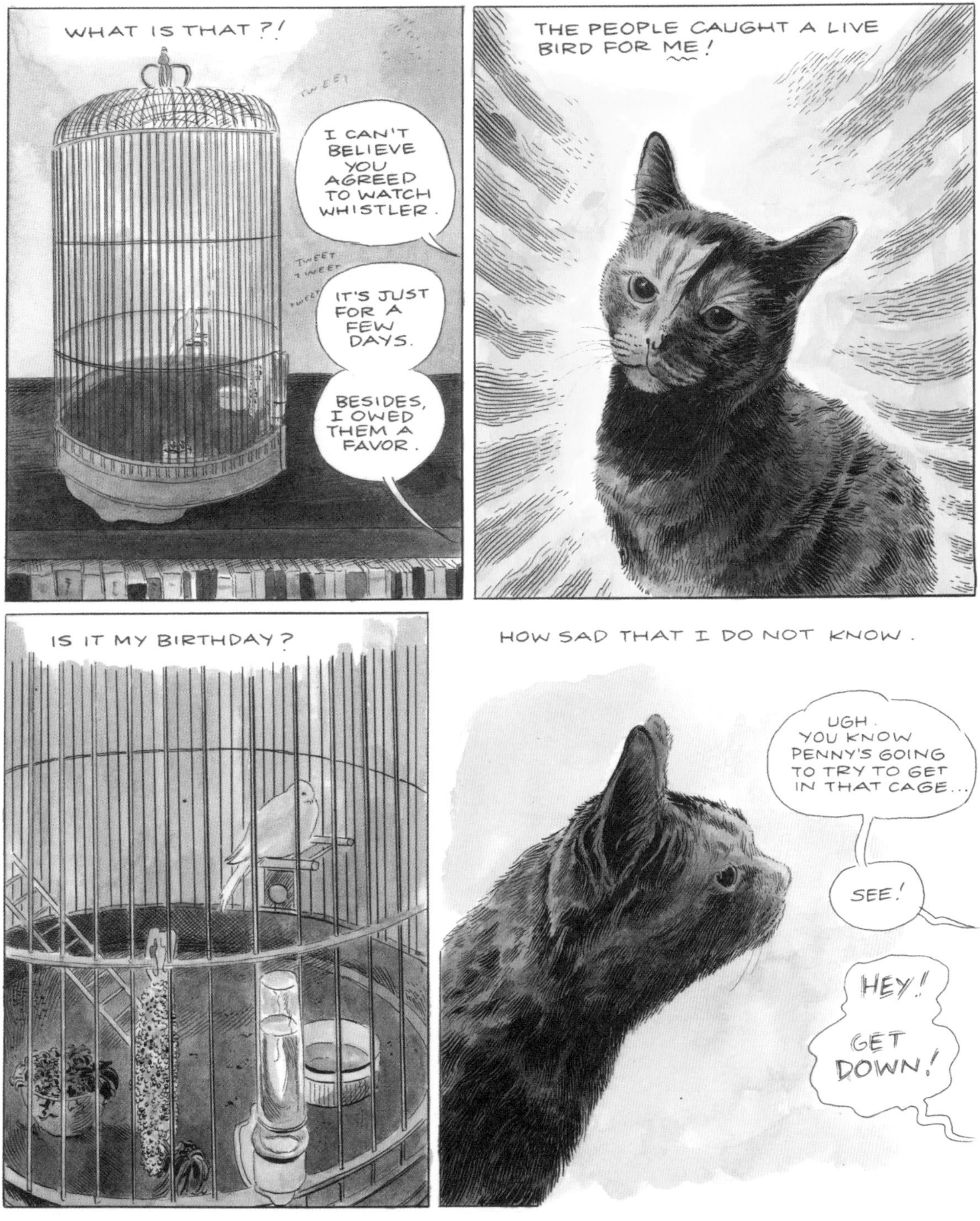
WHAT IS THAT?!
TWEET
I CAN'T BELIEVE YOU AGREED TO WATCH WHISTLER.
TWEET TWEET TWEET
IT'S JUST FOR A FEW DAYS.
BESIDES, I OWED THEM A FAVOR.
THE PEOPLE CAUGHT A LIVE BIRD FOR ME!
IS IT MY BIRTHDAY?
HOW SAD THAT I DO NOT KNOW.
UGH. YOU KNOW PENNY'S GOING TO TRY TO GET IN THAT CAGE...
SEE!
HEY!
GET DOWN!

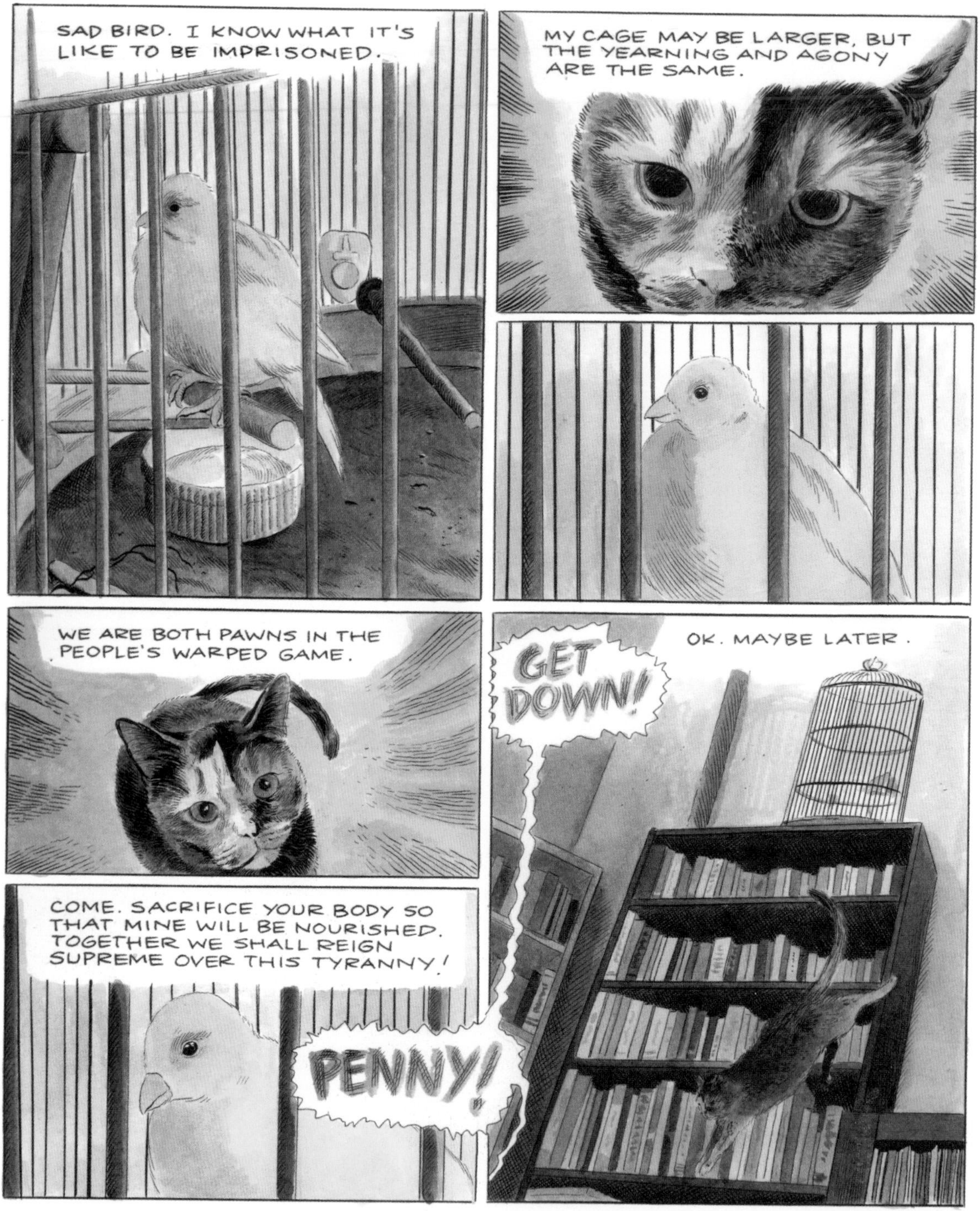
SAD BIRD. I KNOW WHAT IT'S LIKE TO BE IMPRISONED.
MY CAGE MAY BE LARGER, BUT THE YEARNING AND AGONY ARE THE SAME.
WE ARE BOTH PAWNS IN THE PEOPLE'S WARPED GAME.
COME. SACRIFICE YOUR BODY SO THAT MINE WILL BE NOURISHED. TOGETHER WE SHALL REIGN SUPREME OVER THIS TYRANNY!
PENNY!
GET DOWN!
OK. MAYBE LATER.

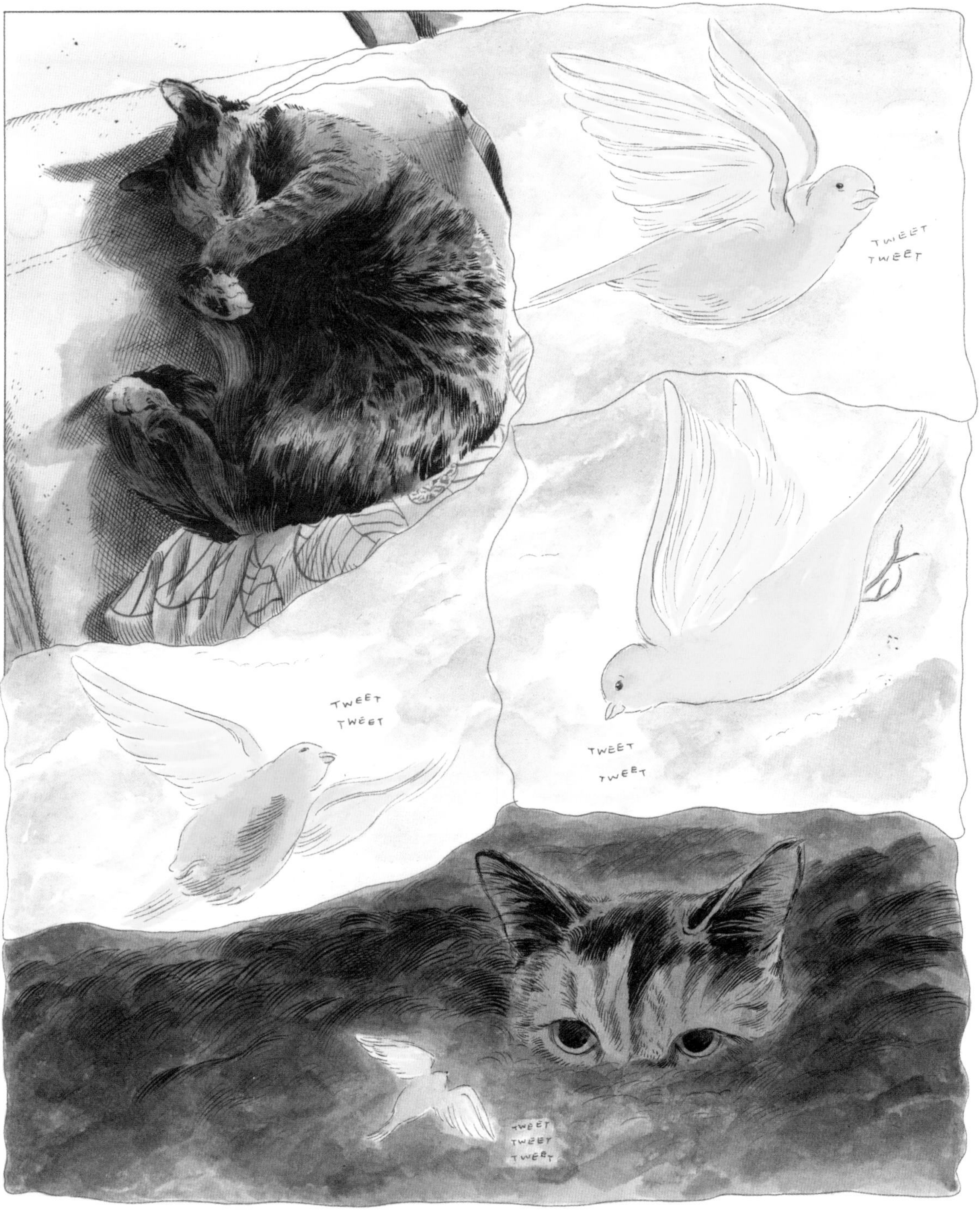
TWEET
TWEET
TWEET
TWEET
TWEET
TWEET
TWEET
TWEET
TWEET

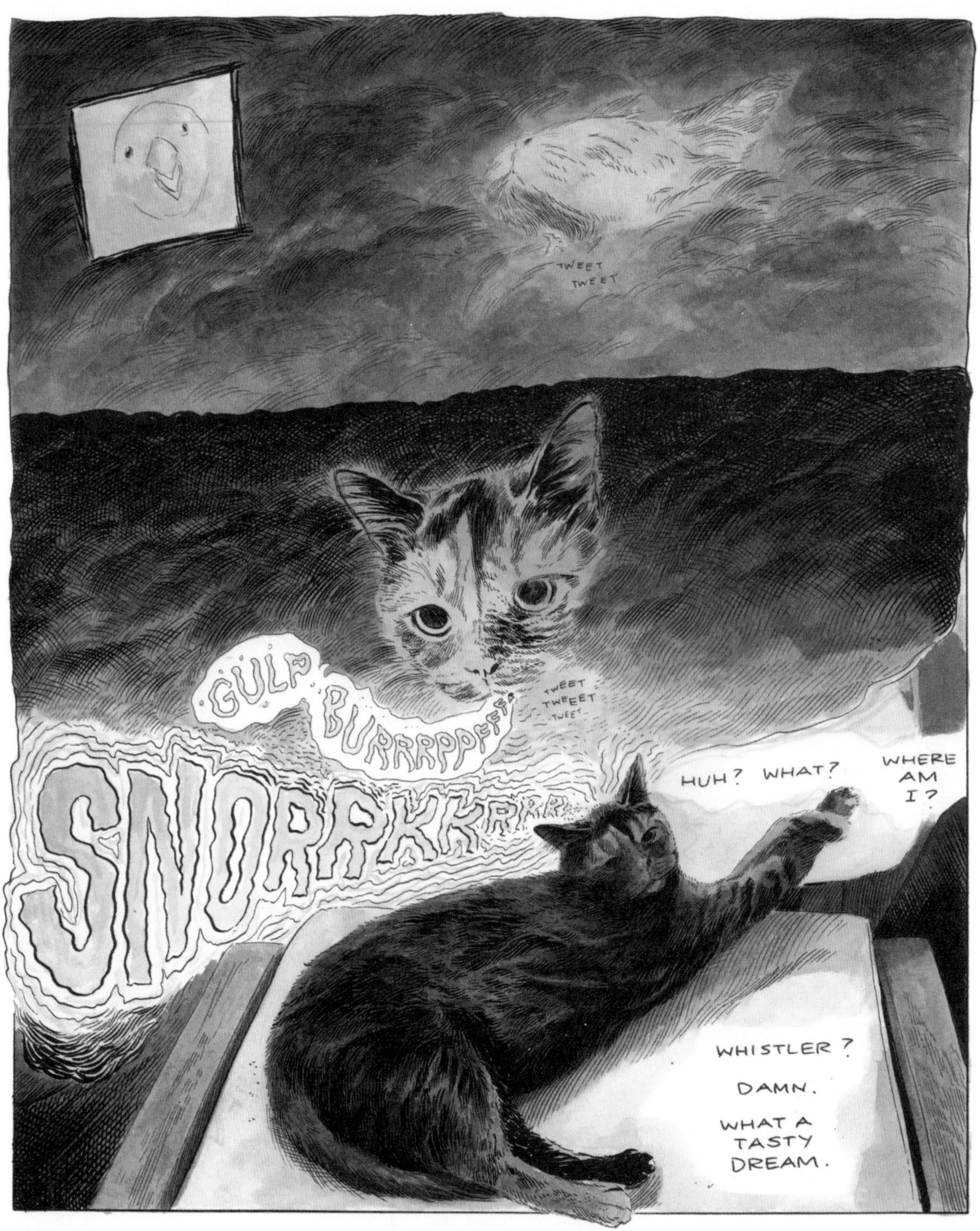
TWEET
TWEET
GULP
BURRRPPFFF
TWEET
TWEEET
TWEET
SNORRKKRRR
HUH? WHAT?
WHERE AM I?
WHISTLER?
DAMN.
WHAT A TASTY DREAM.

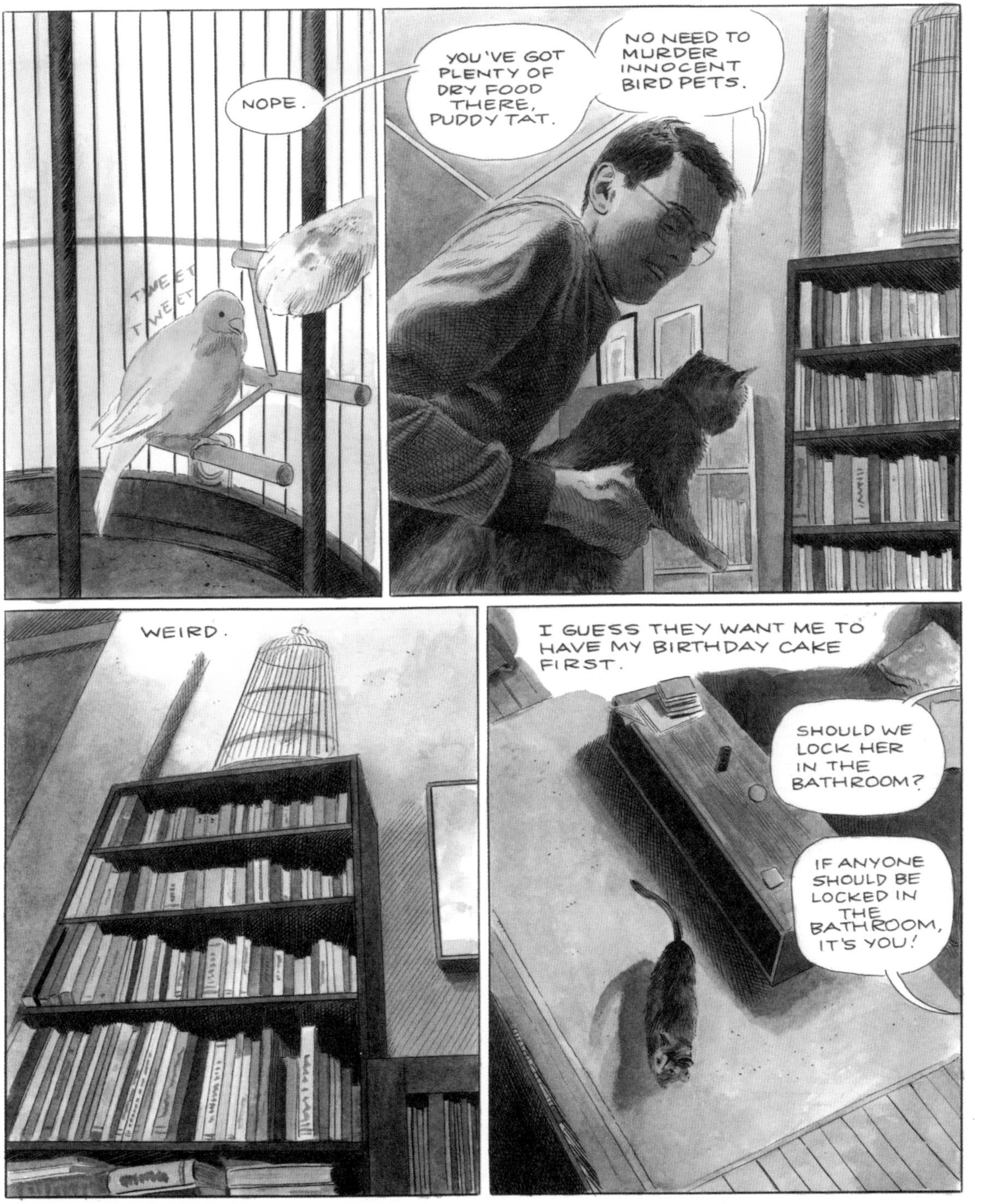
TWEET TWEET
NOPE.
YOU'VE GOT PLENTY OF DRY FOOD THERE, PUDDY TAT.
NO NEED TO MURDER INNOCENT BIRD PETS.
WEIRD.
I GUESS THEY WANT ME TO HAVE MY BIRTHDAY CAKE FIRST.
SHOULD WE LOCK HER IN THE BATHROOM?
IF ANYONE SHOULD BE LOCKED IN THE BATHROOM, IT'S YOU!

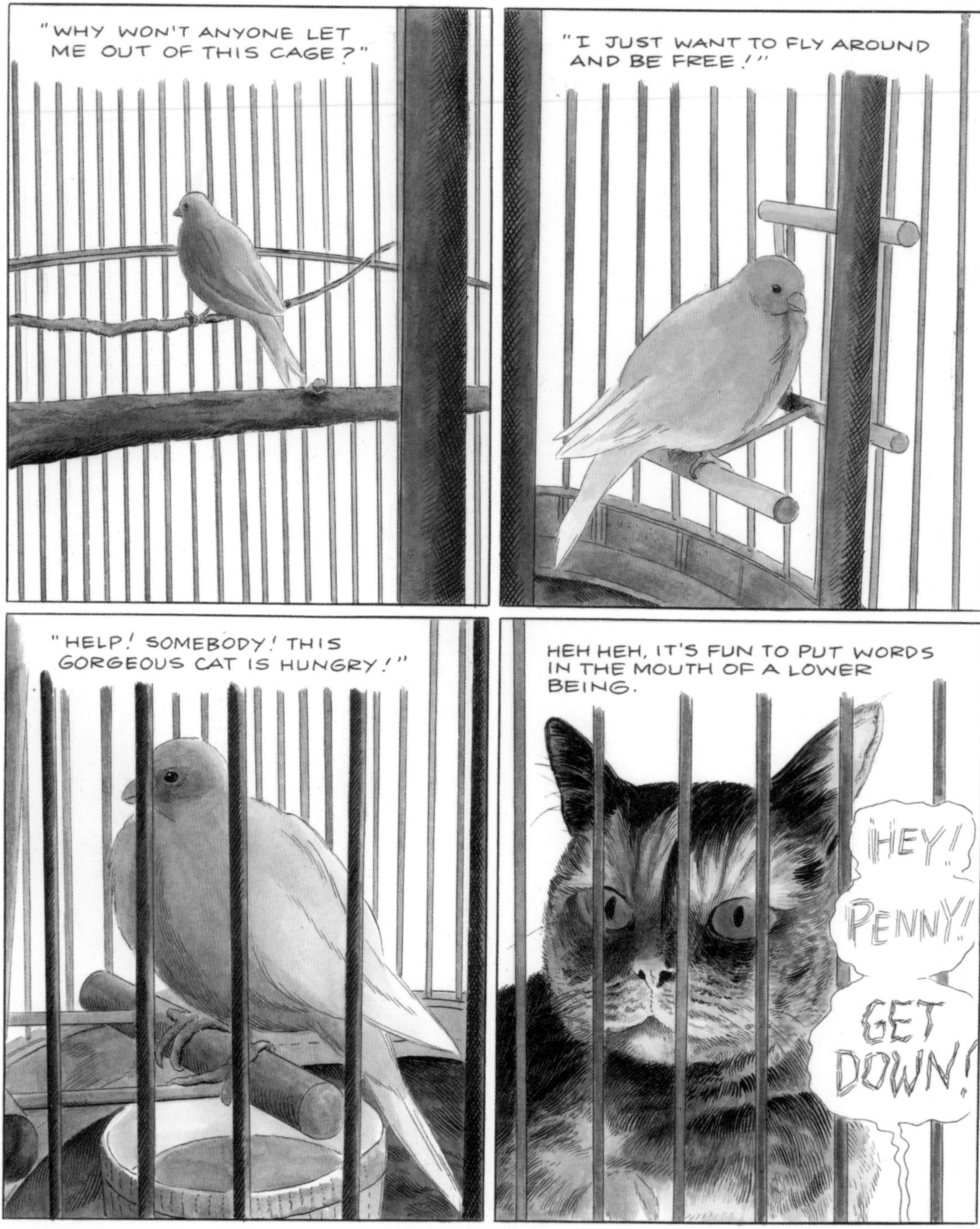
"WHY WON'T ANYONE LET ME OUT OF THIS CAGE?"
"I JUST WANT TO FLY AROUND AND BE FREE!"
"HELP! SOMEBODY! THIS GORGEOUS CAT IS HUNGRY!"
HEH HEH, IT'S FUN TO PUT WORDS IN THE MOUTH OF A LOWER BEING.
HEY! PENNY! GET DOWN!

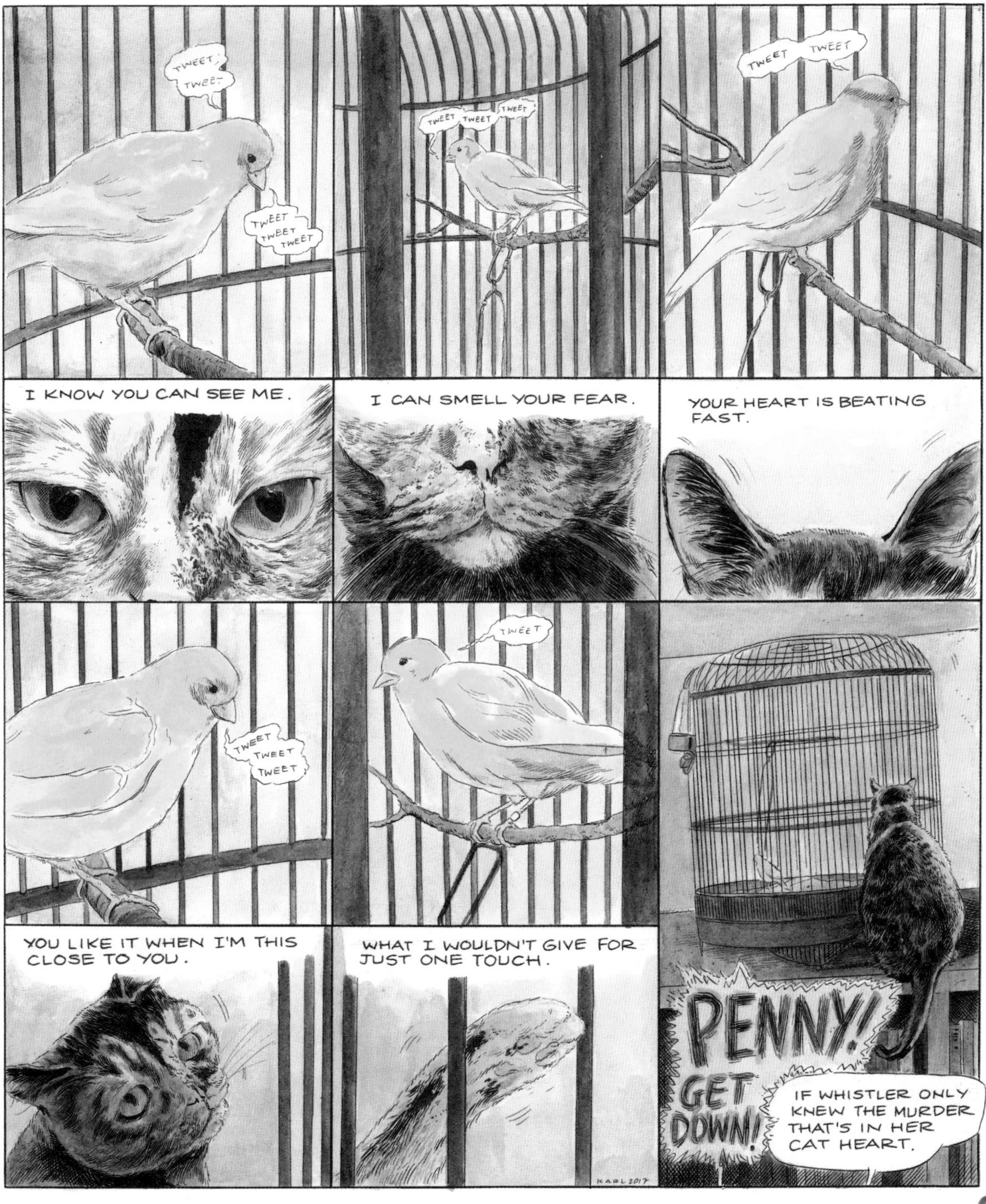

TWEET, TWEET
TWEET TWEET TWEET
TWEET TWEET TWEET
TWEET TWEET
I KNOW YOU CAN SEE ME.
I CAN SMELL YOUR FEAR.
YOUR HEART IS BEATING FAST.
TWEET TWEET TWEET
TWEET
YOU LIKE IT WHEN I'M THIS CLOSE TO YOU.
WHAT I WOULDN'T GIVE FOR JUST ONE TOUCH.
KARL 2017
PENNY! GET DOWN!
IF WHISTLER ONLY KNEW THE MURDER THAT'S IN HER CAT HEART.

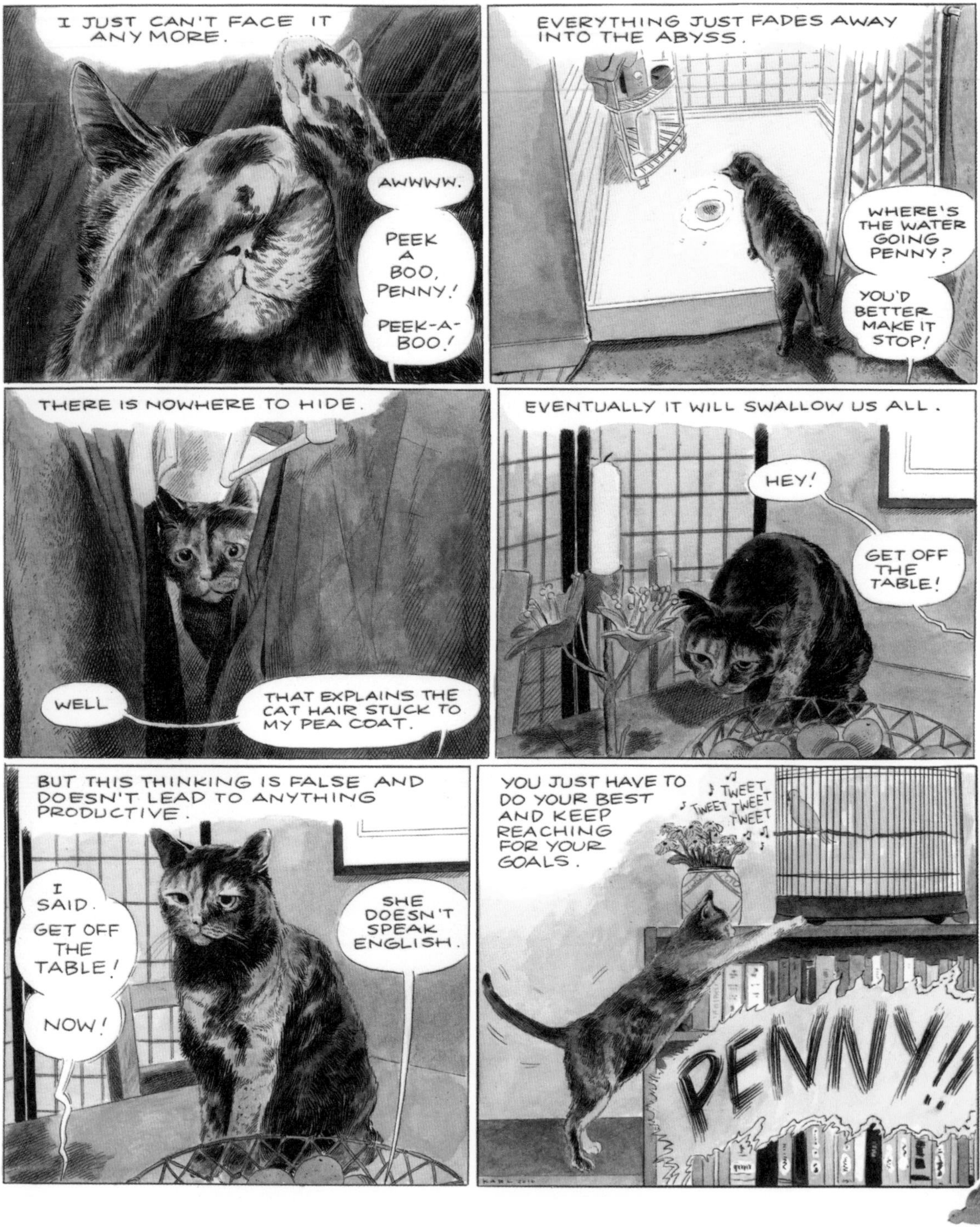
I JUST CAN'T FACE IT ANYMORE.
AWWWW.
PEEK A BOO, PENNY!
PEEK-A-BOO!
EVERYTHING JUST FADES AWAY INTO THE ABYSS.
WHERE'S THE WATER GOING PENNY?
YOU'D BETTER MAKE IT STOP!
THERE IS NOWHERE TO HIDE.
WELL
THAT EXPLAINS THE CAT HAIR STUCK TO MY PEA COAT.
EVENTUALLY IT WILL SWALLOW US ALL.
HEY!
GET OFF THE TABLE!
BUT THIS THINKING IS FALSE AND DOESN'T LEAD TO ANYTHING PRODUCTIVE.
I SAID. GET OFF THE TABLE!
NOW!
SHE DOESN'T SPEAK ENGLISH.
YOU JUST HAVE TO DO YOUR BEST AND KEEP REACHING FOR YOUR GOALS.
TWEET TWEET TWEET TWEET
PENNY!!

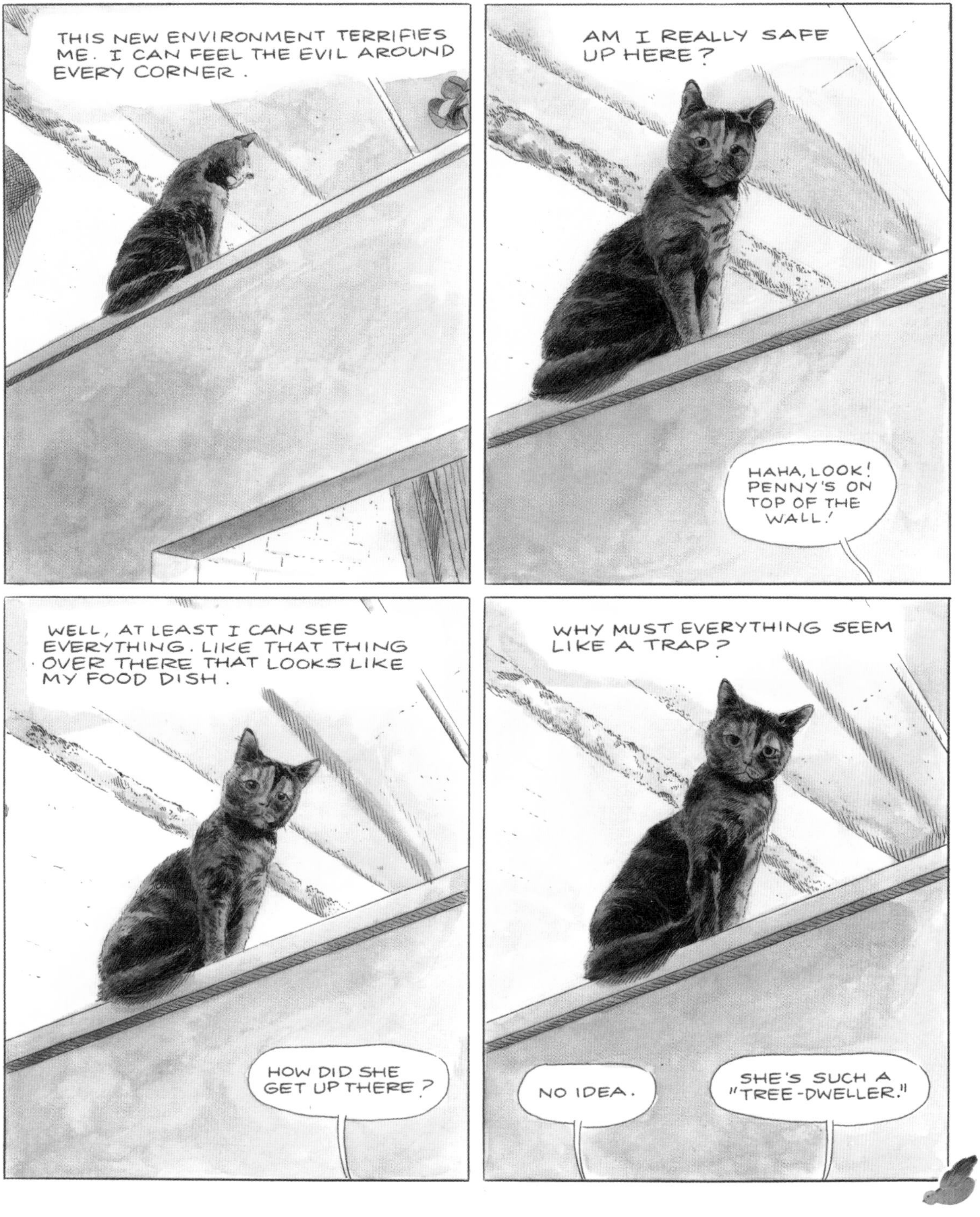
THIS NEW ENVIRONMENT TERRIFIES ME. I CAN FEEL THE EVIL AROUND EVERY CORNER.
AM I REALLY SAFE UP HERE?
HAHA, LOOK! PENNY'S ON TOP OF THE WALL!
WELL, AT LEAST I CAN SEE EVERYTHING. LIKE THAT THING OVER THERE THAT LOOKS LIKE MY FOOD DISH.
HOW DID SHE GET UP THERE?
WHY MUST EVERYTHING SEEM LIKE A TRAP?
NO IDEA.
SHE'S SUCH A "TREE-DWELLER."

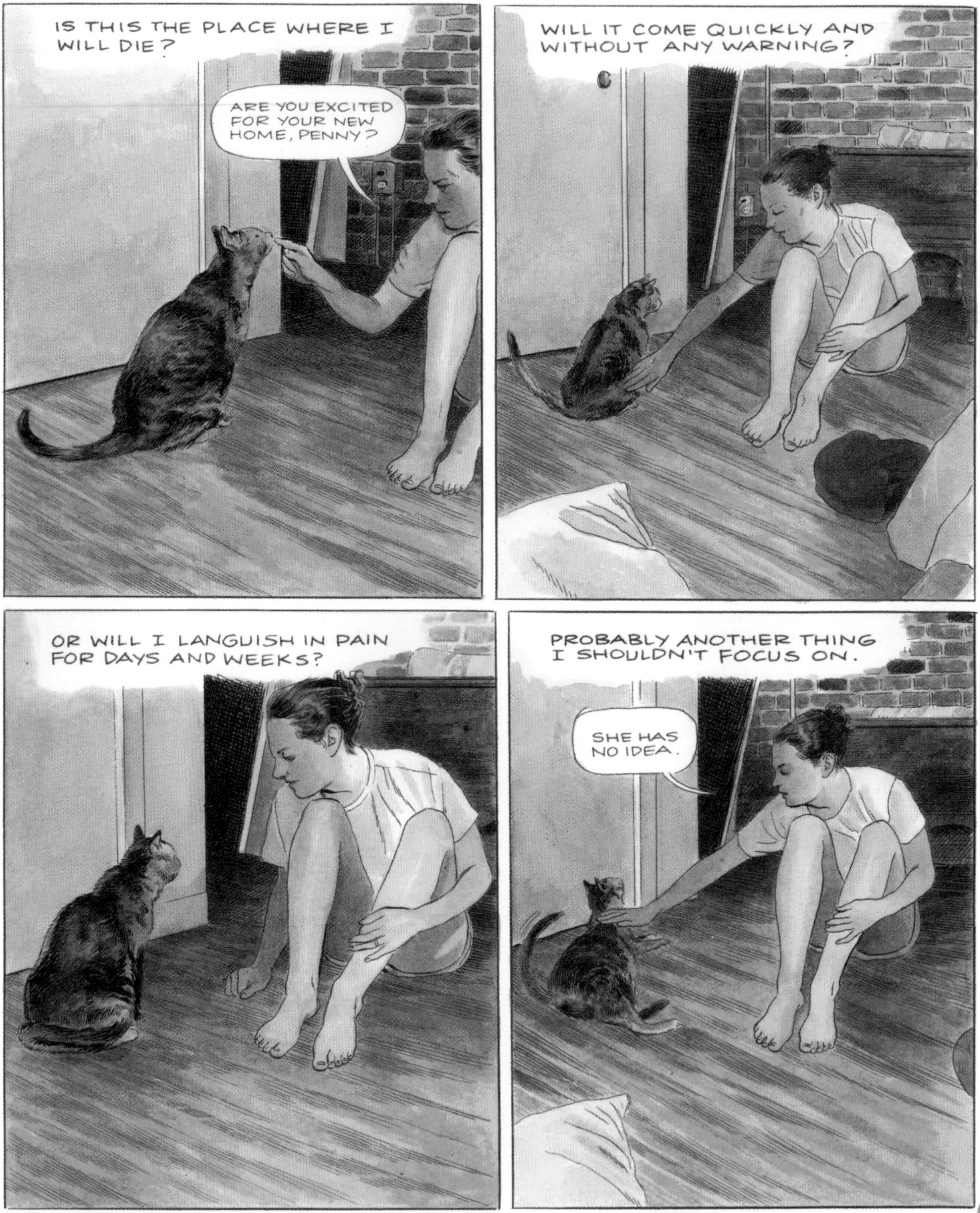
IS THIS THE PLACE WHERE I WILL DIE?
ARE YOU EXCITED FOR YOUR NEW HOME, PENNY?
WILL IT COME QUICKLY AND WITHOUT ANY WARNING?
OR WILL I LANGUISH IN PAIN FOR DAYS AND WEEKS?
PROBABLY ANOTHER THING I SHOULDN'T FOCUS ON.
SHE HAS NO IDEA.

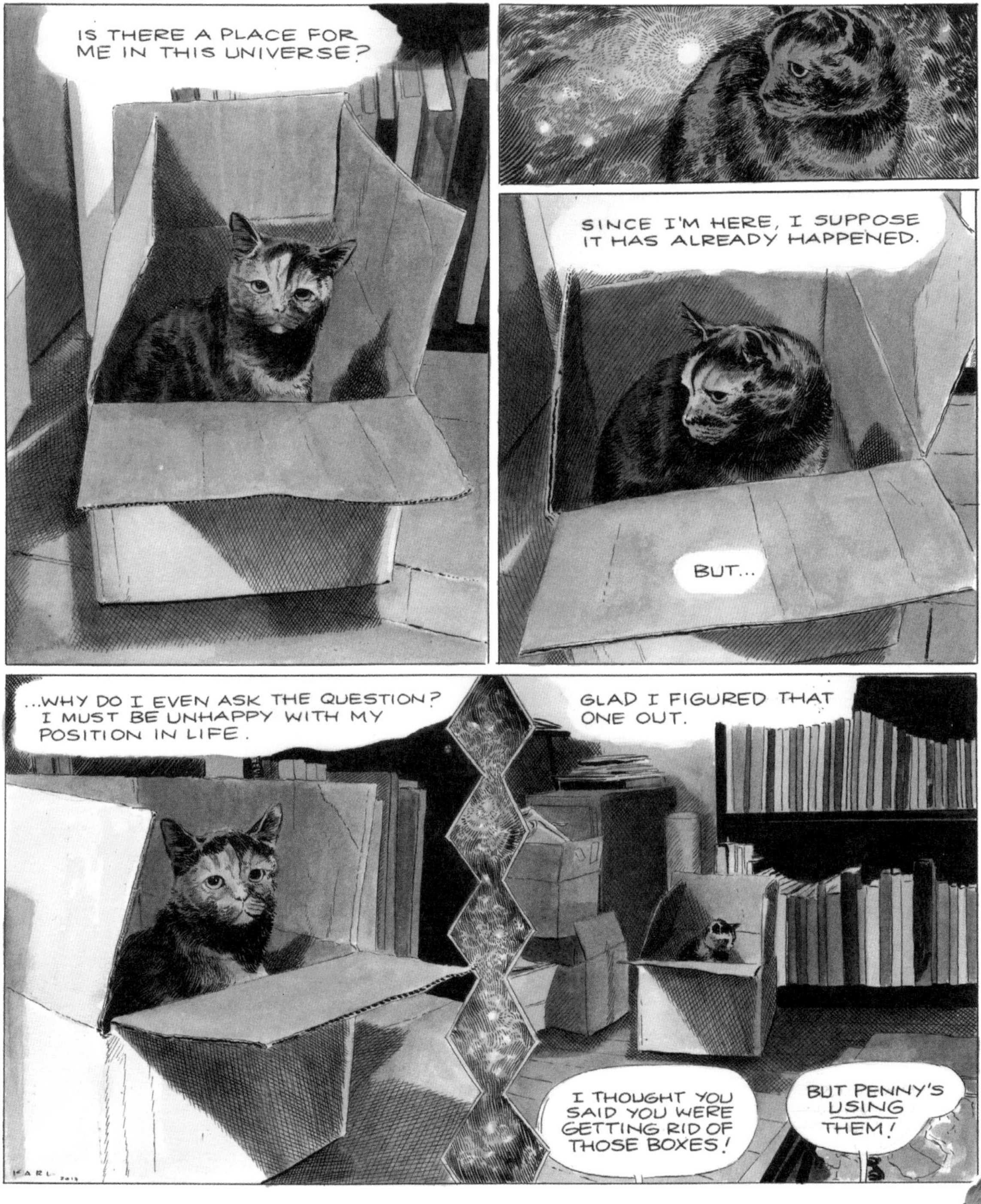
IS THERE A PLACE FOR ME IN THIS UNIVERSE?
SINCE I'M HERE, I SUPPOSE IT HAS ALREADY HAPPENED.
BUT...
...WHY DO I EVEN ASK THE QUESTION? I MUST BE UNHAPPY WITH MY POSITION IN LIFE.
GLAD I FIGURED THAT ONE OUT.
I THOUGHT YOU SAID YOU WERE GETTING RID OF THOSE BOXES!
BUT PENNY'S USING THEM!
KARL

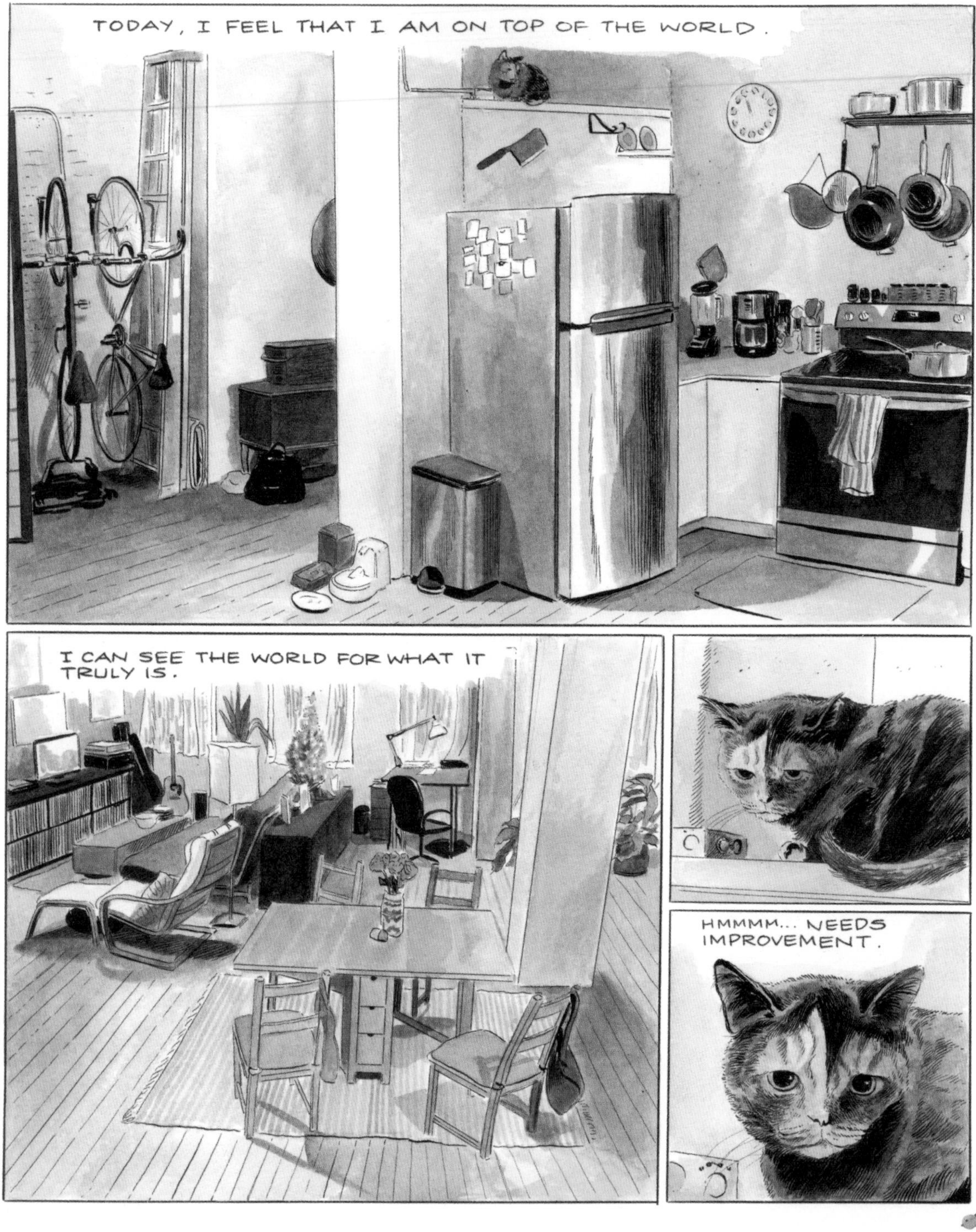
TODAY, I FEEL THAT I AM ON TOP OF THE WORLD.
I CAN SEE THE WORLD FOR WHAT IT TRULY IS.
HMMMM... NEEDS IMPROVEMENT.

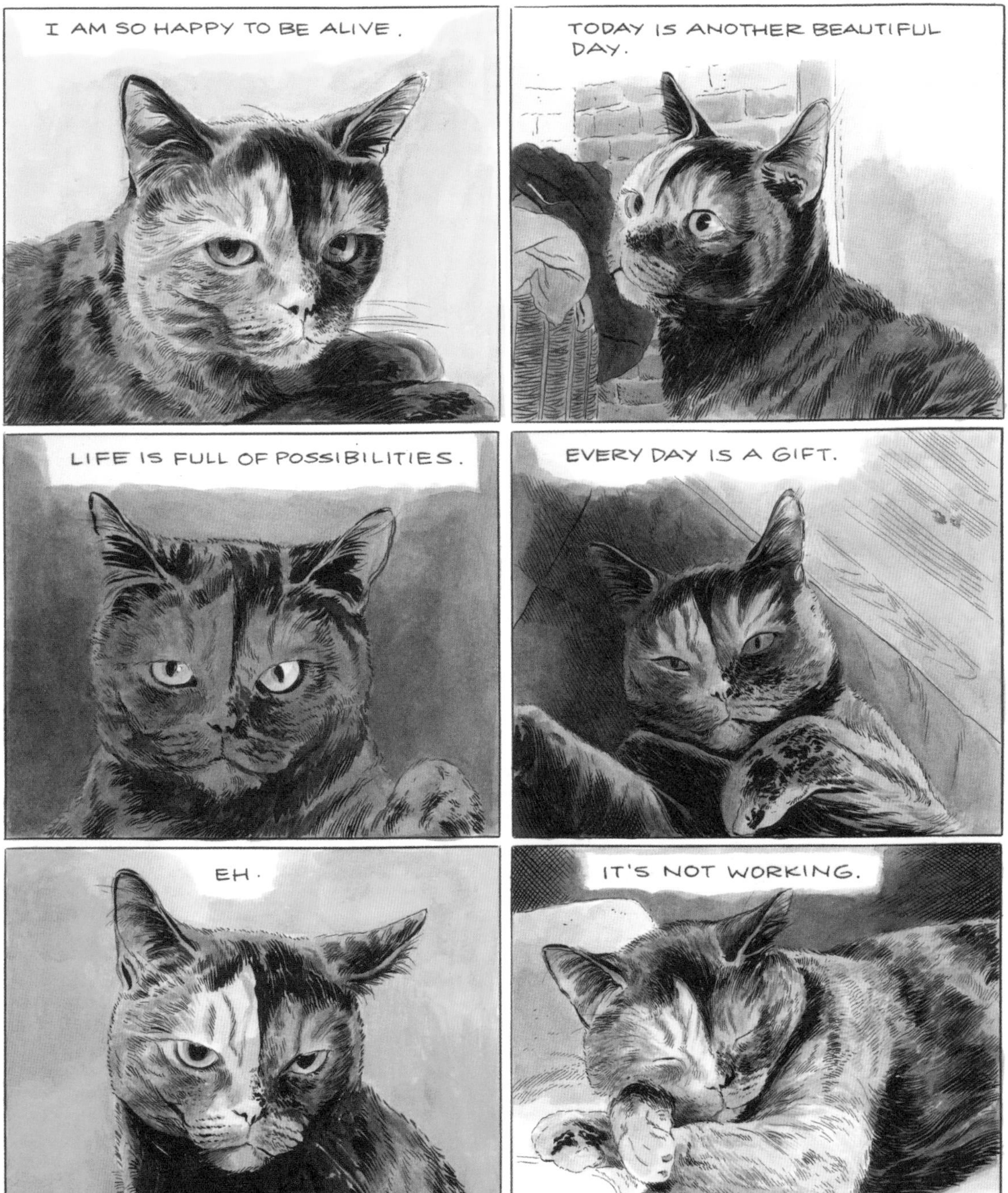
I AM SO HAPPY TO BE ALIVE.
TODAY IS ANOTHER BEAUTIFUL DAY.
LIFE IS FULL OF POSSIBILITIES.
EVERY DAY IS A GIFT.
EH.
IT'S NOT WORKING.

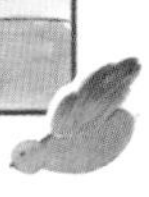

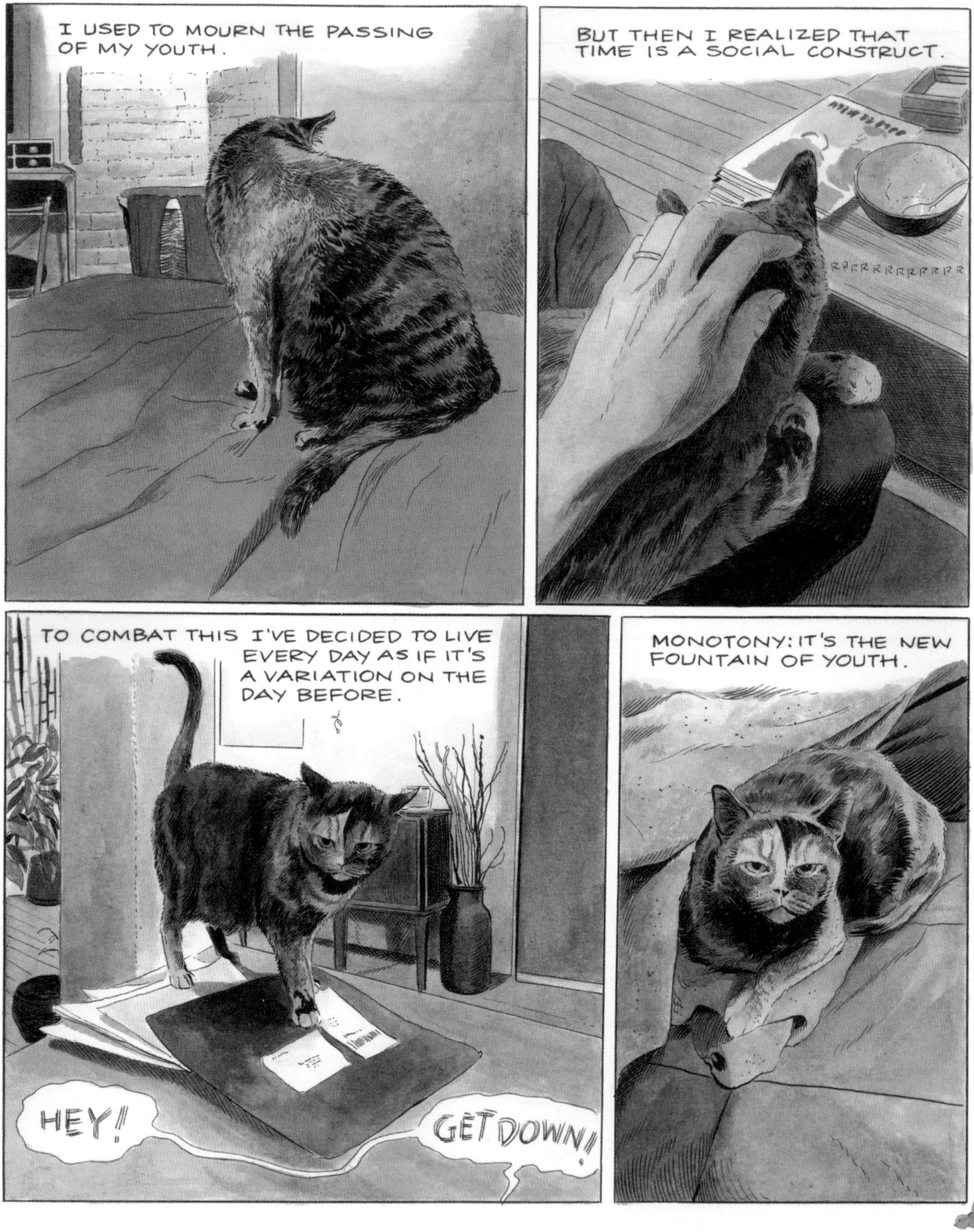
I USED TO MOURN THE PASSING OF MY YOUTH.
BUT THEN I REALIZED THAT TIME IS A SOCIAL CONSTRUCT.
RRRRRRRRRRRRR
TO COMBAT THIS I'VE DECIDED TO LIVE EVERY DAY AS IF IT'S A VARIATION ON THE DAY BEFORE.
HEY!
GET DOWN!
MONOTONY: IT'S THE NEW FOUNTAIN OF YOUTH.

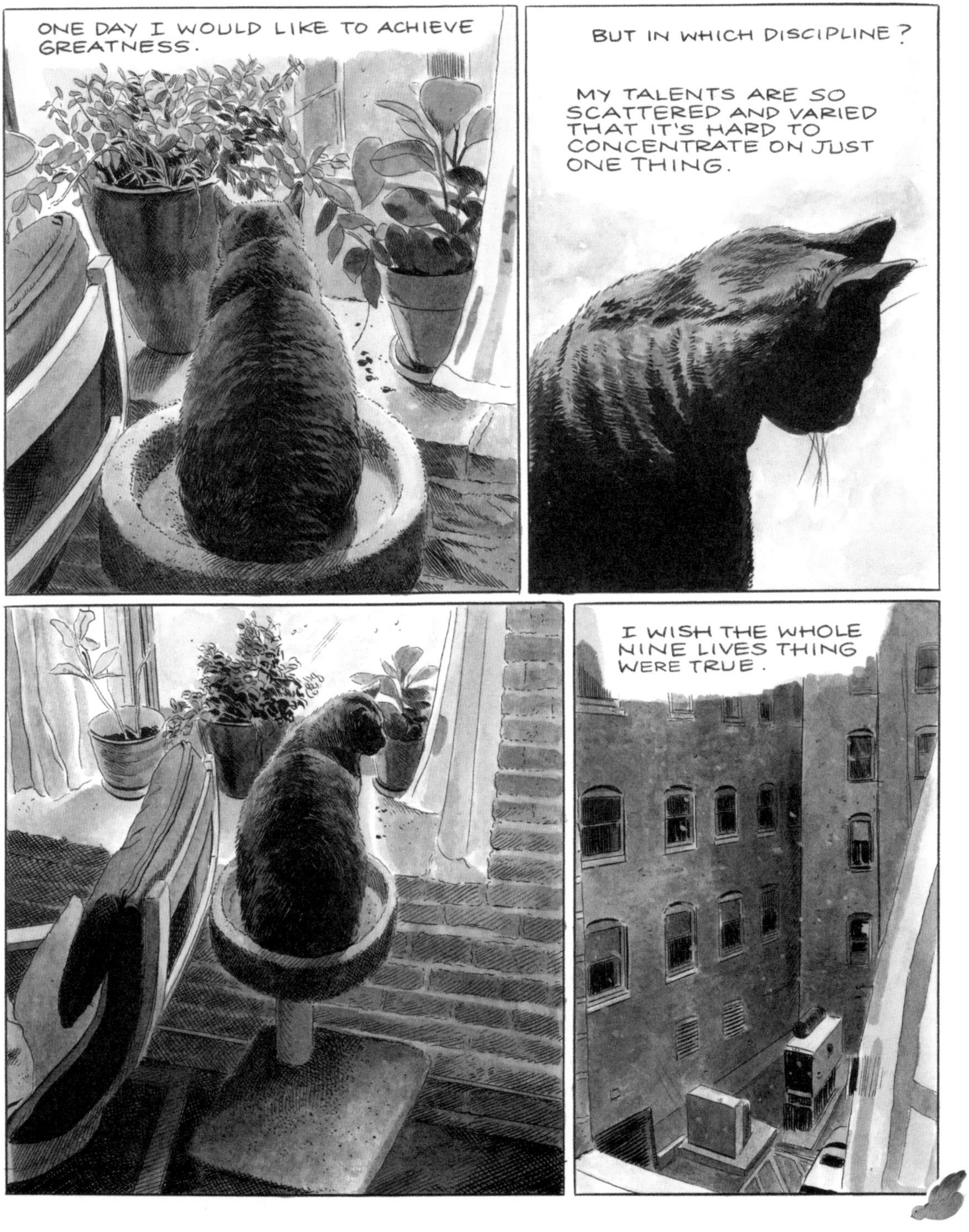
ONE DAY I WOULD LIKE TO ACHIEVE GREATNESS.
BUT IN WHICH DISCIPLINE?
MY TALENTS ARE SO SCATTERED AND VARIED THAT IT'S HARD TO CONCENTRATE ON JUST ONE THING.
I WISH THE WHOLE NINE LIVES THING WERE TRUE.

YOU THINK YOU'RE NOT RESPONSIBLE, RIGHT?

THAT'S WHY YOU SIT THERE WITH THAT DULLARD EXPRESSION PLASTERED ON YOUR FACE.

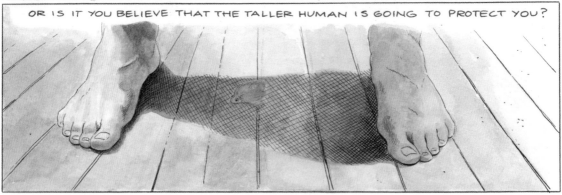

OR IS IT YOU BELIEVE THAT THE TALLER HUMAN IS GOING TO PROTECT YOU?

WELL, JUST SO YOU KNOW, AS SOON AS HE MOVES I'M GOING TO RIP YOU TO SHREDS.

OH, YOU WOULD LIKE THAT, WOULDN'T YOU.

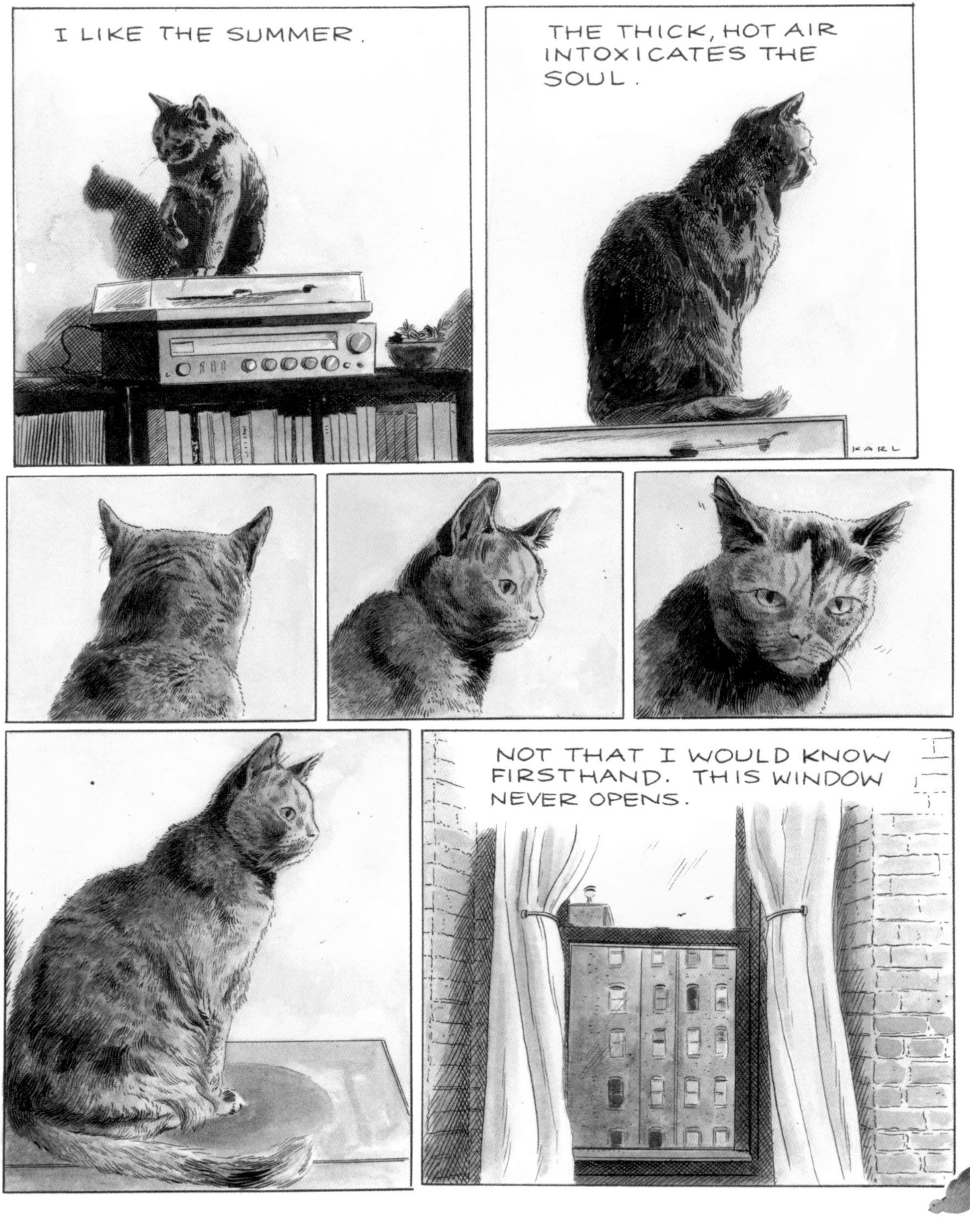
I LIKE THE SUMMER.
THE THICK, HOT AIR INTOXICATES THE SOUL.
KARL
NOT THAT I WOULD KNOW FIRSTHAND. THIS WINDOW NEVER OPENS.

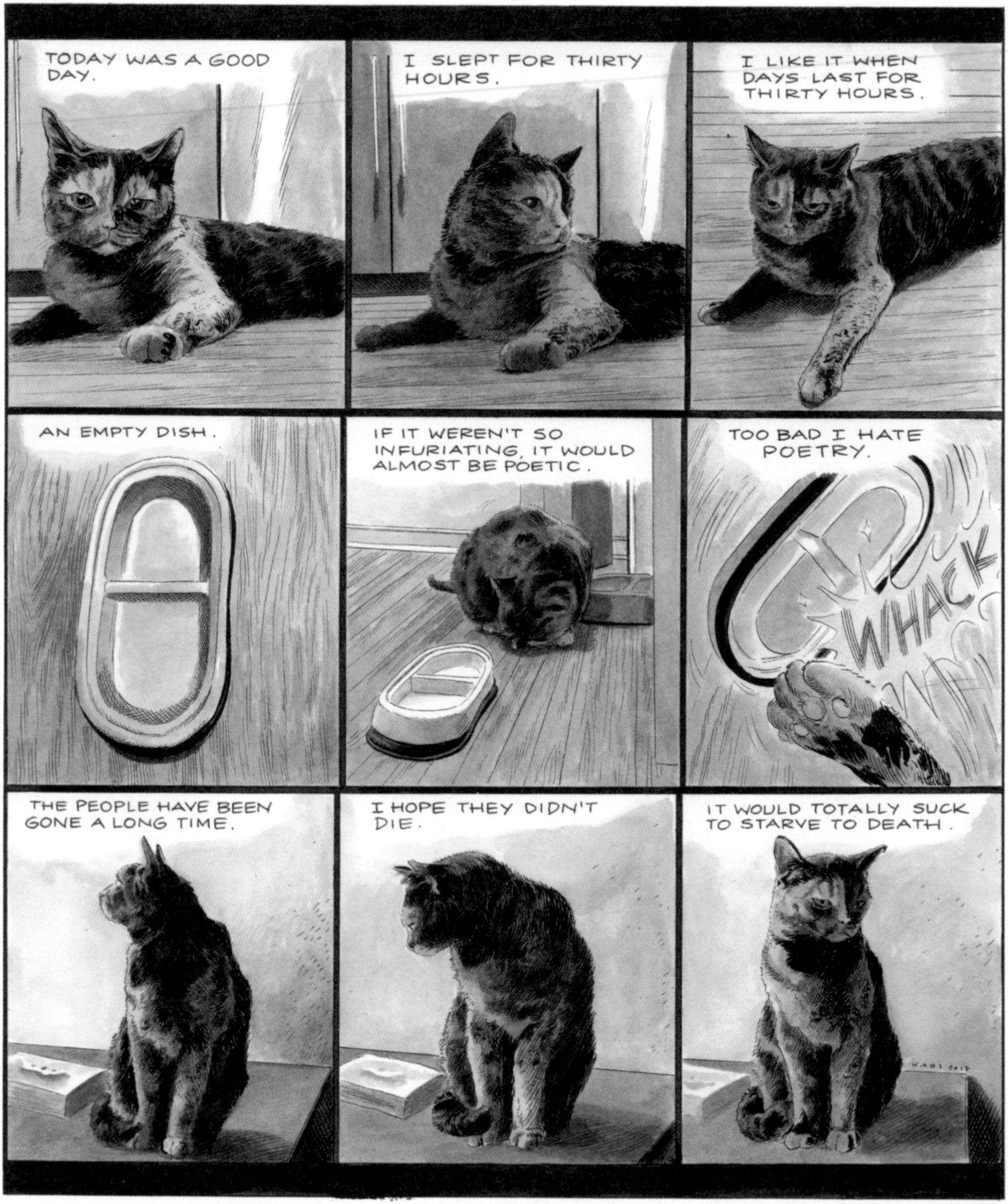
TODAY WAS A GOOD DAY.
I SLEPT FOR THIRTY HOURS.
I LIKE IT WHEN DAYS LAST FOR THIRTY HOURS.
AN EMPTY DISH.
IF IT WEREN'T SO INFURIATING, IT WOULD ALMOST BE POETIC.
TOO BAD I HATE POETRY.
WHACK
THE PEOPLE HAVE BEEN GONE A LONG TIME.
I HOPE THEY DIDN'T DIE.
IT WOULD TOTALLY SUCK TO STARVE TO DEATH.

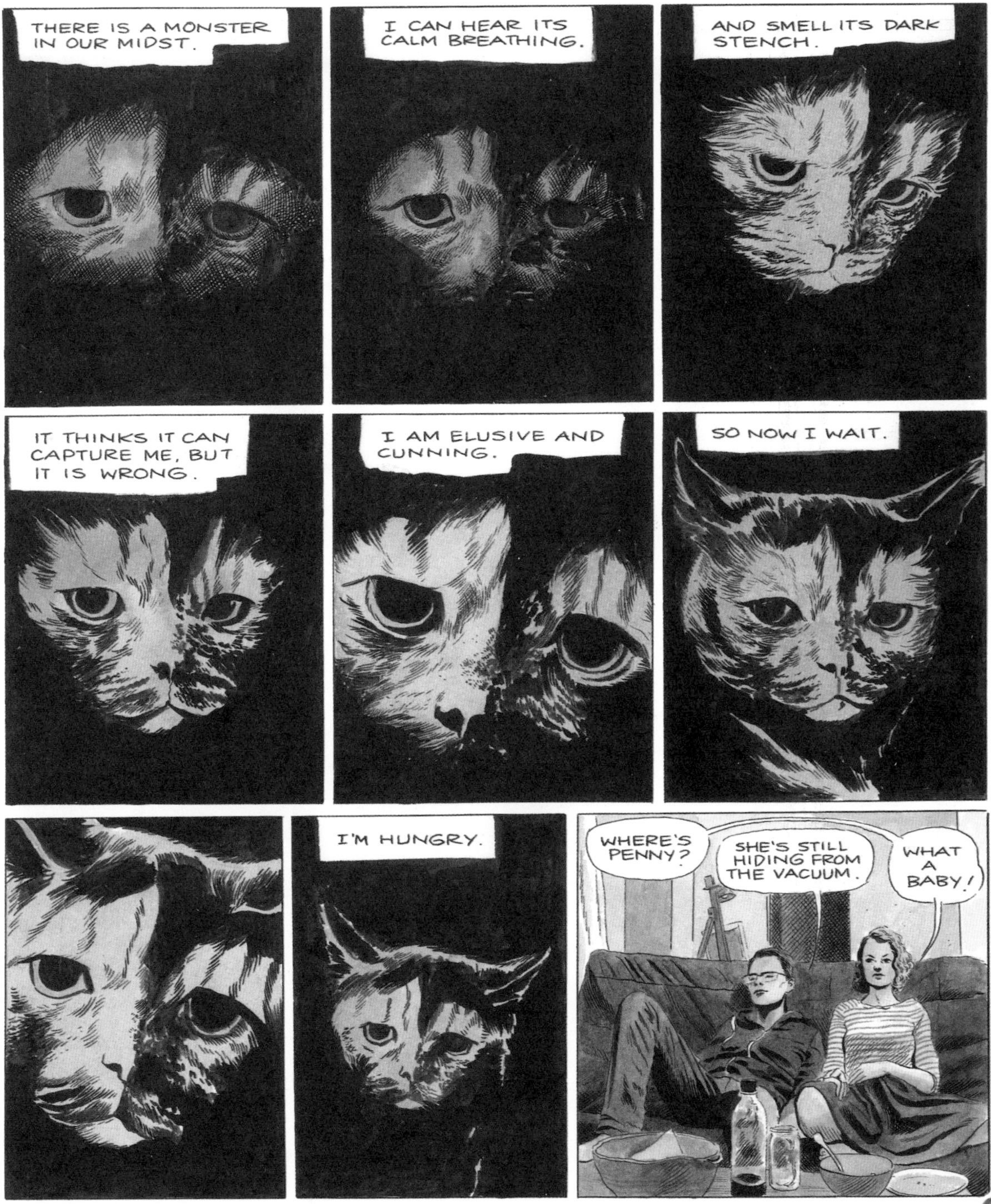
THERE IS A MONSTER IN OUR MIDST.
I CAN HEAR ITS CALM BREATHING.
AND SMELL ITS DARK STENCH.
IT THINKS IT CAN CAPTURE ME, BUT IT IS WRONG.
I AM ELUSIVE AND CUNNING.
SO NOW I WAIT.
I'M HUNGRY.
WHERE'S PENNY?
SHE'S STILL HIDING FROM THE VACUUM.
WHAT A BABY!

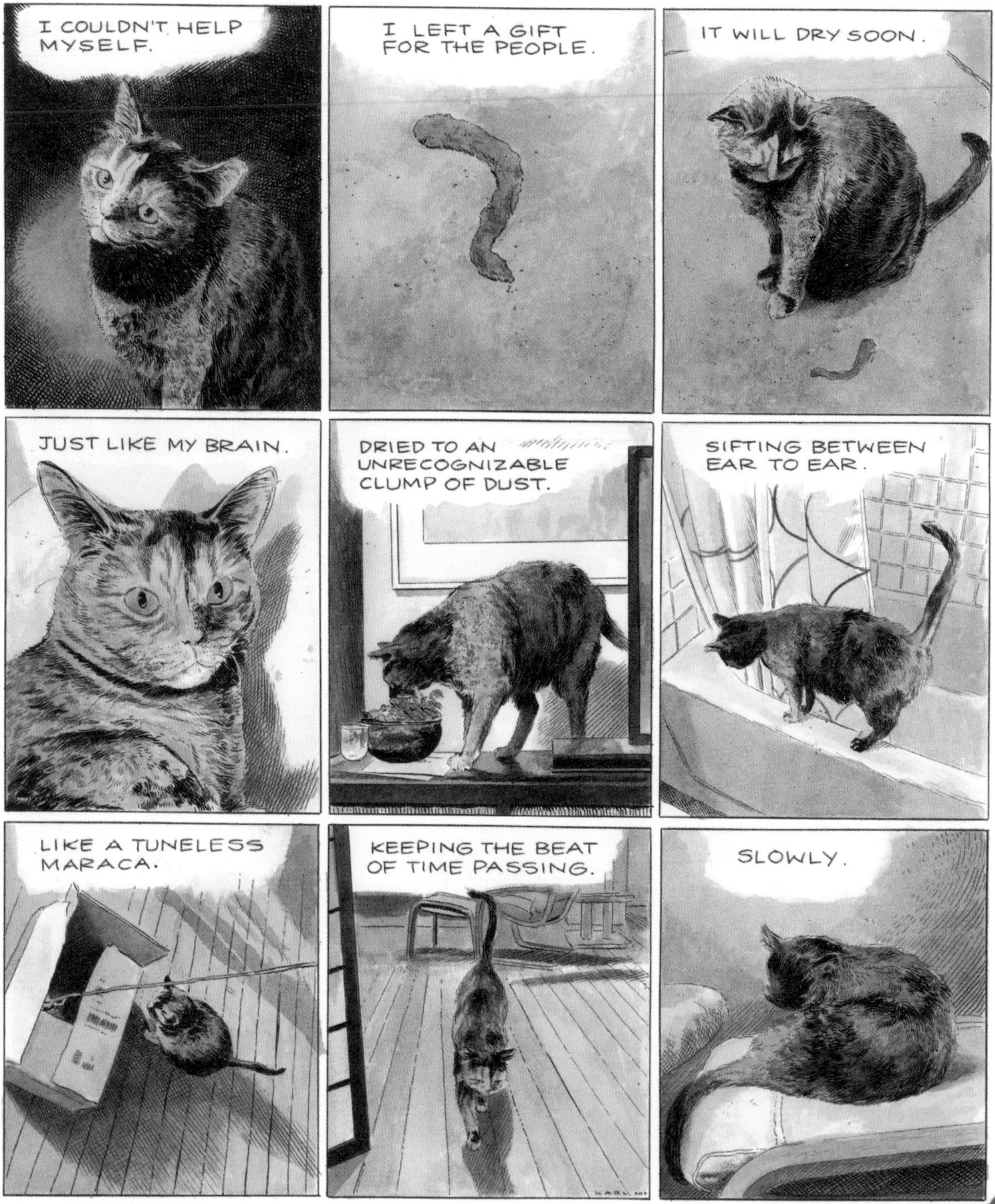
I COULDN'T HELP MYSELF.
I LEFT A GIFT FOR THE PEOPLE.
IT WILL DRY SOON.
JUST LIKE MY BRAIN.
DRIED TO AN UNRECOGNIZABLE CLUMP OF DUST.
SIFTING BETWEEN EAR TO EAR.
LIKE A TUNELESS MARACA.
KEEPING THE BEAT OF TIME PASSING.
SLOWLY.

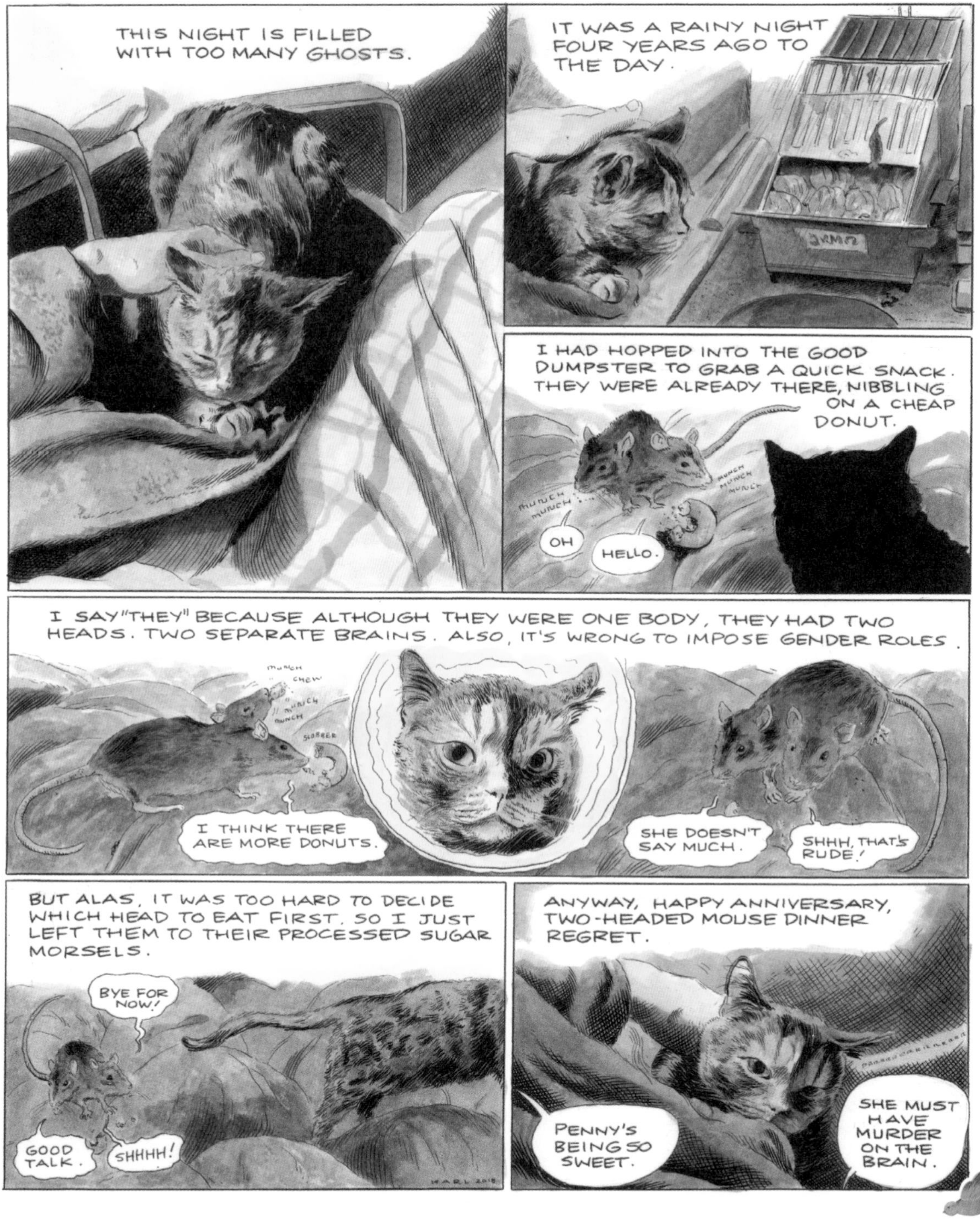
THIS NIGHT IS FILLED WITH TOO MANY GHOSTS.
IT WAS A RAINY NIGHT FOUR YEARS AGO TO THE DAY.
I HAD HOPPED INTO THE GOOD DUMPSTER TO GRAB A QUICK SNACK. THEY WERE ALREADY THERE, NIBBLING ON A CHEAP DONUT.
MUNCH MUNCH
MUNCH MUNCH MUNCH
OH
HELLO.
I SAY "THEY" BECAUSE ALTHOUGH THEY WERE ONE BODY, THEY HAD TWO HEADS. TWO SEPARATE BRAINS. ALSO, IT'S WRONG TO IMPOSE GENDER ROLES.
MUNCH CHEW MUNCH MUNCH
SLOBBER
I THINK THERE ARE MORE DONUTS.
SHE DOESN'T SAY MUCH.
SHHH, THAT'S RUDE!
BUT ALAS, IT WAS TOO HARD TO DECIDE WHICH HEAD TO EAT FIRST. SO I JUST LEFT THEM TO THEIR PROCESSED SUGAR MORSELS.
BYE FOR NOW!
GOOD TALK.
SHHHH!
ANYWAY, HAPPY ANNIVERSARY, TWO-HEADED MOUSE DINNER REGRET.
PENNY'S BEING SO SWEET.
SHE MUST HAVE MURDER ON THE BRAIN.

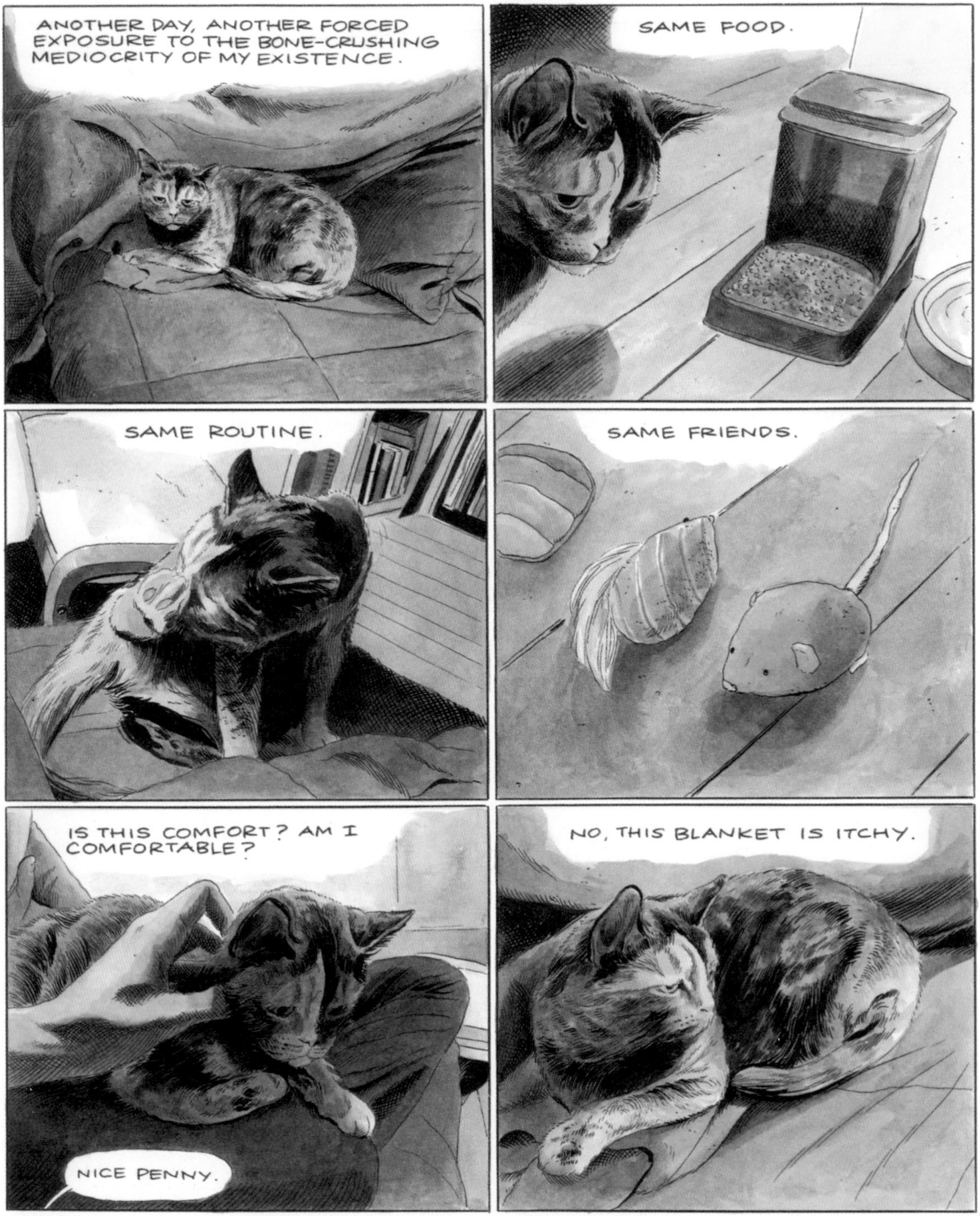
ANOTHER DAY, ANOTHER FORCED EXPOSURE TO THE BONE-CRUSHING MEDIOCRITY OF MY EXISTENCE.
SAME FOOD.
SAME ROUTINE.
SAME FRIENDS.
IS THIS COMFORT? AM I COMFORTABLE?
NICE PENNY.
NO, THIS BLANKET IS ITCHY.

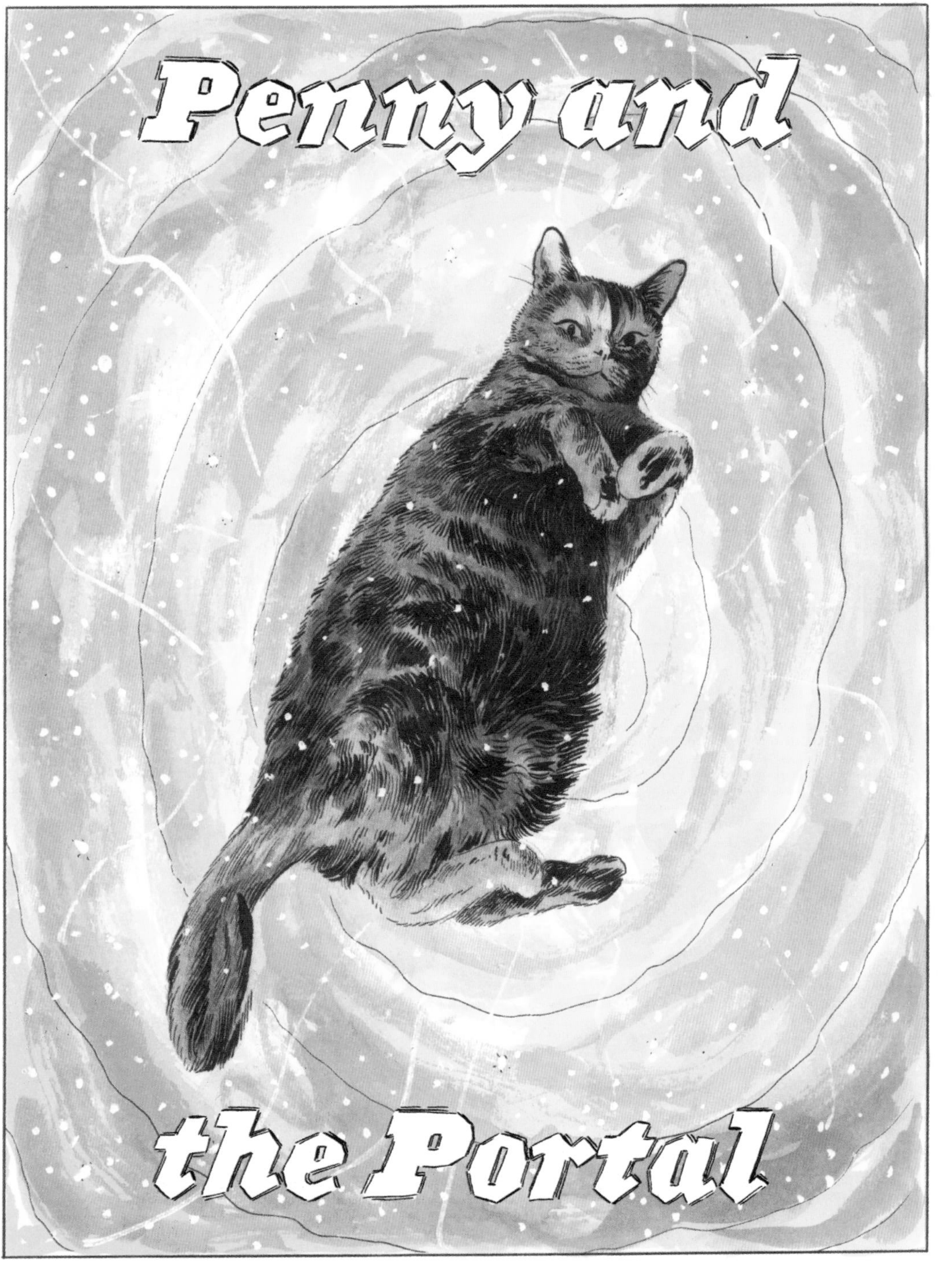
Penny and
the Portal

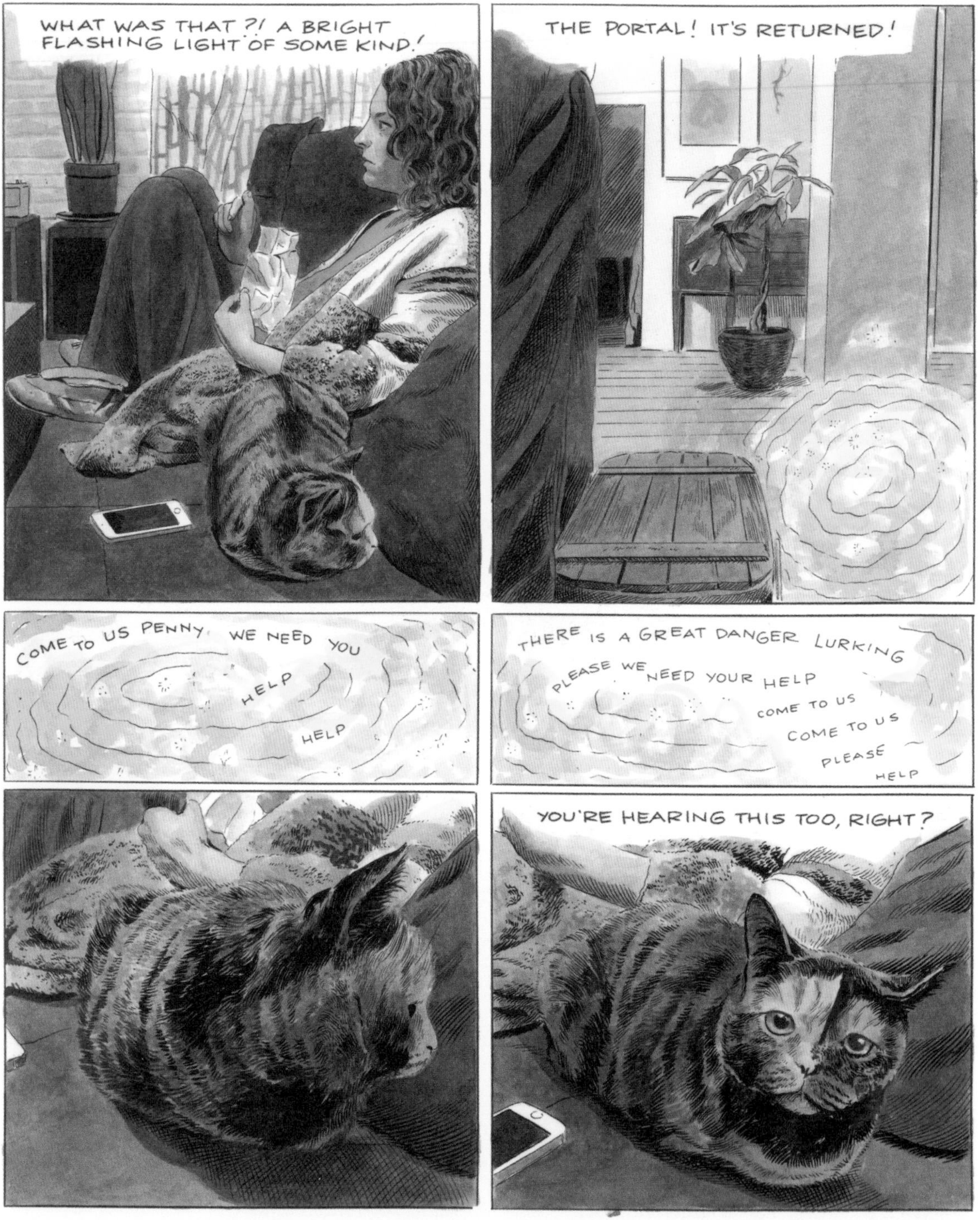
WHAT WAS THAT ?! A BRIGHT FLASHING LIGHT OF SOME KIND!
THE PORTAL! IT'S RETURNED!
COME TO US PENNY WE NEED YOU
HELP
HELP
THERE IS A GREAT DANGER LURKING
PLEASE WE NEED YOUR HELP
COME TO US
COME TO US
PLEASE
HELP
YOU'RE HEARING THIS TOO, RIGHT?

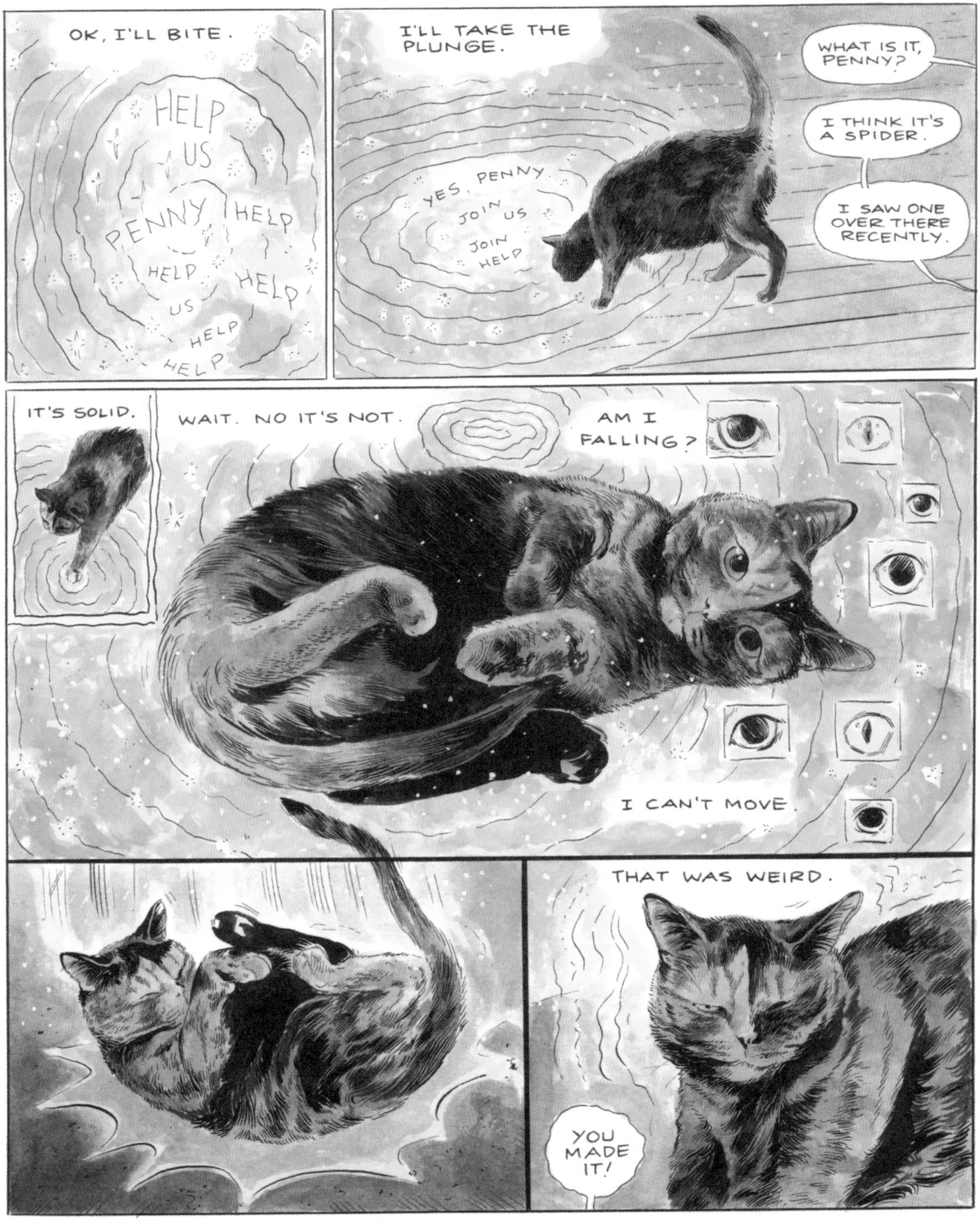
OK, I'LL BITE.
HELP US
PENNY HELP
HELP US HELP
HELP
HELP
I'LL TAKE THE PLUNGE.
WHAT IS IT, PENNY?
I THINK IT'S A SPIDER.
I SAW ONE OVER THERE RECENTLY.
YES, PENNY.
JOIN US
JOIN
HELP
IT'S SOLID.
WAIT. NO IT'S NOT.
AM I FALLING?
I CAN'T MOVE.
THAT WAS WEIRD.
YOU MADE IT!

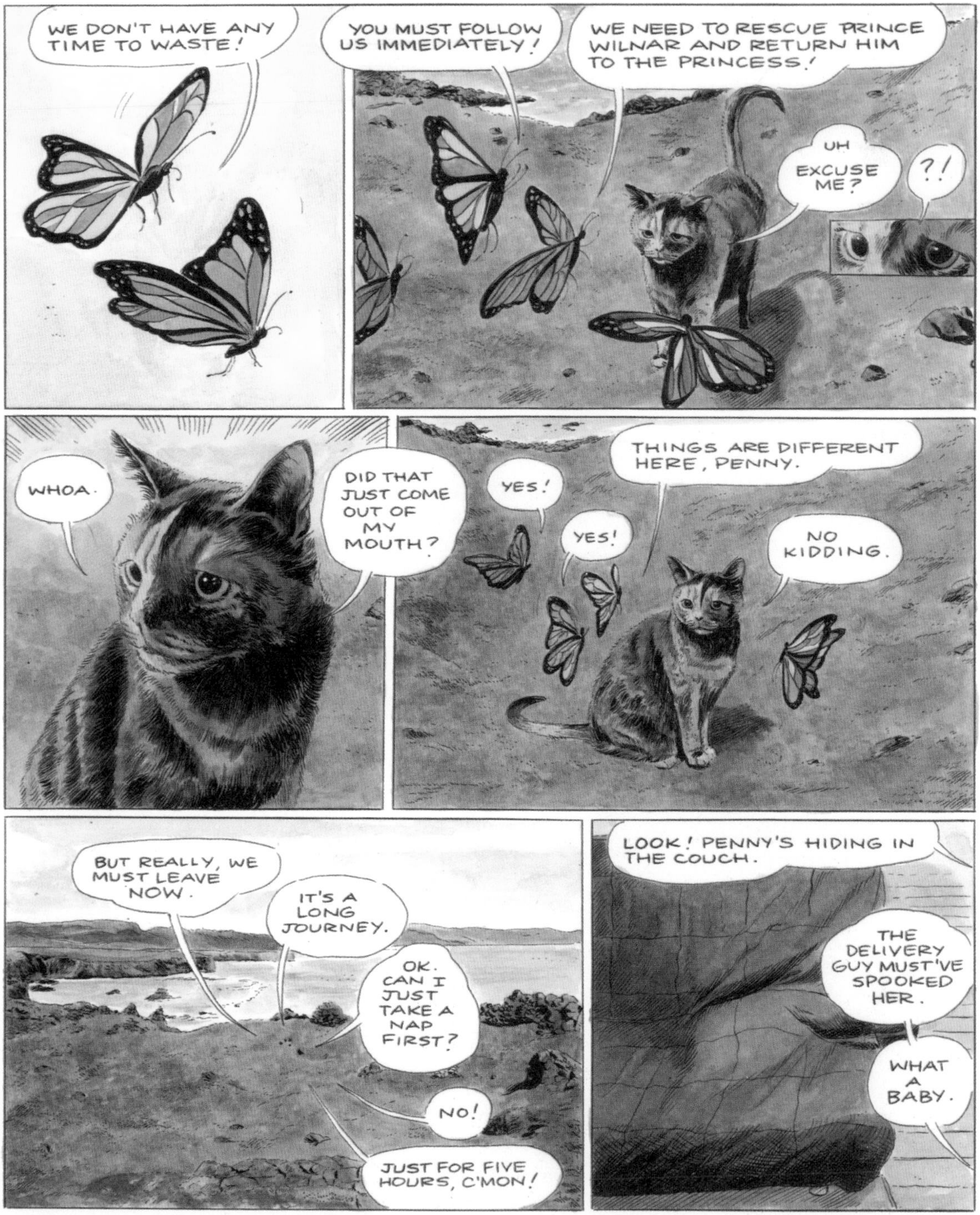
WE DON'T HAVE ANY TIME TO WASTE!
YOU MUST FOLLOW US IMMEDIATELY!
WE NEED TO RESCUE PRINCE WILNAR AND RETURN HIM TO THE PRINCESS!
UH EXCUSE ME?
?!
WHOA.
DID THAT JUST COME OUT OF MY MOUTH?
THINGS ARE DIFFERENT HERE, PENNY.
YES!
YES!
NO KIDDING.
BUT REALLY, WE MUST LEAVE NOW.
IT'S A LONG JOURNEY.
OK. CAN I JUST TAKE A NAP FIRST?
NO!
JUST FOR FIVE HOURS, C'MON!
LOOK! PENNY'S HIDING IN THE COUCH.
THE DELIVERY GUY MUST'VE SPOOKED HER.
WHAT A BABY.

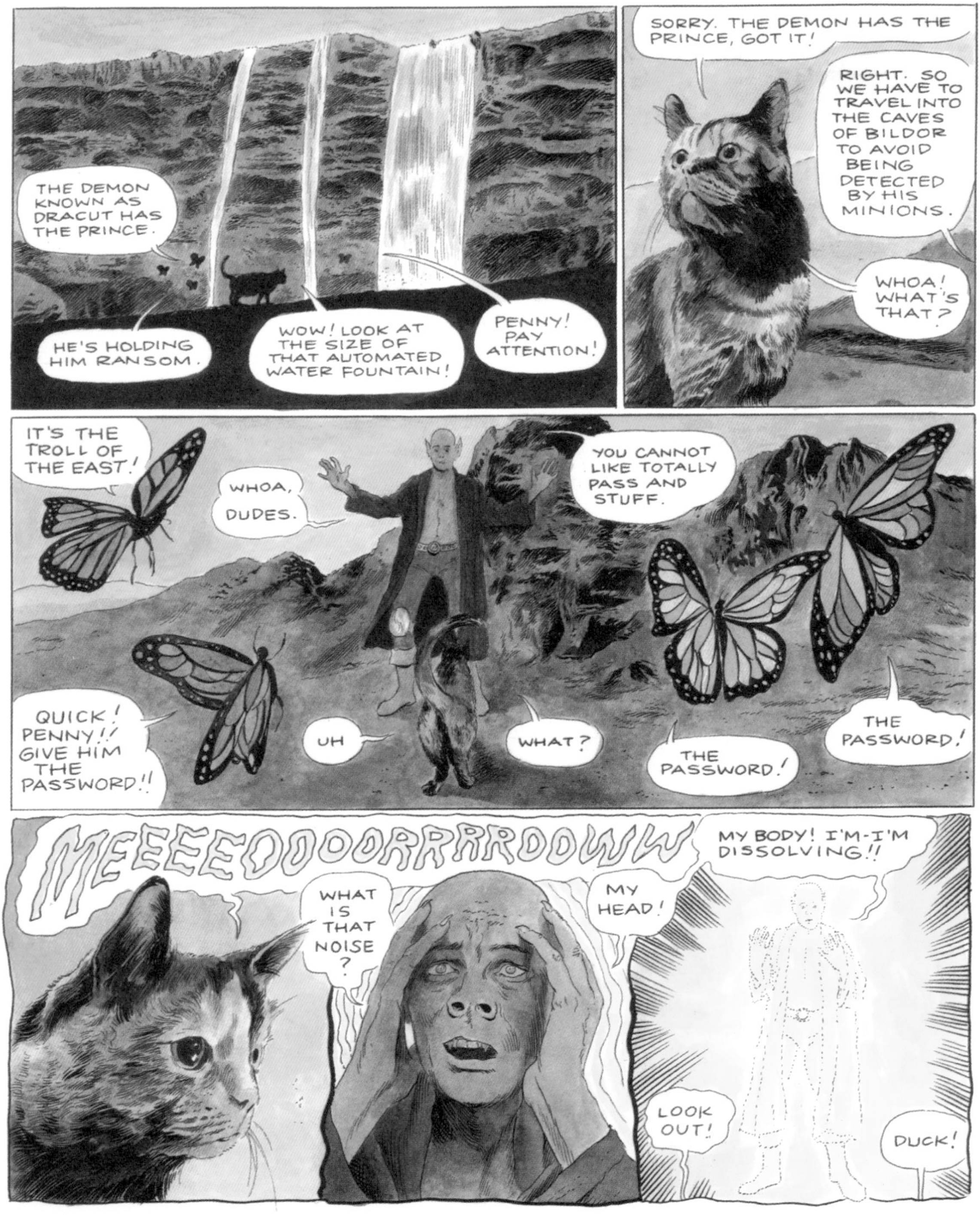
THE DEMON KNOWN AS DRACUT HAS THE PRINCE.
HE'S HOLDING HIM RANSOM.
WOW! LOOK AT THE SIZE OF THAT AUTOMATED WATER FOUNTAIN!
PENNY! PAY ATTENTION!
SORRY. THE DEMON HAS THE PRINCE, GOT IT!
RIGHT. SO WE HAVE TO TRAVEL INTO THE CAVES OF BILDOR TO AVOID BEING DETECTED BY HIS MINIONS.
WHOA! WHAT'S THAT?
IT'S THE TROLL OF THE EAST!
WHOA, DUDES.
YOU CANNOT LIKE TOTALLY PASS AND STUFF.
QUICK! PENNY!! GIVE HIM THE PASSWORD!!
UH
WHAT?
THE PASSWORD!
THE PASSWORD!
MEEEEOOOORRRRROOWW
WHAT IS THAT NOISE?
MY HEAD!
MY BODY! I'M-I'M DISSOLVING!!
LOOK OUT!
DUCK!

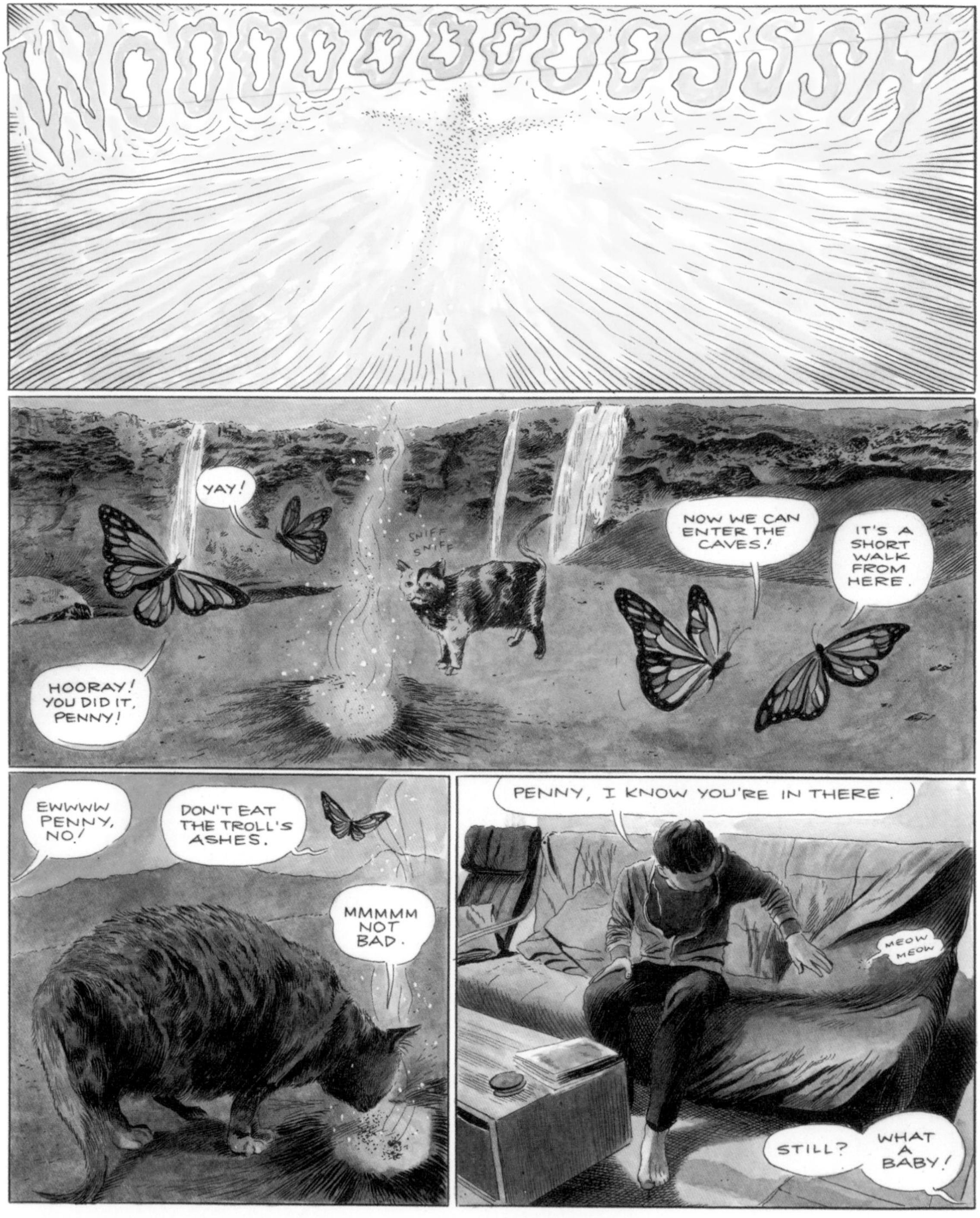
WOOOOOOOOOSSSH
YAY!
SNIFF SNIFF
NOW WE CAN ENTER THE CAVES!
IT'S A SHORT WALK FROM HERE.
HOORAY! YOU DID IT, PENNY!
EWWWW PENNY, NO!
DON'T EAT THE TROLL'S ASHES.
MMMMM NOT BAD.
PENNY, I KNOW YOU'RE IN THERE.
MEOW MEOW
STILL?
WHAT A BABY!

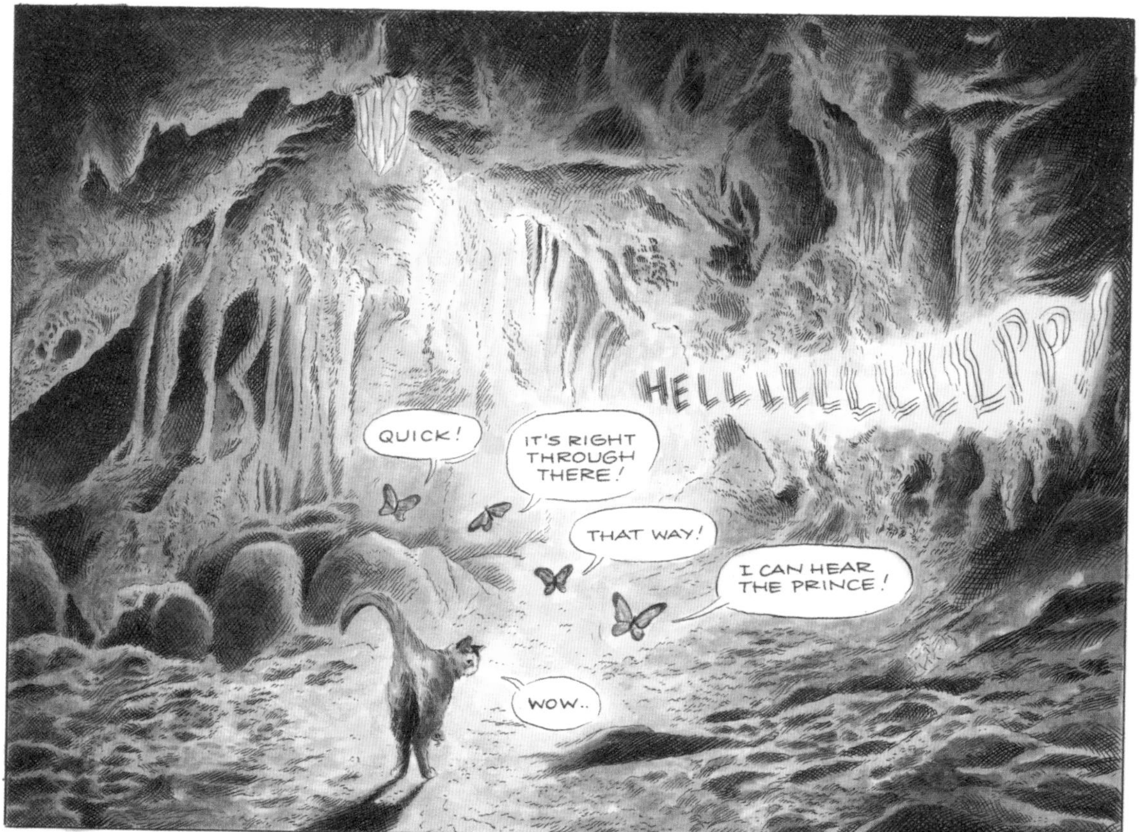
HELLLLLLLLLPP!
QUICK!
IT'S RIGHT THROUGH THERE!
THAT WAY!
I CAN HEAR THE PRINCE!
WOW..

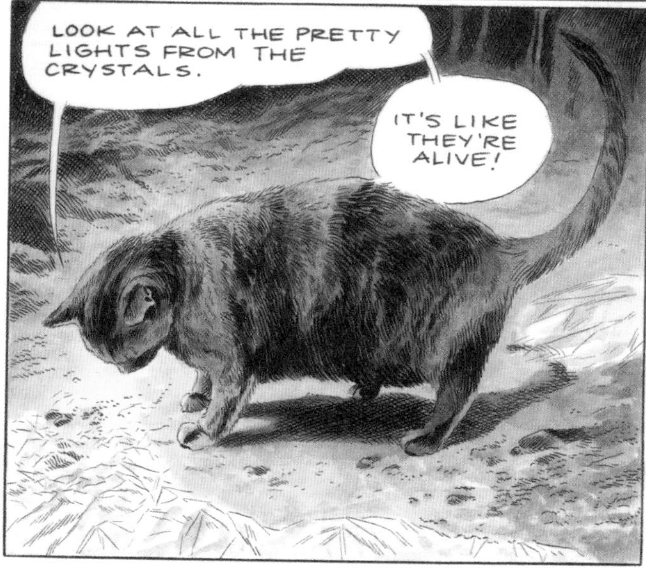
LOOK AT ALL THE PRETTY LIGHTS FROM THE CRYSTALS.
IT'S LIKE THEY'RE ALIVE!

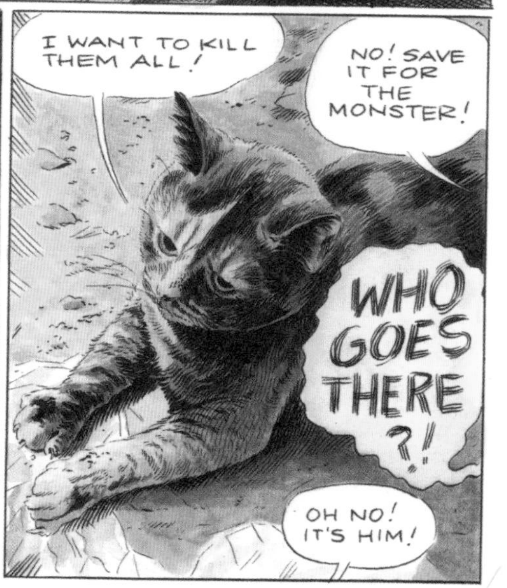
I WANT TO KILL THEM ALL!
NO! SAVE IT FOR THE MONSTER!
WHO GOES THERE ?!
OH NO! IT'S HIM!

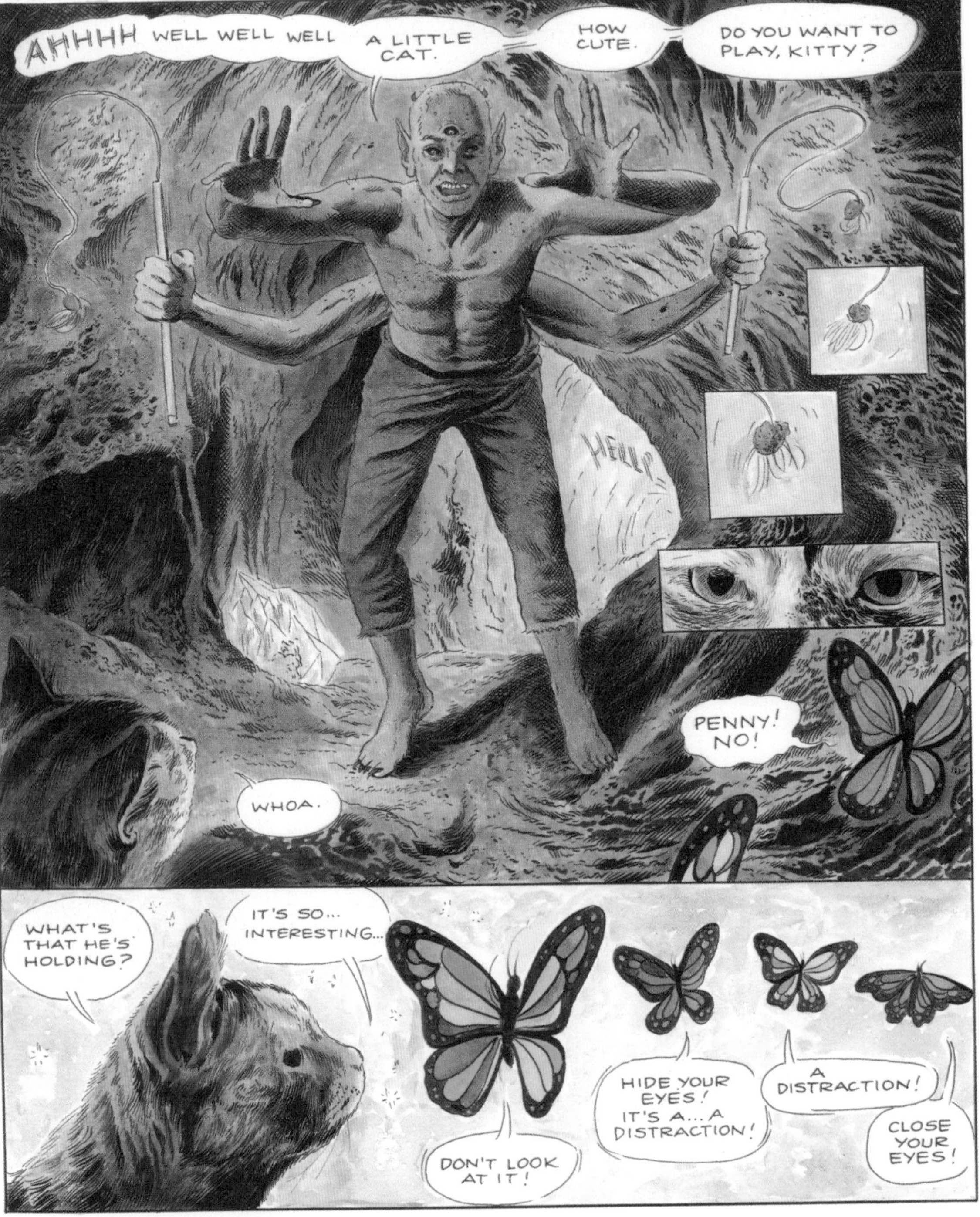
AHHHH WELL WELL WELL
A LITTLE CAT.
HOW CUTE.
DO YOU WANT TO PLAY, KITTY?
HELLP
PENNY! NO!
WHOA.
WHAT'S THAT HE'S HOLDING?
IT'S SO... INTERESTING...
DON'T LOOK AT IT!
HIDE YOUR EYES! IT'S A... A DISTRACTION!
A DISTRACTION!
CLOSE YOUR EYES!

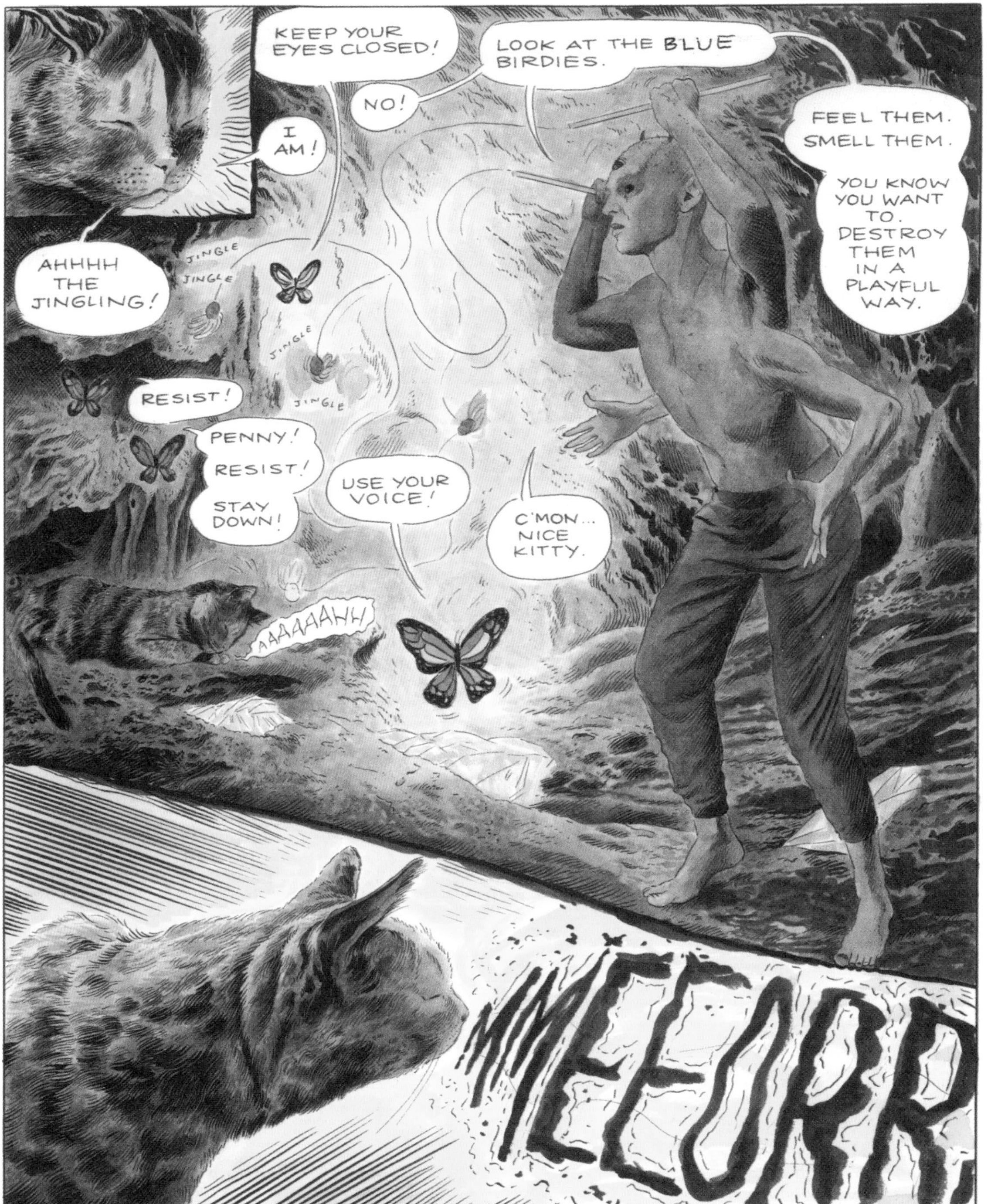
KEEP YOUR EYES CLOSED!
LOOK AT THE BLUE BIRDIES.
NO!
FEEL THEM. SMELL THEM.
YOU KNOW YOU WANT TO. DESTROY THEM IN A PLAYFUL WAY.
I AM!
AHHHH THE JINGLING!
JINGLE
JINGLE
JINGLE
JINGLE
RESIST!
PENNY! RESIST! STAY DOWN!
USE YOUR VOICE!
C'MON... NICE KITTY.
AAAAAAAHH
MMEEORR

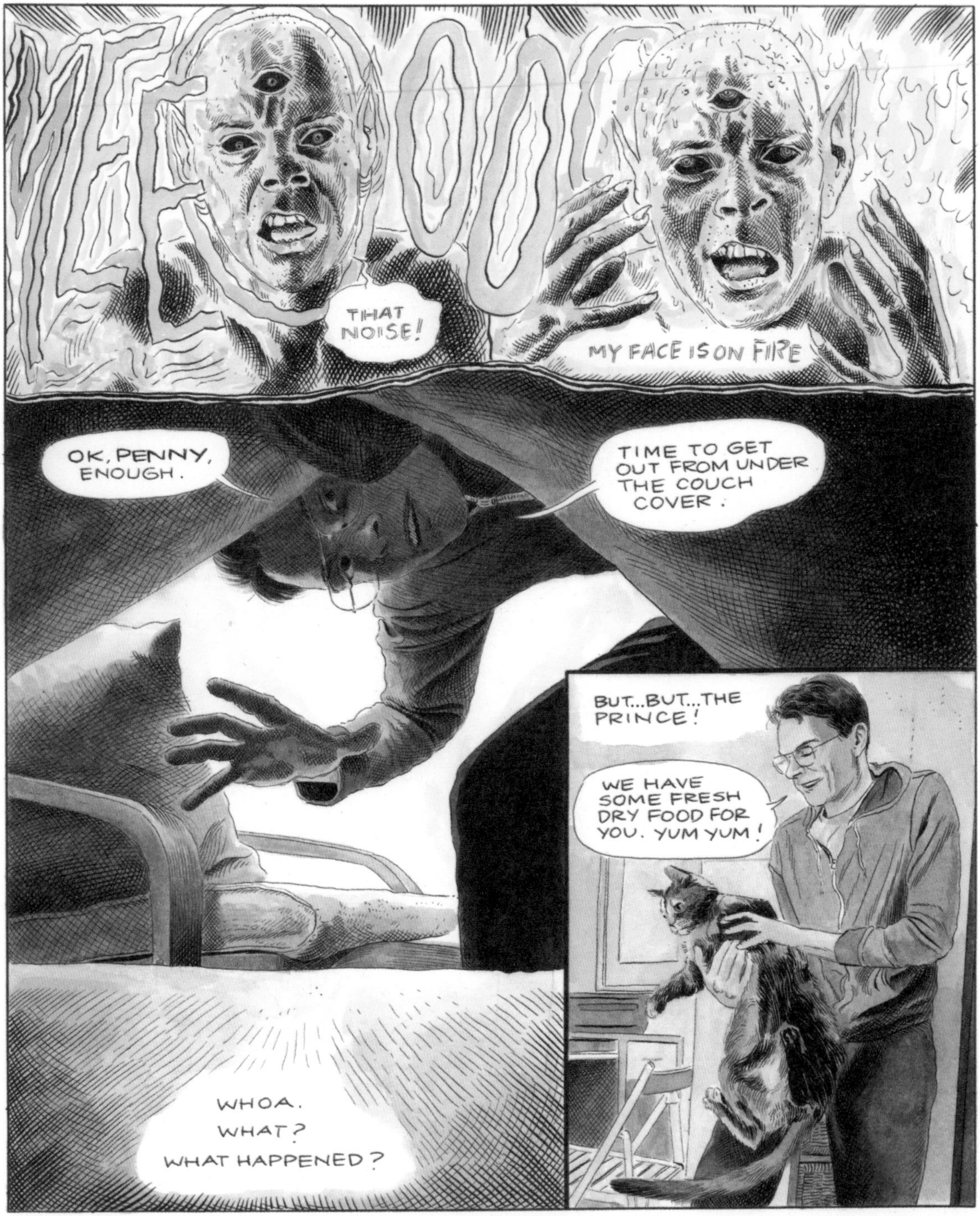
MEOOO
THAT NOISE!
MY FACE IS ON FIRE
OK, PENNY, ENOUGH.
TIME TO GET OUT FROM UNDER THE COUCH COVER.
BUT...BUT...THE PRINCE!
WE HAVE SOME FRESH DRY FOOD FOR YOU. YUM YUM!
WHOA.
WHAT?
WHAT HAPPENED?

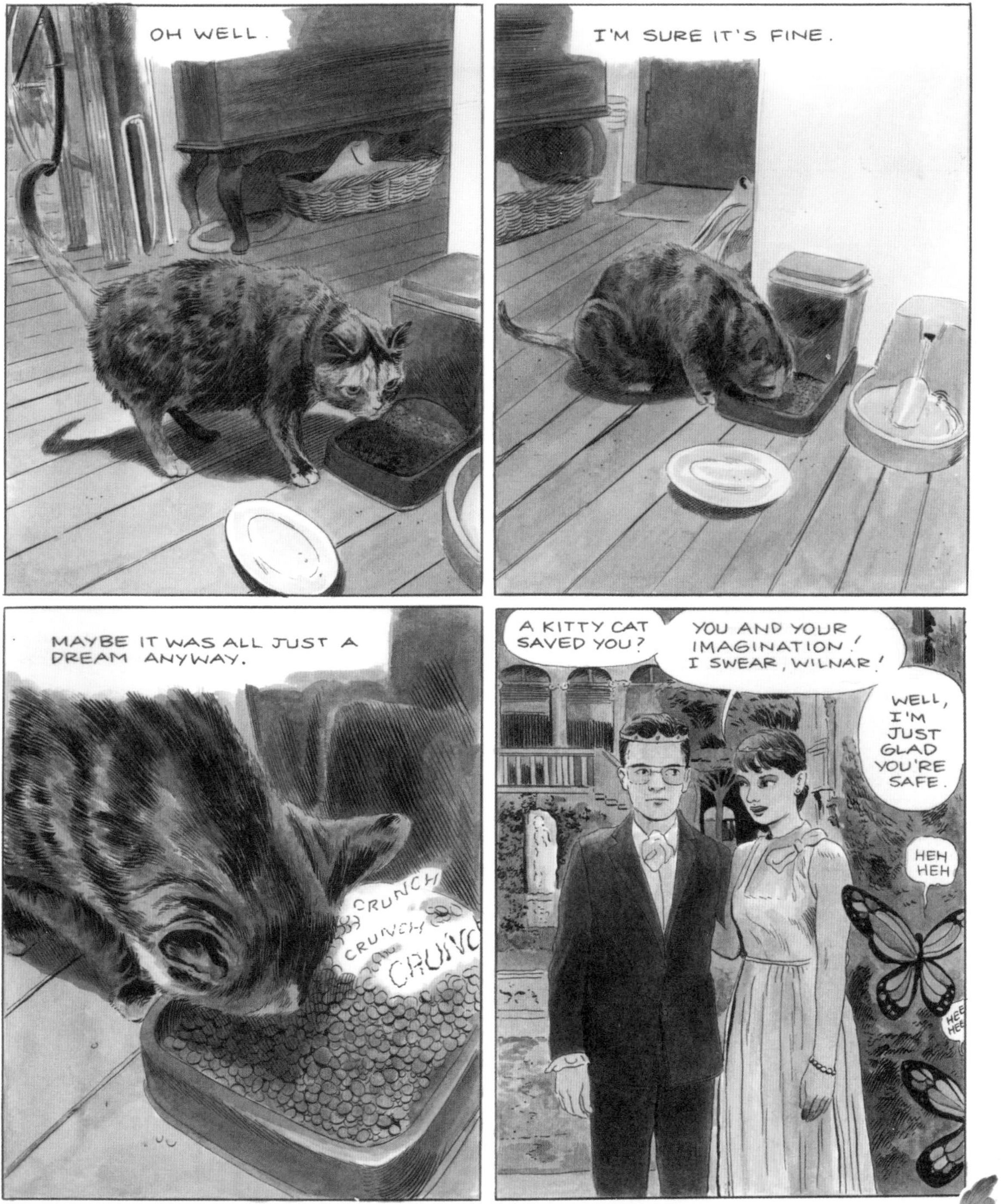
OH WELL.
I'M SURE IT'S FINE.
MAYBE IT WAS ALL JUST A DREAM ANYWAY.
CRUNCH
CRUNCH
CRUNC
A KITTY CAT SAVED YOU?
YOU AND YOUR IMAGINATION! I SWEAR, WILNAR!
WELL, I'M JUST GLAD YOU'RE SAFE.
HEH HEH